"Small Victories"

a legacy of courage and love

Jeff Mercer

xulon PRESS

"Small Victories"
by Jeff Mercer

Printed in the United States of America

ISBN 978-1-60477-263-0

www.xulonpress.com

Contents

"**Small Victories**" a legacy of courage and love

Preface

Foreword

Acknowledgements

1. Introduction "My Son Daniel"

2. Faith, Family and Cancer

3. Angels in Scrubs

4. Small Victories

5. The Heart of a Servant

6. Maintaining a Life and Career in the Face of Adversity

7. Defining Moments

8. Friends Forever

9. I am my Brother's Keeper

10. Gone and Not Forgotten

11. There's no Song in my Heart... Sing Anyway

12. Leaving a Legacy

13. The Next Place

Afterword

Appendix

Daniel P. Mercer – Family Fund

Preface

I am the father of four sons, none of whom arrived with an instructional manual. Most young parents learn through observation and experience. They adopt the disposition that seems best suited to their personalities, beliefs, and values. I am no different.

I am also the father of a son who lost his life far too prematurely. That distinction allows me membership into an unwanted fraternity, a fraternity nonetheless that includes tens of thousands of parents in our country each and every year. In death, as in life, there is no manual. In reality though, responding to the death of a child is far more complicated than raising one.

The writing of this book has, without question, been the single most difficult endeavor of my entire life. Each paragraph sent me headlong into a series of reflections, many of which I did not want to recall. Despite the obvious challenges, I felt compelled to keep moving on this project for two reasons: our community needed a sense of closure that this book could provide, and I believed that I owed it to Daniel to honor his legacy of courage, selflessness, and faith. If, along the way, it brings comfort to others who have been faced with similar tragedies, then all the better.

Over the past couple of years, I have read several books which chronicle stories similar to Dan's. While I gleaned a great deal from each, I found them falling short of sharing what I considered to be the most important messages. So much time is spent telling the story of the main character, but in truth, there are scores of main characters, for a journey such as this elicits the kindness, care, and concern of "the village." If there is truth in the adage that it takes a village to raise a child, so too is there truth that it takes a village to love and support a family who loses one.

With that said, the death of a loved one, especially a child, is in many ways a singular passage. I find that while we provide comfort for one another, we all react differently to our reality. My deepest hope is that this narrative will allow you to know the young man, bring the journey to life, and share the level of commitment and faith that surrounded our family and community.

For the tens of thousands of families who lose a loved one to cancer each year, the question will inevitably arise, "Why has this happened to us?" The answers run the gamut of possibilities from, "They should have taken better care of themselves," to "Our family had a history of this," to "How unlucky we have been!" While I'm sure each of these possibilities has occurred to us at times, it was only for the briefest of moments.

Through this book, I hope to give you a snapshot of the crossing – the crossing from child to man, from belief to conviction, and from life to death.

"Small Victories" a legacy of courage and love

Early Monday, May 29, 2006, soon after midnight with his family by his bedside, our friend, classmate and teammate Daniel Mercer passed from this life and entered God's presence. It was the end of a long and difficult journey for Daniel, his mom and dad, his brothers, his extended family, and indeed for our entire community and so many others who knew and loved him.

I am so honored that Jeff and Pam asked me to pen the foreword for this book. However, I want to make one thing clear to all of you—I have no answers for this. I am not able to tell you why this happened, why it happened to this particular young man and his family, or why a good and loving God allows such experiences to happen in our lives without intervening to deliver those who suffer and die.

Some of you may have the notion that it is a minister's calling to explain such mysteries, that pastors are those who can see into the depths of God's mind and interpret secret knowledge to others who don't have that kind of access. Untrue. Ministers can only teach and share the things that God has revealed. And there are many aspects of life that God has not spoken about or made clear.

Therefore, I would like to focus on some of the truths that have become even clearer to me as I have watched a young man and his family walk this difficult path over the past year and a half. In countless conversations, I have said or heard people say things like, "This is unreal"; "I just can't fathom this"; "I just can't get my mind around this"; "I can't grasp that this is really happening." It has seemed unreal, but in the midst of that apparent unreality, I can testify to you that many things have become even more real to me.

I would like to direct my message to those who are about to read this book—to Daniel's friends, peers, classmates, or those of you who are about to be introduced to him. I'm sure that what Daniel has gone through has or will confuse you, sadden you, make you angry, and will cause you to question all kinds of things about life, about God and about what is real. I don't have all the "answers" for you, but I can tell you about some things that I know now, more than ever, are real.

First of all, I can tell you that I know now more than ever that suffering is real. In my Bible I read these words from Jesus: "In the world you will have tribulation. But take heart, I have overcome the world" (John 16:33).

In the world you will have tribulation. I wish I could tell you differently, but I can't. The Bible teaches that we live in a world that is not right; it has become corrupted by human sin; it has fallen into a state in which people do bad things to themselves and others; accidents and tragedies happen; people at all stages of life get sick and die; nations go to war against other nations and exploit their own citizens; families break up; and it often seems like the bad people win and the good people lose. What happened to Daniel is an example of what happens to people in a fallen, broken world where suffering is real. I too will face things like this, and so will you. It's certainly not something we like to think about or talk about all the time, but let's be realistic and wise about this. Life can be hard. Bad things happen. Suffering is real. Second, I have observed in this situation that love is real. I know you've seen that, too, because so many have been a part of showing that love is real. Countless individuals have practiced genuine love by visiting Daniel or children like him throughout this country, preparing meals for families, bringing special things to sick children at the hospital, helping families with transportation and child care needs, talking with them, laughing with them, crying with them, praying for them and praying with them.

The Mercer family has been a constant exhibit of genuine love. I've observed Jeff and Pam balancing unbelievable demands so that they could show constant attention to Daniel's needs while never failing to fulfill their other obligations. I've watched Jeffrey sacrifice a semester at school and his baseball season to care for his brother and help his family. I've watched Joe and Anthony patiently endure regular disruptions to their young lives.

Their caregivers have also displayed great love. I've seen doctors, nurses, social workers and aides care for Daniel with compassion, personal attention and sacrificial commitment. I've observed a church family that has stepped up to support them in a thousand practical ways. I've seen neighbors, friends, fellow students, an entire community pour out their hearts and hold out their hands to this family, and I'm telling you, love is real. In a world where suffering is real, nothing is more important.

In the Bible verse I quoted earlier, Jesus said, "In the world you will have tribulation." But Jesus goes on to say, "Take heart, I have overcome the world" (John 16:33). How did Jesus overcome the world? You may recall that he did it in a most unorthodox way. He overcame this world of sin, evil and death by loving it and laying down his life for it. He overcame suffering by sacrificial love. He practiced the very thing he had taught his disciples when he said, "Greater love has no one than this, that someone lays down his life for his friends" (John 15:13).

So many of you have followed Jesus' example and laid down your lives in both small and great ways to show love and to bring help and comfort into this situation over the past year and a half. As a result, many very real miracles took place. Laughter was heard in places where sorrow sought to overwhelm. Comfort and encouragement overcame despair. Renewed strength and energy overcame exhaustion. Hundreds of small victories were won. Individuals, families and communities were strengthened. We all learned about integrity, discipline, determination, hopefulness and faith.

Love is real and it's the most important thing in a world where suffering is real. By love, we overcome.The third and final thing I've become convinced of through this whole experience is that God and faith and hope are real. Yes, suffering is real, and yes, love that helps us overcome suffering is real, but I can hear some of you thinking right now, "But didn't Daniel still die? Sure, love helped everyone throughout this terrible experience, but didn't death still win in the end?" And to be honest, I would have to answer "yes" to that question—IF this were the end of the story.

But I am convinced that Daniel's story is not over. For those who believe, death is not like a one-and-out sports tournament where, when you lose you're finished; you go home and there are no more games to play. In fact, what I'm about to say is the greatest irony imaginable. When a believer "loses" the game of life on this earth and dies, he actually is declared the winner of the tournament and is promoted to the next level of competition! Now we all of course feel a tremendous sense of loss through Daniel's death, but in God's eyes, he's celebrating victory and getting ready for an eternity of new games and new hunting and fishing trips and new experiences of laughing and enjoying life forever with his Lord and the ones he loves.

"But how do you know that?" you may ask. If I told you these things and they were just based on wishful thinking, you'd be a fool to believe me. But I'm convinced that God and faith and hope are real not just because I want it to be so. I base my convictions about these things on the fact that a man named Jesus lived and taught and died and literally rose from the dead two thousand years ago. And he said, "Because I live, you shall live also" (John 14:19). He also said, "I am the resurrection and the life; whoever believes in me, though he die, yet shall he live, and everyone who lives and believes in me shall never die" (John 11:25-26). To prove these words, in one of the best-attested facts in history, Jesus himself rose from the dead, and a movement of God, faith and hope spread in his name throughout the world.

The discovery of Daniel's brain tumor came on the week of his confirmation, a time of spiritual awakening in his life. Over the course of his disease, I had the privilege of praying with Daniel and talking with him about his faith, as did several others. Of course, he expressed fears and concerns about his illness and about dying—wouldn't we all?—but I also know that Dan's faith in Christ grew during this time, that he trusted Jesus as his Savior and believed God would welcome him into heaven.

Many years ago, there was a man named Bill Broadhurst. Bill Broadhurst had suffered a brain aneurism as a young man, leaving him partially paralyzed on the left side. But he loved running and sought to emulate his hero Bill Rogers, one of the most famous marathon runners in the world. When he heard that Rogers had entered in the Omaha, Nebraska, Pepsi 10k race, Broadhurst decided to run in the 6.2 mile contest too.

On race day, some finished in 30 minutes; joggers even finished in 60 minutes. But it took Bill Broadhurst much longer. As he ran, his left side got so numb he wanted to quit. After two hours, the cars were back in the streets, it was getting dark, and running through intersections became difficult. One policeman stopped cars to let him across; a nice lady handed him some water. At two hours and twenty minutes, he said the pain was so bad and so throbbing, "I didn't want to make it; I didn't want to go on."

Then he saw the end. They had already taken the banner down that marked the finish line. Broadhurst ran down the street on the sidewalk, saw the banner was gone, and his heart sank because everybody had left. He thought, "What's the use?" But he decided to finish, and when he got to the end, from around a corner stepped Bill Rogers (the man who had won the race) and a large group of people. They had been waiting for him. Rogers opened his arms, welcomed Broadhurst across the finish line, and hugged him. After Broadhurst willed his partially paralyzed body the last few steps to the end of the race, Rogers took the gold medal from around his own neck and put it around the neck of the last runner to cross the line. Rogers said, "Bill Broadhurst, you're the winner; take the gold."

In the eyes of the world, Bill Broadhurst lost the race; he finished last; he didn't win the prize. In the eyes of his great hero, Bill Rogers, he won the race.
Can you picture Daniel in that story? For a year and a half now, he's been limping along, from the world's point of view out of the competition with no chance of winning. But I believe that Monday morning, May 29th, 2006, around midnight, Jesus, the one who died and rose again for him, stepped out with a large group of saints, put his arms around Daniel and said, "Way to go, D, you finished your race. You won."

Suffering is real. But love is also real, and it can help us overcome the pain and sorrow that accompanies suffering. Most important of all, God and faith and hope are real. Daniel ran his race well and finished a winner. Let's follow him and run our races well until the day we see him again.

Acknowledgements

"Small Victories" a legacy of courage and love

It seems that our journey has taken us a million miles with a thousand twists and turns, but regardless of the path, one thing is certain. We have been loved by family, community, and friends, both old and new.

Staggering indeed is the number of kind acts and kind thoughts which accompanied our son's illness. There is virtually no way to recognize all those who carried us when we could go on no longer. However, I would like to acknowledge some very special folks:

To the Mercer and Kieffer extended families for making Daniel feel so loved and for coming to our aid every time they were called upon, and frequently even when they weren't called. A special thanks to Ann Dicken, who gave everything she had to the spiritual well-being of Dan, Pam, and our entire family.

To the hundreds of Daniel's friends, classmates, and supporters who kept vigil at the hospital, at home, and in their hearts. A special thanks to Daniel's best friends Emily Fox and Michael Reese. We love you both! Thanks also to Ben Gordon, Adam Miller, Chris Hawkins, Bart Carter, Brad Gallagher, Danny Cooper, Ashley Adams, Sarah Coudret, and Hilary Fox.

To Daniel's "second" families, Joe and Michele Fox, who loved Dan like their own and were there for us every day for two years; to Mike Carter, whom Daniel loved and admired and who always made him laugh; and to Ann and Larry Gordon, who at times must have felt as though they were raising Daniel, given the amount of time he spent at their home.

To Pastor Mike Mercer who, although not related, seemed like family as he attended to our every need, spiritually and otherwise; and to Carla and Tom Bechman for caring for Anthony and our family.

To the angels in scrubs at Methodist and Riley hospitals who cared for and loved Daniel every day for eighteen months. Special thanks to social worker Erica Short, nurses Emily Parkinson, Tracy Davis, Mary Jo Johnson, Brooke Smalley, Andy Bullock, Missy Etnier, Marti Michael, Jayne Von Bergen, Sally Kirschner, Dr. Michael Turner, Dr. Jeff Goldman and Dr. Lyle Fettig. We love each of you for all that you did and tried to do.

To our employers-- Franklin College, Franklin Community School Corporation, and Clark Pleasant Community School Corporation--who picked up the ball for Pam and me when we could no longer do our part. Special thanks to Dr. Jay Moseley, Dr. David

Brailow, Dr. William Patterson, Pat Hopper, Dr. J.T. Coopman, and the Math Department at Whiteland High School--especially Holly Harlow, Kim Bartholomew, and Janet Garner. In addition, thanks to the two best assistants anywhere in Martha Clark Pfifer and Kay Yoder. God love you both for all you did to support me. And to all our colleagues that sent meals, good wishes, and funds in support of Daniel and our family.

To our church family and community, who were absolutely incredible in their support of our family. Special thanks to Father Tom Schleissman, Father Paul Shikany, Maria Coudret, Tanya Smythe, Dolly Patterson, Linda Cullinan, Mike Pinnick, Chicago's Pizza, and hundreds of others. You name it, and they did it.

To the Athletic Department at Franklin High School, a huge part of Daniel's life. Special thanks to Noel Heminger, Dave Coudret, Mike McClure, Bob Hasseman, Chris Lynch, and Brian Luse.

To our Indiana Bulls family, with special thanks to Dave Taylor, Steve Henke, Scott and Nikki Rolen, Todd Rolen, and David Mundy. Special recognition goes to two of the finest coaches and people anywhere in Dennis Kas and Craig Grow and to the many families and teammates that spent time with Daniel and our family while traveling with the Bulls.

To the University of Dayton baseball program, with special thanks to Coach Vittorio and the team for always including Daniel and for taking extra special care of Jeffrey at a very difficult time.

To Kathy Howard, my good friend, whose editing and guidance helped this book come to fruition.

Lastly, I want to acknowledge the four most important people in my life. To my wife Pam, who was the strength of our family during this ordeal. I love you very much. To my boys Jeffrey, Joe, and Anthony for dealing with the many obstacles which befell you and for loving your brother with all your heart. Your mom and I are so proud of you.

1. My Son Daniel

"A life is not important except in the impact it has on other lives. "

– Jackie Robinson

The journey upon which you have just embarked is one filled with disappointment but not consumed by it, full of heartbreak but not ruined by it, and fraught with emotional distress but not destroyed by it. This is a story of one very special young man, his family, and the finest supporting cast that God ever placed upon on this earth.

"DANIEL!!! Bring the gloves back! What are you thinking? We have a ballgame to play here!" It was 1993 and I was coaching the Indiana Bulls 16-year-old baseball team. The Bulls are one of the country's finest travel baseball organizations, and we were in Detroit, Michigan, playing in a summer tournament. We had just finished our at bat in the 5th inning when I noticed our centerfielder, Brian McMillin, hadn't taken the field. "Brian," I said, "hustle out!"

He said, "Coach, I can't find my glove."
"What do you mean you can't find your glove? You were in the dugout. Where could it have gone?"

"Coach? I can't find my glove either," said Eric Riggs.

"Good lord, fellas, you all were in the dugout while we hit, so how can all your gloves be missing?"

Then I saw the umpire heading my direction. "Hey, coach, let's get your team out there. We have another game after this one."

It was at about that time that my assistant coach Emmitt Carney said, "Jeff, take a look over there." Some 40 feet behind the backstop were my six-year-old son Daniel and 4 or 5 little boys from Detroit playing a ballgame. You guessed it. They were fully outfitted with gloves from half of my starters. How that little rascal slipped into the dugout, took the gloves, and slipped out with no one seeing him is beyond me. I was so mad yet had to chuckle that Daniel had found a creative solution to providing new friends with gloves so that they could play ball like the big boys. I must have known then and there that the fun was just beginning.

There's nothing particularly special about our family aside from the fact that my wife Pam and I have been blessed with four fine sons. The boys are all very different with unique likes, dislikes, and personalities. Our oldest, Jeffrey, is mature and wise beyond his years, an ideal oldest child and one that each of the others can model. Joe is quiet and reserved and rarely puts his feelings on display. Anthony is a kind little fella, forever inquisitive and always on the go. And then, there's Daniel. Daniel is our second oldest and a true "piece of work." This story is about him and I hope you will enjoy getting to know him as much as I did.

Fun he was. Daniel never met a stranger, was never afraid to live life to its fullest, and was simply one of the most entertaining young people I have ever known. It was as if in some strange way he knew he would be on this earth for just a short time, and by golly, he wasn't going to miss out on a thing. In addition to his fun-loving personality, Daniel was absolutely committed to achieving excellence. As a little boy he reveled in showing Pam and me how well he could read, or color, or swing a baseball bat. He was forever commanding our attention so that we could validate his accomplishments. Despite this somewhat annoying tendency, I have to admit he was quite talented, especially in athletics. Pam and I were both college athletes, so his love of sports came honestly, but Dan seemed to elevate that love to a higher level. He could compete easily with older boys, and in fact excelled. It was as if he was on a mission to prove to himself, and to us, that he could achieve the highest levels of excellence in all phases of his life.

Daniel Patrick Mercer ("D") arrived in this world on May 21, 1987, 22 months after his older brother Jeff. I vividly remember that as a little boy he was unwilling to lay his head on my shoulder, even when he was so tired he couldn't keep his eyes open. It was instantly apparent that he was strong willed and stubborn. He had a mind of his own that seemed to frequently frustrate his father...much to his delight, I think. It was that same willful young man that eighteen years later would guide an entire community to seize the

Daniel at First Communion
(2nd grade, St.Rose of Lima Church)

moment, love like there is no tomorrow, and never ever give up.

"Dad?"

"Yes Daniel?"

"What time is it?"

"It's 6:30."

"Dad?"

"Yes Daniel?"

"How long until we're home?"

"Probably an hour."

"Dad?"

"Whaaaat!"

"Did you know that the tallest man ever was Robert Wadlow?"
"No, I didn't D."

"Yep, he was 8' 11"and he died from an infection in his foot. His shoes were too tight. Dad?"

"Whaaat honey?"

"Do you think my shoes are too tight?"

"I don't know. Do they feel tight?"

"Not really, I just don't want to get an infection in my foot."

"I don't think you need to worry about that, Daniel."

This type of exchange took place on virtually every car ride. Sometimes Daniel would repeat "dad" before I even had a chance to acknowledge his first request. So frustrated, I once counted the number of dad's that came from his little mouth, and at the 75 minute mark of a ride home from Grandma's, he had uttered the word dad 86 times. That must have set some sort of a record. Yeah, I'm sure it did. A new Guinness category and one which Daniel would have memorized. Dan loved to memorize the statistics off the back of baseball cards and the incredible but true Guinness Book of Records. For a little guy all of 6 or 7 years old, it was pretty impressive that he could recall facts to the smallest detail. My only concern was that he was determined to share all of them on each and every car ride.

As Daniel grew, he maintained that drive to impress. He evolved from being a walking encyclopedia of facts to being obsessed with excellence in athletics.

"Dad?"

"What Daniel?"

"Can we play catch?"

"D, we just played catch a little bit ago."

"I know, but I'm ready to play again."

"I know you're ready, but I've got some other things to do."

"Like what?"

"Like a bunch of other things."

"Like what other things?"

"OK, I GIVE…I'll play catch."

On and on it would go, day after day. Oh, lest you think I didn't enjoy his love of sports, I was quite proud of that and of his skill, especially in baseball.

Daniel at age 3
(note the coonskin cap and
cowboy "boot")

Participating in baseball in the Mercer family is kind of a foregone conclusion. Beginning with my father Roger, baseball has been the athletic cornerstone of our family. I played in both high school and college and by the time I reached the end of my college career, I had decided to stay in the game through coaching. This love of baseball led me to a coaching career at the high school and college levels, and it also led to my establishing the baseball training industry in Indiana. In the early 1990's, I was training baseball and softball players during the winter season. Daniel and Jeffrey, of course, were always somewhere near the facility we operated in Greenfield, Indiana. Daniel, however, was the one who attracted much of the attention. There he was, sipping on a fountain drink in his cowboy boots, a pair of shorts, no shirt, and a Daniel Boone coonskin cap. People from far and wide looked forward to seeing Daniel each week as they brought their sons or daughters in for their lessons.

Once he had his belly full of popcorn and soda, Daniel would retreat to the batting cage and, as my friend Ron Hounshell used to say, "commence to rippin' line drives" both right and left-handed. He was a talented little fellow who soaked up the atmosphere like a sponge. I've often thought, "What a great place for a little boy to grow up." Unfortunately for Jeffrey and Daniel, in 1995 I sold the business so I could become more involved in all their activities. Daniel cried. We continued our love of baseball, however, and we managed to stay very involved in the game.

In 1996 I was named the head baseball coach at Franklin Community High School in Franklin, Indiana. Our family was excited about the move as we had previously lived in Franklin when I coached at Indiana University. The boys were especially excited because they could hang out with the "baseball boys" at the high school. Pam would bring them by at the end of practice, and they would take ground balls and swing the bat...something they truly loved to do. The high school players were terrific pseudo big brothers and they made hanging around the field a daily adventure for Jeffrey and Daniel.

One of the highlights each season at Franklin was in taking the baseball team to Kentucky over spring break to practice and play in the nice weather. My boys would tag along for all the practice sessions and then join the ballplayers for the rest of the day. I'm sure the players weren't thrilled, but they were always good sports. In the afternoon we would give the ballplayers time to relax and have some fun. Accompanied by some of the parents, many of the boys would trek into the town of Glasgow, Kentucky, to take in a movie or visit the recreational park nearby. Some others enjoyed fishing at the nearby Barren River Reservoir. Jeffrey and Daniel were never ones to pass up a fishing trip, so one afternoon they tagged along with one of our parents, Steve Bowsher, and his two boys. Steve had a knack for catching very large stripers down near the dam, and the boys couldn't wait to take their chances at landing one of those huge fish. As you might expect, if Steve was catching big fish, others were sure to know about it and be fishing very near. This particular day was no different, and Steve and the boys were joined by several other fishermen. Across a small inlet was one such fisherman, who was obviously a grizzled veteran of many such fishing trips--so much so that he kept his fishing worms in his shirt pocket, a point which just intrigued Daniel. OK, you guessed it. Here he goes again. "Mr. Bowsher?"

"Yes, Daniel."

"How come that guy over there keeps those worms in his shirt pocket?"

While coaching third base during a fall league game one autumn afternoon I happened to overhear Daniel "holding court" as he so often did. He was spinning some wild yarn about how fast he could run. Normally, I do not hear what is being said or going on in the dugout when I'm coaching the bases, but the fact that I heard Daniel mention himself and fast in the same sentence, captivated his teammates and even caught my attention. To know Daniel was to know that among the many blessings and attributes he possessed, speed was not one of them. Daniel was boasting to a teammate, Ben McMurray, who is normally very quiet and laid-back, that he (Daniel) was the second fastest kid in his school. Ben looked at Daniel with a bewildered expression, and after a short pause said, "Yeah, if you're the second fastest kid in your school, then you must be home-schooled". Needless to say, the dugout erupted in laughter. I know that I missed the next three pitches trying to regain my composure.

— Ron Hounshell
  Daniel's baseball coach
  at age 11 and 12

"I'm not sure, Daniel, but try not to be so loud. He might overhear you."

"OK. Mr. Bowsher? How come that guy has such a long beard?"

"I don't know Daniel. I guess he likes it."

This whole time Steve had been baiting Daniel's hook in preparation for the first cast. As Daniel whipped the rod tip back to make the cast, Steve reminded him, "Daniel be careful where you throw it." Apparently Daniel wasn't listening because his treble hook flew through the air and burrowed itself deep into the beard of the man with the worms in his pocket. It was not a pretty sight as Daniel began pulling and tugging to free the treble hook while this guy was screaming obscenities at Daniel and Steve. Soon this exchange went from bad to worse, and Steve started yelling back. Thankfully, Daniel's new found "friend" was eventually able to extricate the treble hook from his scraggly beard, and Steve and the boys moved off to another fishing spot.

Have you ever known someone who manages to get himself into the most interesting and entertaining of situations? Daniel was that guy, even when he wasn't trying. The most enjoyable part of these experiences for me was in listening to Daniel and Jeffrey recount these Tom Sawyer like adventures.

"Dad! You should have seen that guy with the worms in his pocket. He was so mad he had tobacco juice coming out of his mouth, and he was calling Mr. Bowsher bad names. Dad? What's a son of a b _ _ _ _?"

"Don't worry about it, Daniel. How 'bout we don't share that one with mom?"

As you must have surmised by now, Daniel stood out from the crowd. He enjoyed being the hub of activity. He was most happy when surrounded by friends and family, especially when the spotlight shone brightly on him. Let me recall a story from a former teacher:

I was sharing the library with the music teacher due to our lack of space. My very first memory of Daniel was during his 3rd grade music class. I was sitting at my desk trying to get some work done. The class was singing and I heard this very loud voice singing above all others. Not only was he singing loudly and totally focused, but he was so OFF KEY! I looked up and saw this adorable little freckle faced boy singing so mono-tone and it was your Daniel. It just made my spirit smile!

— Debbie Lindsey

Many of Daniel's adventures, as with all of our boys, were intertwined with athletics. Daniel was a tremen-dous athlete. He began playing football at the age of seven and was very fortunate to have excellent coach-es in Bryan Stansbury and Jeff Moore. It was obvious that Daniel was following in big brother Jeff's foot-steps and would be quite accomplished on the football field. One thing that was particularly noteworthy was how hard Daniel would hit the other kids. He would run full speed and bowl over the would- be tackler or runner. That never came naturally to me, and I was always impressed with the fearless approach that each of the older boys took to football. As they moved into high school and had the opportunity to play together when Jeff was a senior and Dan was a sophomore, it was enjoyable to listen to them recount all the "big time" hits they had in practice. Daniel's very fine football coach and friend Dave Coudret didn't like to play sophomores at the varsity level. He would how-ever let them play on the special teams. Daniel took particular pleasure in "laying out" unsuspecting kids on the kick-off or kick-off return team. Pam and I, and eventually the fans, would just wait until near the end of the kick-off return for the time when Daniel would zero in on some innocent soul and then proceed to knock the kid three feet in the air, completely parallel to the ground. You just knew it was coming, and it would be quickly followed with an "OHHHH!" from the crowd. Daniel loved the spotlight.

As a junior and in his last sport season, Dan had a great football season. He led the entire Indianapolis area in tackles from his middle linebacker position until the last game of the year when he had to sit out

First year of football
(Greenwood Bantam Bears - age 7)

Daniel
(Franklin football during his
Junior year)

Freshman year of wrestling at
Franklin (189 lbs)

with what we thought was a concussion. It nearly killed him to stand on the sidelines while his team ended their season in the Sectionals. At the completion of the season, Dan was named All-Conference, All-Area, and Honorable Mention All-State.

Daniel also was a wrestler. While he hated the weight loss and preparation required, he loved the matches. He was 29-0 as a freshman on the Junior Varsity team and 22-8 as a sophomore on the Varsity. Franklin Community High School is renowned for its wrestling program, and they are regularly ranked in the top 10 in the state of Indiana. Sometimes the toughest matches were in the practice room at Franklin High School. The kids work so hard it is easy to understand why they were state qualifiers for eight consecutive seasons. Between Daniel's football and wrestling seasons, he lost 35 lbs. his sophomore year. He went from 195 lbs. to 160 lbs. just so he could get into the line-up. Franklin had state qualifiers at 170 lbs. and 189 lbs., so the only way to wrestle in the matches was to go to another weight class. Pam and I remember the agony of watching Daniel try to get down to weight. At 6'1" he just didn't look like he should weigh 160 lbs. It mattered not, as Daniel shot through nearly all of his opponents. Virtually every loss in his sophomore year was to a state-ranked wrestler. I can recall the apprehension that Pam and I would have when he would face a wrestler who was much shorter but appeared to be carved out of granite. It wouldn't be long until Daniel would have his opponent face down on the mat and in total control.

As a fitting end to Dan's wrestling career, his final match came at a pivotal point in the Team Semi-state Championship. Daniel was scheduled to wrestle an inferior opponent when the other team decided to move their outstanding 171 lb. wrestler to 160 lbs. This move was to avoid our exceptional 171 pounder, Jesse Hasseman. Dan's opponent was the 8th ranked wrestler in the state, and he looked very impressive physically. I remember sitting with my brother Tim and my Dad and thinking how proud I was to see Daniel rise to the occasion and manhandle his heavily favored challenger. The final score read 13-2. As Daniel later recalled, there is no greater feeling in the world than standing in the center ring and having the referee raise your hand in victory.

While he loved football and wrestling, Daniel's real love was baseball. He had played from the time he was four, and he just continued to get better and better. Consistent with his personality, he played catcher and occasionally pitched due to his strong arm. As a freshman at Franklin High School, he started every game at the varsity level. Given that I was the head coach, it was a very difficult decision to start my own kid in front of upperclassmen. I truly gave him every opportunity to fail before I reluctantly placed him into the starting line-up shortly before our first game. He rewarded my confidence by hitting .435 for the year. At season's end Daniel was named All-Conference, All-Metro South, All-Area, and the Hoosier Diamond Freshman of the Year in the state of Indiana.

Before Dan's sophomore year, I resigned from the Franklin Community School Corporation to take a new position with Franklin College, and he and Jeffrey played their final year together. Daniel was the starting catcher and Jeff was the number one pitcher. As parents and fans, Pam and I enjoyed watching the two of them work together. There were certainly disagreements, but we could just see the two of them becoming closer as teammates and brothers. Dan again experienced success as he and Jeff led the team to a 20-6 record. Jeff was named All-State and Daniel had his usual string of post-season awards.

In their final year together as teammates, one of the true highlights was in traveling and watching the boys

About to pin another opponent

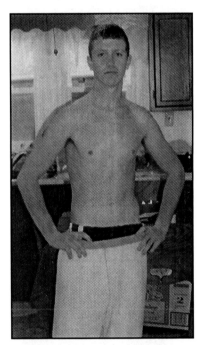
Sophomore year of wrestling at Franklin (160 lbs – too thin!)

My final year of coaching – 2003 (Jeffrey, Me, Daniel)

Daniel sends one on its way!

Their final year together in high school (Jeffrey pitching and Dan catching)

play in the summer. Although he was just 16, Daniel joined Jeff's 18 year-old Indiana Bulls team for the summer of 2004. The Bulls play at the highest level of competition throughout the United States, and they have sent scores of players on to college baseball and the professional ranks. You might recognize some of the names such as Aaron Heilman, Todd Dunwoody, Rob Bowen, Eric Bruntlett, and Scott Rolen. Interestingly enough, Scott Rolen would eventually play a huge role in Daniel's life. Once a Bull, always a Bull.

As the summer of 2004 approached, Daniel was slated as the number two catcher. The number one had been with that group for several years, and we expected Dan to catch the back end of doubleheaders and non-tournament games. Regardless, we were thrilled that the boys were together and had the chance to play for two of the finest baseball coaches anywhere, Dennis Kas and Craig Grow. As the summer drew near, the starting catcher decided he no longer wanted to play; and when he quit, Daniel became the starter. Coach Kas added a second catcher, but unfortunately just before the end of his high school season, he injured his shoulder and had to have surgery. At this point Coach Kas decided to roll the dice and go with one catcher...Daniel. A sophomore playing against all seniors. A tall order indeed.

Typically, in these types of summer travel team environments, each team will carry two catchers and rotate them every other game or every third game. In the hot, humid Indiana summers, it was virtually unheard of to use just one catcher, especially as on tournament weekends the Bulls would play 5 games in 3 days. In my 20+ years as a coach, I had never witnessed a team go with one catcher under these circumstances. But there he was, day in and day out, catching Division I pitchers Chris Fetter, Ryan Hill, Josh Volmer, and his brother Jeff. Coach Kas would ask him if he needed a break and offered to put someone else back there for a few innings. " Nope, I'm fine," he would respond, and on he would go. Over the span of 50 days, Daniel caught 40 games, culminating in a NABF Regional Championship in St. Louis, Missouri, and the NABF World Series in Jackson, Mississippi. Have you ever been to Jackson at the end of July? I thought Indianapolis was hot and humid. It was literally 100 degrees each day with 100 percent humidity. All the other teams were switching catchers every other game, and most were switching catchers in mid-game. Not the Bulls, and not Daniel. He caught every inning of every game just like he had all season. The Bulls' season ended with a loss in the championship game on a Sunday afternoon. Disappointed but not defeated, the boys had a great summer. In retrospect, it was more special than we could know at the time.

Best Buddies!
(Final Bulls season – 2004)

It was, to say the least, a "rich" experience in getting to know Daniel over the past two years through his participation with the Indiana Bulls. I had heard what a good athlete and tough kid he was. He did not disappoint. Daniel quickly put to rest any concern we might have had at losing our previous catcher. I remember vividly the comments made about his endurance at catching every inning the entire season. I especially remember the St. Louis Regional. It was exceptionally hot and Daniel played great defense, and of all the Bulls, it was Daniel who led the way with his bat. I have the two home runs he hit on tape.

I also remember Daniel hogging the front seat so he could control the tape player in the van. It was that summer I really got introduced to country music, especially "Save a Horse, Ride a Cowboy." There is one more memory from that summer that more than anything else impressed me greatly about your boys. We were at the hotel and all four of your boys were playing an adapted game of baseball in the pool. Between all of them they were rough and relentless in their pursuit of victory. However, off to the side was a young man with noteworthy mental and physical handicaps, just watching the game. I distinctly remember Daniel and Jeffrey asking the young man if he wanted to join in, which he did. All of your boys showed this young man great patience and respect for his condition. They allowed him to partici-pate, purposefully altering their game so this individual could enjoy himself when they could have just as easily ignored him. I was impressed by the character displayed by your sons that day more than you could know.

— Bob Rinearson
  the father of Alex Rinearson,
  one of the boys' Bulls teammates

At about 5:00PM following the NABF Championship game, I loaded all the boys into our van and hit the road. We drove straight through from Jackson to our home in Bargersville, arriving at about 4:00AM. At 7:15AM I awoke Daniel to take him to the first day of two-a-day football practice. It seemed as though we were always chasing our tails. At least until November 4, 2004, when life would take a decidedly different twist.

2. Faith, Family and Cancer

"Great occasions do not make heroes or cowards;
they simply unveil them to the eyes of men.
Silently and imperceptibly, as we wake or sleep, we grow strong or weak;
and at last some crisis shows what we have become."

– Brooke Foss Westcott

Thursday, November 4, 2004
(excerpt from my online journal)

Today my son Daniel was diagnosed with a brain tumor. Quite a shock, given that we thought he had been fighting a concussion from playing football. He will be operated on today to relieve pressure in his brain and to take a biopsy. Thanks to our entire community for your support. To be honest, I am braced for the worst. However, cancer has seen few opponents as tough as the one it will face with Daniel, our family, and this entire community.

It has been said that "a journey of a thousand miles begins with but a single step." On November 4, 2004, my son Daniel Patrick Mercer took a single step that would begin a journey sure to test his strength, courage, character, and faith down to the last fiber of his being. His family, friends, community, and the world came along for the ride.

Daniel's incredible journey actually began on November 3, 2004, with his confirmation into the Catholic faith. Confirmation is a momentous occasion for all young Catholics; although we didn't know it, for Daniel it held far greater significance. The ceremony was officiated by the most reverend Archbishop Daniel Buechlein. Some eighteen months later, the Archbishop would once again enter our lives, but this time under much less pleasant circumstances.

The evening of November 3rd began as it normally does for the Mercer family when we prepare to go anywhere: Pam running late, the boys squabbling, and Dad trying to corral everyone so that we could get to the St. Peter and Paul Cathedral in Indianapolis somewhere close to on time. The church was quite full when we arrived as families from St. Rose (Franklin) and several other parishes were there to share in the special evening. My boys were well dressed and handsome, especially Daniel and Jeffrey (who would serve as Dan's sponsor). Surrounded by his friends and confirmation partners, Daniel was particularly conspicuous, tall and well-chiseled with a huge smile and his trademark baby blue eyes. He seemed particularly happy before the ceremony began as he joked with his friend Adam Miller and Adam's brother Todd. Every occasion for Dan was an opportunity for fun, and this one was no different.

Although I'm not Catholic, Pam has made sure the boys have been raised in her faith. It was something that she and I had discussed prior to getting married, and I agreed that this is what we should do were we to be blessed with children. I have long admired her devotion to the Catholic faith and to making sure that our boys have a solid foundation in the church. This dedication, I am ashamed to say, came with very little help from me at times.

Jeffrey had also been confirmed at the St. Peter and Paul Cathedral just two years earlier, so I was not totally unfamiliar with the proceedings. This ceremony seemed to hold more significance for us since Jeff and Dan were reunited as sponsor and confirmed. Not quite three months earlier, Jeff had left home to pursue college and baseball (not necessarily in that order) at the University of Dayton in Dayton, Ohio. As Jeff and Dan grew older, they had grown noticeably closer, and tonight they seemed to be thoroughly enjoying one another's company. The ceremony was very nice and moved along swiftly. I remember thinking at one point how much Daniel must be enjoying his favorite church song, "Wade in the Water." The choir really cranks it up for that one, so Daniel always felt compelled to crank it up as well, much to the chagrin of all sitting near him.

Once the formal ceremony was complete, the newly confirmed and their families moved across the street to the Catholic Center to enjoy cookies and punch. We stayed for nearly an hour, and then decided it was time to head home, given that the boys had school the next day. Joe and Anthony were hurried off to bed well past their bedtime while Pam, Jeff, Daniel and I stayed up talking and laughing. At some point, as was frequently the case, Jeff and Dan began to roughhouse. Daniel picked Jeffrey up, all 215 lbs. of him, controlled him in midair, and placed him on his back in the middle of the living room floor as if they were on the wrestling mat. I remember thinking, "Uh oh, Jeffrey, I believe he has caught up to his big brother." We were all having so much fun spending time together, but soon it got late and we all headed off to bed

Confirmation on November 3, 2004
(8 hours before Daniel fell ill)

Adam Miller, Todd Miller,
Jeffrey, Daniel

about 11:00PM.

I quickly drifted off to sleep and remained that way until our bedroom door swung open at 4:30AM. I remember vividly Daniel on all fours. "Mom, my head is killing me." Pam and I, still half asleep, leapt out of bed to see what was wrong. Little did we know that this scene would replay itself scores of times over the next year-and-a-half.

I asked Daniel, "Where is your head hurting?"

"All over," he replied. "I think I'm going to get sick." Off to the restroom he scurried.

Pam and I quickly decided that she would take Dan to the hospital, and I would stay home to get the little boys ready for school. She drove quickly to St. Francis Hospital about 25 minutes away in Greenwood, and then she called me to say that they were taking Dan back to examine him. I hustled Joe and Anthony along and dropped them off at school. I was about halfway to St. Francis when Pam called. She was crying. "Jeff, the doctor says Daniel has a brain tumor." A brain tumor? How could that be? He was supposed to have a concussion.

My mind was racing, half in shock and half in terror. This couldn't be right. Last night he was body slamming Jeffrey in the front room and now he's totally incapacitated from the pain of a brain tumor? In retrospect it all began to make sense. Daniel had been forced to sit out the last football game of the season due to what we thought was a concussion. He had experienced some headaches and had been out of sorts in his last football game against Beech Grove. After the game our trainer, Marcus Davis, determined that Daniel had probably gotten his "bell rung" and sustained a concussion. Daniel was an outstanding middle linebacker, and for him to play below par against Beech Grove was completely out of character. He and I talked about it after the game, and he said, "I just kept getting knocked off balance. I must not have stayed in a good stance or something."

As I continued driving to St. Francis, I kept thinking, "Oh my God, oh my God, this can't be happening." I called Jeffrey, who had stayed at home, and told him he needed to get to the hospital as soon as possible. "Dad, what's wrong?" "Just be careful "J", but get here as soon as you can."

When I reached the emergency room and was led back to Daniel's cubicle, my first impression was how visibly upset Pam was. Dan was lying on the bed, asleep from all the pain medication they had administered. Pam and I looked at one another in disbelief. We were stunned. I can't even describe the emotion other than feeling as if someone had just hit me in the stomach with a ball bat. A few minutes later Jeff rushed in. "What's going on?"

Pam said, "The doctors did a CT scan and have found a tumor in Daniel's brain." Jeffrey immediately began to cry and ask if they were sure.

About that time the emergency room doctor walked in. He woke Daniel and told him, "Son, you have a brain tumor."

Football dinner
(Ben Gordon, Adam Miller, Daniel)

I thought to myself, "Nothing like slamming the kid upside the head with a 2 by 4. Couldn't he be a little bit more compassionate?" Dan didn't say anything but began to cry. Since he was little, I don't think I had ever seen him cry. Not when he was spanked, not when his team lost or he played poorly. Ironically, in the remaining eighteen months I saw him cry only one more time. I guess I cried enough for both of us.

The doctor recommended that we take Daniel to Methodist Hospital in Indianapolis as they were much better equipped to handle this situation. We chose to transport Daniel ourselves rather than take an ambulance because I knew it would be quicker. Dan and Jeff rode with Pam while I drove separately. I remember little about the ride other than calling my brother Tim to tell him the news and make sure he contacted our dad and the rest of the family. "This must be a nightmare," I thought. "Surely they can't be right. This is the healthiest kid I know. Even if they are right, Daniel will beat this like a drum. He can make it. He can do it. He has never allowed anything to whip him in his entire life. He's so damned tough and determined. He'll be a survivor. I just know he will. Oh God! This is not a dream. This is real, and it's my son. You have to be kidding me! Oh no! They'll have to open his head and remove the tumor, and this is the same kid that can't stand needles and mice. The toughest kid in Franklin but needles and mice render him an invalid. I've got to get to Methodist ahead of Daniel so I can ease him into the thought of needles. He'll be a basket case, but what can I do? This one is out of my control. For the first time in my life I won't be able to make things all better." I cried so hard I nearly had to pull off the inter-state. "Get it together. Daniel can't see me like this. If he thinks I'm afraid, he will go to pieces."

Pam and I helped Daniel into the emergency room at Methodist. I had taken each of the boys to the emergency room in Franklin at various times for broken bones, stitches, etc. This, however, was the "big leagues." There was a waiting room full of people with various ailments; I remember how cavalier the receptionist was as she listened to our plight. Just another patient to her, I'm sure. By this time his head was beginning to hurt again. It was taking what seemed like forever to get him processed. With our patience nearly gone, they finally called us back to the examination area. There were rows of cubicles and beds with people of all ages and illnesses. It was impossible to know how many more times we would come through those doors. I eventually grew to detest the emergency room, and if I never had to visit again, it would please me greatly. In actuality, emergency room doctors and nurses are special people. I have no idea how they handle the stress of that environment day in and day out. God bless each and every one of them.

Daniel was placed on a bed, and a team of nurses and doctors converged upon him. They were busy taking our insurance information, and I drifted into and out of awareness as if immersed in a horrible nightmare. The nurses took Dan's vitals and got him started with an IV so that they could administer his pain medication. Dan hated needles so I knew this was uncomfortable for him, but by now his head hurt so much that he gladly accepted the poking and prodding that accompanies an intravenous line. Soon the emergency room (ER) doctor came in and told us that they were intending to get Daniel comfortable and then transfer him to the PICU (Pediatric Intensive Care Unit). Dan was being assigned to

a neurosurgeon named Dr. Michael Turner. The ER doctor assured us
that Dr. Turner was one of the finest pediatric neurosurgeons in the
entire country and that Daniel would be well cared for.

I felt so inadequate. This new reality--ICU, neurosurgeons, morphine,
CT scans-- was so far out of my comfort zone that I felt totally useless.
Pam must have felt the same way. We were just hanging on for dear life.
It wasn't too long before the ER team had Daniel's pain under control;
he was drifting in and out of sleep. The worry on Pam and Jeff's faces
was evident, as I'm sure it was on mine. Nearly three hours after we
arrived, Daniel was transferred to PICU. He had a corner room with
enough space for two patients, but for the moment he was by himself.
As I walked down the PICU corridor, I was startled to see so many other
kids hooked to machines with tubes running everywhere. "These kids
are really, really sick. What are we doing here? Less than twenty-four
hours ago, my kid was the picture of health, and now he is on a ward
full of critically ill children." I came to appreciate the plight of the
many families we encountered over the next eighteen months. I would
see the "newbies" arrive with the same terrified, exhausted look that I'm
sure Pam and I displayed on November 4th.

It was instantly apparent that the battery of nurses on PICU was well
versed in stress-filled, highly critical situations as they shot into action
with Daniel. They quickly hooked him to machines that would track his
vital signs and slipped him out of his clothes and into the hospital attire.
The efficiency of this group gave us great comfort that Daniel's needs
were being met. I just didn't want him to be in pain, and right now he
appeared to be resting comfortably. I asked Pam if she wanted to go
downstairs to the cafeteria to get something to eat as by now it was well
after lunch time. She said she wasn't hungry. I concurred, and we sat
and waited for the next directive.

Through the door he scurried--Dr. Michael Turner entered, outfitted in
surgical attire complete with the light blue cap and gown. He appeared
to be very sure of himself and he was somewhat short in his assessment
of our situation. "I've had the opportunity to study Daniel's CT scan. It
appears that Daniel has a fairly significant tumor located at or near the
third ventricle. The tumor has grown to the point that the ventricle is
partially blocked and the fluid in Dan's brain is causing a substantial
pressure increase. That is what has caused his pain and vomiting." Dr.

Turner went on to say that he suspected the tumor was called a germino-ma. This is a fairly common type of tumor for someone Daniel's age, and while serious, it was far less serious than some other varieties. He did qualify his initial assessment by saying that to be sure they would need to perform brain surgery to relieve some of the pressure and secure a piece of the tumor in order to evaluate the type of growth. He said he would have a much better idea of Dan's situation after the surgery. "We'll schedule it for tomorrow afternoon. I'll be back in the morning to check on Daniel and answer any questions you may have." Just as quickly as he had entered, he shot out the door and on to his next destination. Stunned silence accompanied his exit. Jeffrey and I sat motionless, as if momentarily bewildered. Pam clutched a Kleenex and dabbed her moist red eyes.

Dan continued to drift in and out of consciousness as his "pure as the driven snow" system struggled to handle massive doses of pain killer. I thought, "What do I tell him when he wakes? How do I tell him that in less than 24 hours they are going to make a 2" incision into the top of his head and probe deep into his brain to extract a tissue sample?" As a small boy, Daniel had been hit in the head by the claw end of a hammer swung by his brother Joe. Dan had crept too close to Joe, who was attempting to drive a nail under the watchful eye of his Dad. Joe nicked Daniel's scalp. The cut appeared deep enough that I thought I should take him to the hospital. You'd have thought that I was suggesting a limb amputation. Dan instantly went into hysterics and absolutely refused to go to the hospital. At age 6 he was going to lose that argu-ment, but it took him and me nearly 2 hours and a trip to the Pizza Hut buffet to coax him to the emergency room. Twenty minutes and 1 stitch later, he and I were on our way, but the memory of that day came rush-ing back. "He may not handle this news very well."

At about 5:30PM, Dan awoke enough to speak to us. Pam said, "Dan, do you know where you are."

"Methodist," he replied.

"Yes," she continued, "and do you know why?"

"I have a brain tumor."

"Yes, honey, you do. Dr. Turner, the neurosurgeon, came in a little while ago and told us they are going to have to do a biopsy tomorrow." Daniel stared as if he didn't understand what Pam meant. She continued, "Dr. Turner is going to make an incision in the top of your head to relieve the pressure in your brain and take a piece of the tumor so they can find out what it is."

"Is that why my head hurts so bad?" Daniel asked.

"Yes, sweetie, the pressure in your head is caused by the tumor, and they have to relieve it or it will continue to hurt." Dan nodded as if he understood and drifted off to sleep.

Pam and I stepped out into the hallway and left Jeffrey with Daniel. "Look, we need to get ourselves together here and map out the next day or so," I said to her. We were interrupted by Deborah, the PICU desk attendant, who announced that Joe and Anthony were there with my brother and sister-in-law. "Thank you," I said. "Do you mind sending them back?"

Pam looked at me with those big brown eyes, which were obviously weary from the events of the day, and said, "What do we tell them?"

"We tell them the truth. We have no choice."

Soon the boys, Tim, and Karen made their way down the long corridor. I could see that Karen had been crying, but she was trying to do her best to hold it together. The boys both had blank looks on their faces, as if they didn't know what to think or feel, and believe me, I knew that feeling. Karen hugged Pam, and I retreated, without speaking, into Dan's room. Tim and the boys followed.

"Is Dan dying?" asked Anthony.

"Of course not," I replied. His little heart was breaking as he couldn't make sense of what was happening, and here I was--very little help--not really knowing what to say. Tim asked the normal questions, ones which I would become accustomed to answering over the next few weeks. "What happened"? "Are they giving you any indication of what it might be"? "How are they going to proceed"? I answered dutifully as if disconnected from the body which was answering. "I don't really know, he just woke up with a terrible headache". "The doctor said they will do surgery tomorrow to relieve the pressure and take a biopsy". "They should have an idea of what they're dealing with after that, but the doctor thinks it's a germinoma...common in kids Dan's age."

Deborah poked her head into the room, saying, "Can I see you and Mrs. Mercer for a minute?" She went on to say that the lobby was completely full and wondered if it might be possible for us to come out and speak to everyone.

I looked at Pam, took a deep breath, and said, "We really need to go out there."

"I'm not sure I'm up to it," she said.

"I know honey, me neither, but we really need to go out there." Reluctantly, we made the long walk while trying to determine what we might say about a situation that even we didn't understand.

The lobby for PICU is a narrow, rectangular room probably 30 feet in length and 15 feet wide. I swung the automatic door to face the group and couldn't believe what I saw. The entire room, and I mean the entire room, was packed with kids and adults from Franklin, standing shoulder to shoulder. Their worried looks showed their great concern. Dan's best friends, Emily Fox and Michael Reese, stepped forward. Emily fell into Pam's arms sobbing. It broke my heart to see her and the others so devastated, but I wasn't prepared to offer much in the way of encouragement. Twelve hours ago I was the father of four boys and just another face in the crowd in Franklin. Now, I was the face for an entire community and beyond. I'm not sure I fully understood at the time, but it wouldn't take long to firmly grasp that reality.

Many years earlier I had written a book on baseball which eventually led to the production of eleven videos. I became somewhat seasoned at being "on stage." That experience coupled with my teaching and coaching background had helped prepare me to handle the duties of spokesman for our family, a skill that would be tested over and over in both oral and written forms. I think I understood clearly at that moment how very important our response to Daniel's situation would be to our entire community. They were struggling for understanding just like we were, and it was our responsibility to provide hope for them and for Daniel. Pam and I didn't have the luxury of baring our emotions. I felt confident that I could do it, as that had been my approach through many years of coaching. Pam, on the other hand, was the wildcard. I had often thought over the years that she might struggle with difficult situations like this. The few unsettling circumstances that she and I had been thrust into over our twenty-one years of marriage had not gone well for her. Interestingly enough, she would prove "up to the task" over the next two years, and in fact was much stronger than I. My belief that a mother is the backbone of any strong family was never more evident than in our family.

Darkness came and went far too quickly, and before we knew it, they were prepping Daniel for surgery. He had been awake a few times during the morning, and of course expressed his displeasure with not being able to eat. Now that the pain was temporarily under control, his stomach was out of control. Despite his pleas, the nurses would not consent, and he was relegated to ice chips as a pre-surgery protocol. Pam and I had a few short discussions with Dan prior to his surgery. He was naturally concerned and asked us about the procedure. We tried to dwell on the positives and shared that this might provide some relief from the pressure in his head. In addition, we needed to know what type of tumor we were dealing with so that we could set about treating it. We related that Dr. Turner was confident that the tumor was a germinoma, a type of tumor that frequently just dissolves after it is removed.

"Who is Dr. Turner?" Dan asked. No sooner had I answered than through the door he came. Dr. Turner had obviously just come from surgery, still outfitted in his surgical garb. He gave the appearance of a brain surgeon. Bespeckled and studious, he both looked and acted the part, and at this point we were looking for any assurances we could find. Dr. Turner almost always came into a room with authority. Blasting through the door. A man obviously on a mission and with a short time frame. We would get a kick out of Daniel describing these entrances: "He would come exploding through the door with smoke billowing around his body. Hair net firmly in place with flames shooting from his mouth." It's understandable why Dr. Turner's presence would be intimidating for Dan. I'd be intimidated, too, if every time someone came through the door he was likely to cut my head open.

As Dr. Turner was finishing his conversation with us, two interns slipped into the room and waited until he completed his instructions. They had arrived to transport Dan to the surgical holding area. When Dr. Turner concluded, the interns sprang into action. "Hi Dan, we're here to take your downstairs, OK"? Unhooking monitors and the IV machine seemed like a brief moment before they were ready. "We're going to take him downstairs," the female intern shared. "You're welcome to come with us." We traveled down the hallway in stunned silence, my heart so heavy that I could feel each beat. The tension was palpable. We followed along into the elevator, down to the second floor (surgery), and into a holding room where we stayed with Dan for about 20 minutes. The anesthesiologist stopped by to introduce himself and explain what the procedure would be.

"Are you allergic to anything?" he asked.

"Only to needles," Dan joked. I found it incredible that he could joke at a time like this, but I think it was his mechanism for dealing with his stress and fear. It wasn't long until a nurse stepped into our cubicle and told Dan it was time to go.

To this day I retain the vision of the look on his face. It said, "Dad, can't you do something? I need you to make this all better. Get me out of this place." Tears welled up in my eyes as we said our goodbyes, and I watched as they wheeled him around the corner and out of our sight.

Dr. Turner had notified us that the surgery would take about two hours, so we made our way to the waiting area where we were joined by Tim and Karen and Mike Carter. I don't recall uttering a single word in the two+ hours we waited for news of the surgery. Paralyzed by the fear of the known and unknown, I sat slouched over, staring at the floor. "Mercer?" The desk attendant loudly called our name, and Pam went up to collect the news. The surgery was just beginning, and Daniel was doing fine was the message. I breathed a heavy sigh of relief, much the same as everyone else I'm sure.

Nearly two hours later, Dr. Turner emerged and walked briskly toward us. Heart in my throat I awaited what could easily be the most important conversation of my life. "Everything went fine with the surgery," said Dr. Turner. "He's doing fine and will be in recovery for an hour or so, and then we'll move him to a room on the 8th floor." The tumor was tougher to get to than we thought it would be, but we were able to get enough to biopsy. Our initial findings indicate it is not a germinoma. We think it's a PNET. I won't even go into the technical name, but it's not the positive news we were hoping for. However, the survival rate is still 60/40, so we have a fighting chance. As soon as the biopsy results are confirmed I will let you know. It will be sometime in the next couple of days."

We spent the next few days becoming acclimated to our new surroundings and allowing Daniel time to rest and recover. By Sunday afternoon, three days post-surgery, I made the decision that Dan had lain in bed long enough, and Jeff and I managed to get him up and literally drag him up and down the halls of PICU. His system, not at all used to massive painkillers, was rebelling, and he was moderately incoherent. Coupled with a dose of self pity, he was not a very happy camper. That attitude wasn't going to help us get better, I surmised, so Jeff and I won the battle and off we went. Fortunately, it seemed to work because by Sunday evening Dan was sitting in the lobby with his friends, eating White Castles and chatting. His friends were relieved to see him interacting again, and I think Dan was thrilled to be able to feel somewhat normal again.

The following day we brought Dan home for what would become the first of many return trips home. He seemed genuinely pleased to be back in familiar surroundings. A new level of appreciation infiltrated our entire family. For Dan it was just being home, and for us it was having him there in order to complete our family. Funny how we can lose track of things that are vitally important yet somehow take for granted. Quickly we were moving to a newly heightened sense of awareness and appreciation for the small things in life. The next day brought one of those small, or in Dan's case, big things. Scott Rolen (St. Louis Cardinals third baseman) and Dave Taylor both friends of mine stopped by the house to see Dan. The look on Daniel's face as Scott walked through the door was priceless indeed. It was terrific to see him smile and laugh again.

Our jubilation was short lived as Dan experienced the first of what would become a long series of setbacks. Early in the afternoon the following day, the incision in Daniel's head began to leak spinal fluid. We could track his heartbeat in the incision area, a good indication that intracranial pressure was beginning to build. Later in the afternoon the vomiting began again. Every time he would get sick the spinal fluid would spew from his incision, so we quickly determined that we needed to get back to Methodist. I have wondered if other families have experienced a similar phenomenon, but it seems as if any condition requiring medical attention always occurs on the weekend. Off we went to the emergency room driving, as fast as I could while helping Dan hold a bucket in which to vomit. The 45 minute drive seemed like 3 hours. Upon arriving at the emergency room, we once again encountered the "sit and wait" routine. I'm sure all of the patients in there felt their case was the most important, but this was my kid, and I just couldn't stand to see him in pain. Yet we waited and waited. Over ninety minutes after we arrived, they took Dan back. After our first few visits, this would become a routine we would know all too well: vitals, insurance information, endless medical history questions, multiple nurses and doctors making appearances and assessments, and finally the morphine.

For anyone who has had to experience an urban emergency room late on a Saturday afternoon/evening, you know how disconcerting it can be, but especially so for a seventeen-year-old kid who's scared to death. While we waited for Dan to be processed and treated, multiple car crash victims were wheeled in with two of them screaming and crying. In addition, a heart attack victim was in the next cubicle. The cubicles at Methodist consist of a paper thin drape, so aside from not being able to see what's going on, you might as well be in there with the person. Little is left to the imagination. I would eventually become somewhat hardened to this environment but never completely, and Daniel hated it.

After what seemed like hours, a neurosurgeon stepped into our cubicle. "Since Dr. Turner is not here today, I will be taking care of you tonight," the doctor said. "Let's take a look at what we've got here." I told him how the incision began leaking earlier in the day and that Dan had begun to vomit periodically. He said he thought we needed to re-sew the incision where it had begun to leak. Almost immediately he gave Daniel a shot of painkiller, and the sewing began. I know the painkiller had not had time to take full effect, but to his credit Dan didn't even flinch. No sooner than the doctor finished sewing than Dan announced, "I'm going to get sick," and headed for a restroom. A nurse pointed us in the right direction, none too soon. To my surprise, shortly thereafter Dan was released to come home, so I piled him into the car and we headed south down Hwy. 37 toward Bargersville.

Dan and I arrived home at about 11:00PM. We hadn't been there 30 minutes when his head began to throb again. Off we went, back to Methodist and a repeat of the earlier episode. This time a two hour stay in the waiting room preceded Dan's admittance into the emergency room. At this point I was nearly frantic. He was in such pain. I can't even begin to describe the sense of helplessness I felt as the hospital attendants seemed to work at one speed—slow--while every passing minute must have seemed like hours to Dan. They finally took him back and began the same arduous process: vitals, insurance information, endless medical history questions, multiple nurses and doctors making appearances and assessments, and finally the morphine. During this entire time, I just couldn't take my eyes off Dan. He never once cried out. He just went to another place in his mind, his defense mechanism to address the pain he was destined to incur. After a five hour ordeal, Dan was transferred to the 8th floor Pediatric Critical Care Unit. In the span of a few days, we had come full circle, and the "Angels in Scrubs" were waiting.

3. Angels in Scrubs

"They whom we love and lose are no longer where they were before.
They are now wherever we are."

– Saint John Chrysostom

"Hi, Dan. I'm Missy, and I'll be taking care of you today. How are you feeling?"

"My head is killing me," he said.

"OK, I'm going to check with the doctor to see what I can get for you." She was back in an instant to let us know that they were going to try Fentenol. This was to become Dan's drug of choice for nearly eighteen months and was one of the few painkillers that seemed to make a difference for him. At this point, nearly 7:00AM, Dan was totally exhausted from enduring the pain and not having had any sleep. He tried to sleep but the pain made it difficult. Over the next two hours, Missy stayed alongside Dan and worked to get his discomfort under control. By about 9:00AM she was beginning to win the battle. However, another problem had arisen…Daniel's temperature began to rise…100…101…102…103. Missy worked tirelessly in an attempt to gain control of Dan's fever. She tried everything. At about 5:00PM his temperature peaked at 103.1 and then began a steady descent.

Somewhere along the way Pam arrived and allowed me a couple of minutes to catch a nap. Meanwhile, Missy continued her relentless pursuit of comfort for Dan. During this time, unbeknownst to us, Missy had broken protocol and called Dr. Turner on this, his day off, and at about 6:00PM, through the doorway he came. Dressed in a pair of jeans and a sweatshirt, he had obviously been enjoying a well-deserved day away from the hospital. "Well, Dan, it sounds like you're causing trouble again," he joked. "Let's take a look at you." Dr. Turner was rapidly becoming a bastian of hope. It was so comforting to have him around even if he was the frequent distributor of bad news. He pulled Pam and me into the hallway and told us that the pressure in Dan's head was going to have to be relieved and that he was going to insert a metal rod into his temple through which a flexible tube could be introduced so that the spinal fluid would drain. He also told us he suspected that Daniel had contracted an infection in his brain, and he was going to take a culture to assess the type of infection. After a few minutes of preparation, Dr. Turner was ready to get started, and he performed the rod insertion right in Dan's room. Dan was so sedated I don't think Dr. Turner used much if any anesthetic. In retrospect, it didn't make much difference as Dan experienced almost instant relief. Within two hours he was awake and requesting food, and that was music to our ears!

Missy stayed through the procedure with Dr. Turner and then turned her shift over to another nurse. Their 7:00AM to 7:00PM work shift would be taxing on anyone, but especially so when working in highly critical and pressurized situations. Missy would become a good friend and trusted caregiver to Dan and our family, and as we were about to find out, there was a team of angels on our side.

Sometime later in the evening, an unfamiliar face joined us in Dan's room. "Hi, my name is Erica Short, and I am the social worker on the 8th floor. I'm here to help you with questions, concerns, or anything else I can do to assist." Erica had a friendly face and a calm, yet outgoing demeanor. We liked her instantly, and she became a wonderful sounding board, especially for Pam. Erica introduced herself to Dan and asked if she could do anything for him.

"Yeah. Do you think you could get me some Steak and Shake? I'm starving." Serious as he could be, I had to remind Dan that Erica wasn't our waitress and that I would be happy to go get him something. True to form for Erica, though, the next day she brought Daniel Steak and Shake: a patty melt and cheese fries with extra cheese, exactly what he had requested.

Little by little over the next few days, Dan began to feel better. The pain had begun to subside, and he started to display some of his personality and wit. On the third day in the hospital, he met his equal in Nurse Emily Parkinson. Emily was tall and thin with short red hair. She was perky and upbeat and always up to the "Daniel" challenge. They hit it off instantly and established a strong rapport. She was semi-fluent in all things athletic and could conduct a meaningful conversation with Dan about daily happenings in the sports world. She appreciated his sense of humor and gave as well as she received.

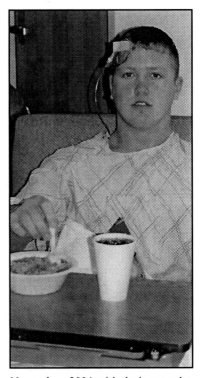

November, 2004 with drainage tube to relieve pressure

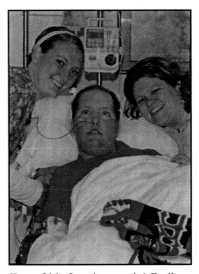

Two of his favorite people! Emily Parkinson and Erica Short in the late stages of Dan's illness

"Hey, Em, have you ever seen 'guns' like these?" referring to his biceps.

"No, I don't think I ever have," she would chuckle. "Let me see one of those biceps. It's time for your shot!"

"Oh, my Lord!" he would retort. "I hate shots. Don't you have something I could drink instead?"

"Nope, sorry. OK, you're going to feel a little stick."

"A LITTLE STICK? OUCH THAT HURT!"

"Oh, quit being such a weenie," she would say. Dan loved all his nurses but he especially enjoyed it when Emily was on duty.

Over the next couple of days it was determined that Dan did, in fact, have an infection in his brain. Chances are it came from the incision opening and leaking. Regardless, Dr. Turner placed him on two weeks of antibiotics. Pam and I shared time with Dan over the next several days. One would stay with him until the other could provide relief. We were reluctant to leave him alone even for a short time as the possibility of complications were always on the horizon.

Within a couple of days, Daniel seemed to be getting better, and we were so pleased to see him regain his appetite and demeanor.

Anyone who has dealt with the realities of cancer would likely concur that your life is no longer framed by days, weeks, and months, but rather by trips to the surgeon or oncologist for pathology status reports.
Though not even two weeks into Daniel's illness, two separate diagnoses had been shared: germinoma and PNET. We were about to receive a third.

Pam and I left Daniel's room early on Wednesday, November 17, to meet with Dr. Turner to discuss the pathology report from the biopsy. We suspected some sort of difficulty as it had been nearly twelve days since the pathologist had received the tissue sample. Surely it didn't take this long as a general rule? Dr. Turner had originally indicated that it could take 4 or 5 days, and even he had no explanation for the delay, or if he did, he wasn't sharing.

The sensation one experiences in anticipation of this type of news is nearly unbearable. The need to know is offset by the desire to turn and run. The first two diagnoses had been preliminary, based not on thorough research and analysis but rather on gut instinct rooted in years of experience. This new diagnosis, however, was based upon a litany of tests performed by the finest physicians available at Methodist Hospital. The awareness that these tests could unveil Dan's future was almost more pressure than I could stand. I felt almost physically ill as the nurse ushered us into a tiny room to await Dr. Turner's arrival.

As he entered the room, I could tell that the news was not good. His eyes diverted to the floor as he began to speak. "The initial pathology report indicates that Daniel has what is called an ependymoma. This type of tumor is very serious, and the long term prognosis is not good if it cannot be removed completely. Daniel's situation is complicated by the location of the tumor. It is buried almost in the center of his brain, making accessing it very challenging. In fact, I'm not sure that surgery is even an option at this point."

The tears began to well in Pam's eyes as they did in mine. The hope we had maintained when we entered the room had been replaced by hopelessness. Though Dr. Turner didn't come out and say so, it was apparent to me that Daniel had just been issued a death warrant. Short some sort of miracle, my son was beginning the final chapter of his life. How in God's name could this be happening?

While I observed Pam as she received this horrific news, there was no way I could understand what she was feeling. However, if she felt anything like I did, the sheer panic reverberated deep into my soul. Like any normal father, the love I feel for my children cannot be adequately captured, and now it appeared pos-

It was a normal day at work for me and Dan was one of my patients for the day. As he was lying in his bed, he seemed to be pondering something, just looking off into the distance…thinking. It was then Dan asked me a question I will hold in my heart forever. I had my back to him, getting his morning medicines together, when I heard, "Em, do you know anywhere I can get a good tattoo?"

"What? A tattoo?" I replied.

"Yeah," he answered.

"What on earth do you want to get a tattoo of?" I asked.

"I want to get a tattoo of all my family members' names over my heart so that they will be with me always," he said.

Tears began to stream down my face, the first time I had cried in front of Dan. It was an emotion that all of us nurses had hidden from him. When I turned around, he saw the tears. He just looked at me in a way that said, "I am okay, Em, I will be okay." It is that memory of Dan, his thoughtfulness and love for his family that is strongest for me.

Emily Parkinson
Methodist Hospital Critical Care Nurse

sible if not probable that one of them would be snatched from me. How could I respond to my own feelings of despair much less to those who depended upon me? Societal obligations dictated that I remain strong. At that moment, there was nothing about me which felt strong, nor safe, nor secure. For the first time in a long time, I felt completely alone. Sure, Pam was sitting next to me and loving Daniel just as much as I; however, she was of no help to me right then and I of no help to her.

Dr. Turner finished what he had to say, but I wasn't listening. He left the room in near silence except for Pam's soft sobs. I had nothing to offer but an arm around her shoulder. It was an embrace fraught with misery and total isolation.

In a shared daze, we made our way across the hospital to deliver the news to Daniel, who was awaiting the results. Along the way, we stopped and sat on a marble bench to discuss how we would break the news to him. "We can't take away his hope. We need to tell him the truth but also share with him that through treatment we have a fighting chance." Pam sat quietly and listened but did not respond.

She finally said, "I'm going to stop by the chapel downstairs before we go to see Dan. Do you mind waiting on me?"

"Not at all," I replied. "I'm going to take a short walk, and I'll meet you back here in fifteen minutes."

I arrived back at the chapel and waited for Pam to emerge. When she came out, she flashed a half-hearted smile and said, "When I went into the chapel, there was no one there so I went up front to the altar and knelt down. There was a bible there and it was open. It was opened to the Book of Daniel. God is watching over us." I nodded approval, and we proceeded to the elevator, pushed the familiar button "8," and began the short journey to a lifelong odyssey.

Dan received the news as he had all other times: quiet...reserved...reflective. I'm sure his heart was broken and he was scared to death, but he never let on. Erica made her way into the room as she had been awaiting our arrival. She had a keen sense of timing, always allowing just enough time for us to be alone with Dan but never too far away when we needed her. Brooke Smalley, Dan's nurse for the day, was scurrying around the room cleaning, organizing, and monitoring his progress. Because she was always smiling and cheerful, I was pleased that she was on duty this day as she seemed to brighten the mood.

I sat quietly next to Dan and observed the activity in his room like so many other rooms on the 8th floor at Methodist Hospital: parents, grandparents, brothers, sisters, aunts and uncles shuffling in and out with the same look of despair that must have covered my face. It seemed as if we were all living someone else's life. I had read about things like this but had never been faced with anything similar either personally or from afar. I spent a lot of time contemplating how we might respond to the insanity, and while the answers were not at all clear, there was an overwhelming awareness that we weren't in this alone. At the end of the day-- when family, friends, and colleagues had long since retreated to the security of their own surroundings-- we were embraced by the kindness and compassion of the "Angels in Scrubs." Special indeed are those who can forsake their own sanctuary to immerse themselves in someone else's pain and anguish.

The next several days found us by Dan's side. Each of us attended to our work responsibilities as we could, but in large part we devoted ourselves to Daniel's needs. Through it all, our newly found friends and confidants at the hospital were there to provide sympathy, advice, comfort, a kick in the fanny, or anything else we might have needed.

Daniel was somewhat the oddity on the pediatric ward. He was 17 when he fell ill, and the age maximum on the ward is 18. Naturally, he was the oldest patient and one with whom the nurses could converse. His wit and personality began to win over each of them. Frequently, those who weren't assigned to his case on a given day would stop in during their break just to check on him. "How are you doing today, Daniel?"

"I'm as good looking as ever." After a good chuckle and a five minute conversation, they would be on their way back to their respective patients. Ever the social butterfly, Daniel enjoyed the attention and looked forward to the distraction created by lots of nurses. While we were reeling from the news of the diagnosis, it was really nice to see Daniel's attention deflected, if only briefly.

Early in the morning on Tuesday, November 23, Dr. Turner stopped in to see Daniel, as he did nearly every day. After speaking with Dan, he called Pam and me into the hallway and announced that he, in consultation with his partners, had determined that they felt they could get to Dan's tumor. My heart raced! He went on to explain that rather than enter the brain from the top, they believed they could go in through the back of his head, up and over the cerebellum, and into the third ventricle area. The surgery would be highly difficult and very risky but the alternative (to do nothing) was far worse. We were elated with the news and thanked him profusely. "The surgery is planned for the day after Thanksgiving at 10:00AM," he stated as he moved down the hallway.

Pam and I looked at one another and uttered a collective "Thank God." We hustled back into the room to share the good news with Daniel.

Over the next two days, we experienced a wide range of emotions with Dan. The thought of a surgery of this magnitude petrified him and us, as one could expect. A huge advantage for us arrived the day before when Jeffrey came home for Thanksgiving. Jeff spent the next couple of nights alone with Daniel. Pam and I decided that the two of them probably needed some time apart from the rest of us. Dan would open up more and share his feelings, and Jeff would be there to assist, guide, and advise. Our strategy seemed to work as Dan's spirits were better by the 24th. He issued a mandate that he would be having Thanksgiving the next day and preferably at home. Well, the part about having Thanksgiving at home wasn't going to happen, but we could certainly bring "home" to Daniel. So, the next day saw both my family and Pam's hosting a huge Thanksgiving dinner in an unused conference room arranged, of course, by the nurses on the ward. The room wasn't really available for those types of events we were told, but "What the hospital administrators don't know won't hurt them," according to the nurses.

Daniel had a great Thanksgiving Day enjoying his grandparents, aunts, uncles, and cousins. He loved nothing more than being with his family, especially after he fell ill. I think he sensed that each one of these events might be the last, so he wanted to soak up all he could. He hung in there until he was totally exhausted and, with the help of the nurses, we returned him to his room for what promised to be a short night.

Daniel was awake by 7:00AM. Pam, Jeff and I took turns taking showers to prepare for the long day ahead. Dan was not allowed to eat prior to surgery, so of course he was grumbling somewhat, but I suspect as much as anything to distract himself. Mike Carter arrived shortly before 8:00AM and brought along a copy of The Daily Journal (our local paper). Upon the front page was a picture of Daniel and an article written by Sherri Coner. Dan picked up the paper and began reading. He wasn't a third of the way through the article when he began to cry and put it down. It broke my heart to see him upset. At times like this I just wanted to shout out, "God, why must he go through this? Please let me take his place!" Unfortunately, this was Daniel's journey and no amount of pleading would change that.

We were all doing our best to maintain our composure when Dr. Turner stepped into Dan's room. "Well, we're all set downstairs. They'll be coming to get you in a few minutes. Dan, let me explain to you how this will work. They will take you to the surgery prep room and shave small circles into your hair. In each of those circles they will attach electrodes. Those electrodes will allow us to be guided in large part by computer. I expect the surgery to take between 4 and 6 hours, and then you will go to recovery before you come back up here to your room. Do you have any questions?" Dan shook his head no. "OK then, I'll see you all after the surgery." He left the room to com-

Thanksgiving at the hospital (November 2005)

plete silence. What to say? What to think? What to do?

Franklin football player prepares for brain surgery
(Daily Journal — Sherri Coner) 11/26/04

From around the corner, Daniel Mercer can be heard laughing with Jeff, his older brother. He's finished a morning shower and taken some time to shave. Jeff Mercer good-naturedly makes jokes about Daniel having only a few whiskers anyway. There is hardly a need for a razor.

Then Daniel steps out of the bathroom. He pulls an IV pole along behind him and climbs back into his hospital bed on the pediatric unit at Methodist Hospital. For a few moments, Daniel Mercer was a regular 17-year-old guy. A football player. A jokester, poking fun at his brother. But now, Daniel's head hurts again. A brain tumor causes the pain. He covers up with a football-patterned blanket from home. He asks a nurse for pain medication.

Daniel's brother has been sleeping on the roll-away bed against the wall. Daniel's friends visit every afternoon. They play football games together on a Playstation 2 near Daniel's bed. At least 20 students from Franklin High School shaved their heads to show support for their friend. But at night, when the hospital wing is quiet and lights are turned low, Jeff talks with his younger brother about his feelings and fears.

"I say things like, 'Are you worried about this? Are you scared about that?'" Jeff says. "I tell Daniel, 'You can give up. You can roll over and quit right here. Or you can make this a dog fight.'" Shortly after the nurse brings Daniel some pain medication, a hospital volunteer walks in. Daniel and Jeff bow their heads for prayer and accept communion with the volunteer. A while later, the family's priest, the Rev. Paul Shikany, stops by to say hello.

Two weeks ago, Daniel woke at 4:00AM on a Thursday with an excruciating headache. For more than a month, he was bothered by a constant, throbbing headache. He and his family believed the head pain was the result of a concussion suffered on the football field. As the pain intensified that particular morning, Daniel became nauseous. His mother Pam Mercer, a math teacher at Whiteland Community High School, drove Daniel to the emergency room at St. Francis Hospital in Indianapolis.

By the time Daniel's dad, Jeff Mercer Sr., dropped off Daniel's younger brothers,

Joe 14, and Anthony 9, at school in Franklin, Pam Mercer had stunning news. Test results revealed a dime-sized mass on Daniel's brain. "I drove 150 miles per hour to the hospital," says Jeff, 19, a student at the University of Dayton.

Heavily sedated, Daniel woke later that day. His family was gathered around his bed at the hospital. "I said, 'Why is everybody here?'" Daniel says. "And then the doctor came out and told me, 'You have a brain tumor.'" None of it seemed real, Daniel says. "You don't expect at 17 years old to have something like that come along in your life." Daniel says. "One day, you just wake up and you've got a brain tumor. It kinda hits hard."

Later that day, Daniel was transferred to Methodist Hospital. One day later, he underwent surgery to relieve a build-up of spinal fluid and biopsy the tumor. With an incision from the top of his head to his right ear, Daniel returned home a few days later. It was only after the surgery that he started to deal with the reality of his situation, Daniel says. But there wasn't much time to get settled back into his home. There wasn't much time to work toward accepting what he faced initially.

Twice, spinal fluid leaked on Daniel's pillow while he slept. Twice, Jeff and Pam Mercer rushed Daniel back to the hospital. The surgical incision was not healing as expected. Testing on the spinal fluid revealed that Daniel had a staph infection. Again, he was hospitalized. Last Wednesday, Daniel underwent another MRI. "It was really bad news," Jeff says softly. "Every time they did more tests, the news got progressively worse."

This particular cancerous tumor, called an ependymoma tumor, is extremely rare, says Jeff Mercer Sr., director of new program development at Franklin College. Because the tumor is located "right in the middle of Daniel's head, the doctors gave us no hope of getting it out," Jeff Mercer Sr. says. "The best chance you have is to get all of it out of there and then start zapping it."

By Tuesday morning, surgeons changed their minds. After discussing Daniel's case with other specialists and studying X-rays, "they realized the tumor was poking out enough that they could get it, " Jeff Mercer Sr. says.

Thanksgiving Day, Daniel's family members gathered at the hospital for a traditional dinner. This morning, Daniel Mercer will undergo surgery to remove the tumor. After a couple weeks of recovery time, he will begin chemotherapy and radiation treatments. "He's a fighter," Jeff says with a smile as he looks at his

Surprise birthday party for Dan
at the Fox's (May, 2005)
Derry Carter, Mike Carter, Daniel

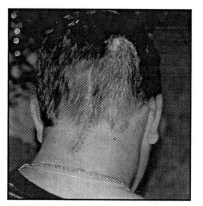

Incision to remove tumor and
another to insert Dan's shunt

brother. "He won't give up."

Mark Pieper entered the room just after Dr. Turner left. Mark is a good friend and one of Dan's baseball coaches. He had no more said hello to Dan than the nurses arrived to take him downstairs. They told us we could all go down to the prep room and stay with Dan until surgery. So within a few minutes we all started down the hallway, followed by Mike, Mark, and several nurses who were wishing Daniel well. Once we arrived in the surgical prep area, they began to shave circles into his hair. Aside from being painful, multiple circles shaved into your hair aren't terribly attractive and prompted Mike to suggest that Dan not pay for that haircut. A much-needed chuckle. Mike always had a way of making Dan laugh. The anesthesiologist came out and asked the required questions. Then it was time for Dan to go. So much emotion, so many tears. This could be the last time I would see my son alive. Everyone said their good-byes, and then I hugged him, told him that I loved him, and promised that Dr. Turner was as good as it gets and that everything would be fine. He nodded and the nurses took him away. Pained, I watched as he disappeared down the hallway and into God's hands.

Dan went to surgery at 8:35AM. It took until 10:00AM to get him prepped, and the doctors began work at 10:05AM. We moved on to the waiting room where we were joined by my brother Tim, his wife Karen, Joe, Anthony, and Pam's mom and dad. Every half hour or so the attendant at the desk would call out "Mercer," and Pam would go up front to receive the latest update. My mind tends to be at work virtually all the time anyway, but this day it raced through every conceivable variable and possibility. Few if any appeared to be good. I didn't speak. I didn't listen. I just contemplated. At 1:20 PM my meditation was shattered as they called Pam up front to tell her that Dan was out of surgery.

About 30 minutes later, Dr. Turner appeared through a set of doors to our left. He walked quickly, as if on a mission. "Everything went well," he said. "I was able to get the tumor down to the clear margins, but there was a portion that was wrapped around an artery. I had to be very careful or risk causing Daniel to have a stroke. We'll know more once we take another MRI. He'll be in recovery for a couple of hours and then they'll move him back up to the 8th floor." Dr. Turner's news brought great relief as at least Daniel had made it through surgery. At nearly 5:00PM they notified us that Dan had been returned to his room and we could go back up to see him.

Pam and I went back first and peeked into the dimly lit room which housed Dan. He was surrounded by a host of nurses who were making sure that monitors were working and that he was comfortable. Missy Etnier, one of his nurses, announced to him that mom and dad were there. He wasn't interested. He opened his eyes briefly...long enough for me to see that they were not working together. His left eye rolled down to the left while his right eye moved up to the right...all at the same time! It almost made me sick watching it. He was having great difficulty following the nurses' commands. "DAN! Can you move your right leg for me? Can you squeeze my hand?" It was a struggle for him to obey, though it was apparent that he was trying. His head was completely bandaged and his eyes were turning black and blue. He was obviously in excruciating pain; I just couldn't stand to watch. Pam and I moved up and down the hallway for the rest of the night, pausing to check on him periodically. Dan was sick from probably 5:30PM until after midnight, probably from the anesthesia. At about 9:00PM they were concerned that he had internal bleeding and took him for a CT scan. Fortunately, the results came back negative, and he rested reasonably well the remainder of the night.

Over the next two weeks, Daniel had his ups and downs. Good days followed by bad days. Increased intracranial pressure followed by another surgery to install a shunt designed to divert spinal fluid from his brain to his abdomen. Through it all, the nurses and doctors performed as trained--with precision, confidence, and compassion. In over thirty days, the "Angels in Scrubs" had become our lifeline, both for our family and for Dan. They treated Daniel as if he were one of their own, and they treated us as if we were family. God love each and every one of them!

4. Small Victories

"No individual is shaped by a single moment in time,
but rather we are sculpted by a series of thousands of small moments
when someone or something has influenced who we become."

– Jeff Mercer

I knew he was coming to visit. My good friend, Dave Taylor, had called me earlier in the day and informed me that John Theil, one of my former players at Indiana, and Scott and Nikki Rolen wanted to visit Daniel in the hospital that night. While it's always great to see Dave, John, and Nikki, the man of the hour was Scott. There was a purpose to his visit, and he carried with him a message--more appropriately, a mantra--one which Daniel and our family would come to live by.

Scott Rolen, raised in Jasper, a small town in southwestern Indiana, has gained fame as a perennial All-Star for the Philadelphia Phillies and St. Louis Cardinals. Many years ago Dave Taylor had arranged my initial meeting with Scott as he was preparing to arrive in the major leagues. A former Indiana Bulls player, Scott wanted to work with me on his hitting. The season before, Scott had been struck by a Steve Traschel fastball that had ended what should have been his rookie season. He was excited to once again get started and took this opportunity to have someone else critique his swing.

A relative unknown in 1996, Scott arrived in Franklin for the initial session. Jeffrey and Daniel begged to be there to meet a real major leaguer. "Dad, can we get his autograph?" Dan asked.

"D, remember he is here to work. Maybe when we're done he'll have a minute to sign your baseball. We'll see." The boys had done some research and knew that Scott was expected to be the Phillies next third baseman, and it was a big deal to have him here in our own facility. As instructed, they sat quietly for nearly two hours as Scott, Dave Taylor and I analyzed and worked on his swing. When finished, Scott took a moment to speak with the boys. He flipped his batting gloves to Jeffrey and signed Daniel's baseball. We would repeat similar sessions over the next couple of years, and we enjoyed watching Scott attain All-Star status.

One is instantly drawn to Scott Rolen. He is a physically imposing figure, quick witted, and extremely intelligent.

"Dad, did you see the guns (biceps) on him?"

"Yes, Daniel, I did. Now you see how much hard work goes into being a major leaguer," I stated. It's hard to teach 6'4", but Scott had worked incredibly hard to develop a physical presence that impresses even the most seasoned major leaguer. Fortunately for our family and Dan, being a Hall of Fame caliber baseball player is but one part of what makes Scott Rolen a special person.

In 1999 Scott tagged along with teammates Rico Brogna and Kevin Sefcik as they visited the cancer ward of the Temple Children's Hospital in Philadelphia. Although the children they visited were terminal, these players were not greeted with despair and illness. They were greeted with smiles and appreciation. According to Scott, something magical happened in each room. For 20 seconds, 2 minutes, 10 minutes, that child was not ill. Physically, yes. Emotionally, no. There was hope in those rooms. Scott knew instantly he was called to "make a difference" in the lives of those he could touch. Shortly thereafter, he and his wife Nikki founded the Enis Furley Foundation and Camp Emma Lou. The vision of the foundation and its many programs is to bring joy and happiness into the lives of very sick children. Without fanfare, Scott hosts scores of children and their families each year when they visit the Cardinals ballpark. He brings them onto the field before the game to live out what will surely be an unforgettable dream. As if they didn't know who he was, he starts, "Hi, I'm Scott Rolen, and I'm so happy you could come," he would say to the frail little boy standing before him. "Let me introduce you to Albert Pujols," or Tony LaRussa, or any other player or coach he could corral long enough to make this day even more special for the child.

It was December 14th and here he was, at Methodist Hospital, just to see Daniel. His 6'4" 240lb. frame filled the doorway. Tears filled my eyes as the look of astonishment spread across Daniel's face. "Hi Daniel," Scott said. "It's good to see you again. Your dad tells me that you've not been feeling well, and we wanted to visit and tell you how much we've been thinking about you."

Stunned, Daniel didn't really know what to say. "Thanks, Scott," was all he could utter.

When Dave Taylor had called earlier in the day to tell me that Scott and Nikki would be visiting, he asked if there was anything special Scott could do to cheer up Dan. I seized this opportunity to work on Daniel's mental state. He had been struggling. Shortly removed from major brain surgery, Dan had become quite discouraged. The 7" incision down the back of his skull and the horseshoe-shaped cut on the back right of his head where they inserted a shunt to divert spinal fluid to his abdomen were nothing compared to the emotional scars--the awareness that he would never again snap his helmet in anticipation of that next big hit on the football field, never again don the "tools of ignorance" and squat behind home plate set to receive a 90 mph fast-ball, so much a part of his life and now just a distant memory.

I noticed in Scott's left hand what appeared to be a jersey. Scott sat down on the side of Dan's hospital bed and began to talk. "I brought this for you," he said, extending the Cardinals jersey. "I had to sneak this out of the clubhouse," he joked, "and I wanted you to have it." A little more than a month earlier and pre-illness, Dan and our family had enjoyed watching Scott and the Cardinals compete in the World Series. Despite losing the Series 4 games to 0 to Boston, we were thrilled that Scott had this experience. As I watched Scott hand the jersey to Dan, I thought back on a much happier time, a time without cancer, without surgery, and so full of hope and promise.

Daniel and Scott Rolen

"Thank you very much, Scott," Daniel said, and he held it up to look at it. "Rolen" was on the back, and as he turned it to look at the front, I noticed letters etched in black marker: "Daniel…Small Victories…Stay Strong."

I had shared with Dave in our conversation earlier that Dan had been really down. "I can hardly get him to eat, and he won't get out of bed to do his exercises like the doctor wants. We should have been home three days ago! It's almost as if he's given up, and that is so unlike him."

Dave said, "I'll make sure Scott knows, and I'm sure he will address that."

Address it he did. "Daniel, how about taking a walk with me?" Scott said.

"OK," Dan replied as he swung his feet down onto the floor.

"Wait a second, Bud," I said to him. "Let me unplug your IV machine." Truthfully, I was scared that Dan would fall and hurt himself due to his weakened state and/or poor equilibrium, but I was also overjoyed that he willingly complied with Scott's request. It took what seemed to be forever to get him prepped to leave his bed, to unhook the IV machine, to organize the endless supply of tubes and cords, to put on his hospital socks, to give him a small dose of morphine through his intravenous line, to disconnect his vitals monitor so as not to set off the alarms. (OOPS. Too late.) Several of his nurses came in, alerted by all the commotion and the beeps emanating from his monitor. He assured them that he was fine. Slowly but surely we made it out into the hallway. Scott walked next to Dan, holding his right arm to help steady his gait. I tagged along, pushing his IV machine and listening intently to what Scott shared with him.

"Dan, did you read what I wrote on the front of the jersey?"

"Yeah," Dan responded, "small victories and stay strong."

"That's right, and let me tell you what that means. It means you have to celebrate all of the small victories you have each day." He went on to say that sometimes when faced with the challenges, we have a tendency to dwell on the things that have been taken away. "I challenge you to be proud of all the small victories you are achieving each day." I could see Dan soaking in everything Scott said, and knowing him the way that I do, I could tell he was really contemplating the message. "You've been dealt a tough hand, and yet you aren't complaining. You have a family that loves you; nurses and doctors that are well trained to take care of your situation; you are still able to do your rehab and regain your strength; you have a great deal to be thankful for."

Each floor at Methodist Hospital is designed in a square. The goal each day with Dan was to coax him to make several laps to help him regain his strength. Until Scott arrived, the most we could wrangle was one trip around the square. This had gone on for several days, but this night would be different. Before we knew it, Dan had made four trips around the square under his own power. He was so captivated by Scott and his message that I think he lost track of the "small victory" he had just achieved. As we made it around the last corner, I could see Dan was beginning to wear down, but I also observed how hard he was trying to finish strong. We made a right turn into his room and plopped him down on his bed. We were now joined by his nurses who had watched with interest as Scott motivated Dan to do something he had not pushed himself to do. They snapped into action, reconnecting his tubes and monitors as Scott finished his visit.

Scott said, "I want you to regain your strength, and once our season starts, I want you to bring your family to St. Louis for a game. How does that sound?"

"That sounds great," Dan replied.

Scott shook his hand, as did the others, and out the door they went. I stepped out into the hallway and thanked them all for taking time to visit. "This meant more to Dan than you can know," I said. I silently hoped that I was correct.

I spent the night with Dan, sleeping on a cot in his room. We talked about how neat it was that Scott would come in just to see him. I could tell he was reflecting on the significance of the visit because he was unusually quiet for the remainder of the evening.
11:32...1:27...2:40...4:15...with each passing hour an alarm would sound or the nurses would come in to take his vitals. Whoever said the hospital is a restful place has never spent time in one. At about 7:30AM Dan was wide awake. "Dad?"

"Yes, honey?"

"Do you think I could have some breakfast?"

"Absolutely!!! What would you like?"

"I'd like six pieces of bacon, some Rice Krispies, a sausage biscuit with cheese, and some milk."

"You got it!"

Excitedly, I called in the order. It was the first time in days he had expressed any interest in eating. I was even more excited to watch him "wear out" that breakfast. Soon, Dr. Turner burst through the door as he did most days. " Well 'Dan the Man,' how do we feel this morning?"

"I actually feel pretty good," Dan replied.

"That's great. How about going home today?"

"Do you think I'm ready?" Dan asked.

"You look good to me," said Dr. Turner. "I'll have the nurses get the paperwork started. Let's get you out of here." That was certainly music to my ears. It became such a blessing each time we were able to bring Daniel home.

I must admit, I was just flabbergasted. Not even twelve hours earlier Daniel had been discouraged, disappointed, and maybe even defeated. In steps Scott Rolen, and Dan does an about-face. He became determined, resolute, even enthusiastic about heading for home.

"Hey, Dad? Do you think we could go to Chicago's Pizza on the way home?"

"Are you serious, D?"

"Yeah, why wouldn't I be?"

"Well, you just haven't seemed interested in doing much eating lately," I said. "Let's see how you feel on the way home." I quickly stepped out into the hallway to call Pam who was at school working. "Dan's coming home," I eagerly shared.

"You're kidding!" said Pam. I could sense her getting emotional over the phone.

"I'll let you get back to class, but I just wanted to let you know. By the way, we're going to stop by Chicago's Pizza on the ride home."

"I don't believe it!" she said.

"Me neither," I replied.

As is typically the case, it took forever to get checked out of the hospital, so we weren't able to leave until nearly 11:00AM. Several nurses stopped by to wish Daniel well. They were always so supportive and kind to Dan and our family. It was as if we were part of their family, and they were part of ours.

I pulled the car around to the front of Methodist, and Nurse Andy Bullock brought Daniel down in a wheelchair. We eased him into the car, thanked Andy, and were on our way. I purposely drove slowly at first, checking to make sure the jostling wasn't hurting Daniel's head. He assured me he was fine, so we picked up the pace. Soon, I wheeled into the Chicago's parking lot in Bargersville. I came around to Daniel's side to help him out. "Are you sure you want to do this?" I asked. "I want to make sure we're not overdoing it."

"I'll be fine," he said.

I helped Dan across the parking lot and through the door. As soon as we entered, most of the patrons turned to see Daniel. While we knew few of the customers, most of them knew of Dan. They had read about him or heard of his story from someone else. This was really the first time I had been out in public with him since he fell ill, and it was an odd feeling to have everyone stare at us. Dan took it in stride, though, and he eased into a booth. "Tell me what you want, D, and I'll get it for you."

"OK. I want 3 breadsticks, 2 pieces of cheese pizza, and some cheese sauce...don't get the hot kind."

As I departed for the buffet line, I noticed Petunia Daylily (a name that Dan actually coined for her, but in reality, a Chicago employee whose name is actually Rose) making her way to Dan. Rose is an elderly lady. Kind and gentle, she said to him, "I've been following your progress and praying for you every day." They talked for a moment, and when she departed, she said, "I love you, Dan."

He said, "I love you too." I was touched by their affection for one another, especially given that Dan had been a handful for Rose over the years. Dan and Michael Reese would stop in during football or wrestling season, eat from the buffet, sleep in a booth for an hour, wake up and start eating all over again. It's a wonder the owners or Petunia didn't kick them out, but that's the beauty of a small town in Indiana where they know you and care about you. Now, in his hour of need, the folks at Chicago's really cared about him. They would periodically send gift certificates for him to use, or when someone would stop by to pick up a pizza for Dan, the manager wouldn't charge them. Special folks.

I have always been proud of each of my boys. Each of them has a unique blend of traits that make him special in his own way, but none of them had ever been tested in the way that Daniel was being tested. He had now endured three brain surgeries, weeks in the hospital, excruciating head pain, enough needle sticks to qualify him for "pin cushion" status, and emotional upheaval beyond comprehension. But here he was at home, feeling reasonably decent for the first time since he fell ill. Buoyed by Scott Rolen's visit, Pam and I felt it was time to again discuss his reality and the impact it was having on his friends and our community.

"Hey, D, let's talk a little bit, OK?" I said, "Let's discuss the reaction you're going to receive now that you're home and starting to hang out with your friends."

"I don't know what you mean," he said.

"Well, you haven't really been able to see firsthand all the things that people have been doing for you and for us, but when you get out with your friends, I don't want you to be surprised by the response. This is the first time that most of these folks have seen you since you got sick. They don't know quite what to expect or what to say. You need to put them at ease that you are still the same old Daniel, albeit with a 'reverse mullet.'" I frequently joked with Dan about the strip of hair they had removed from the back of his head to create the 7" incision. He was a good sport about it despite being very self-conscious. I went on to tell him, "You remember when we used to run the baseball camps for the little kids in Franklin, how all the little ones would run up to see you and the other ballplayers when you arrived? Well, I think when you get out into the community, it's going to be like that again. But I want you to remember that their stares and attention are merely a form of affection. They want to make sure for themselves that you're doing OK."

I could see Dan processing the implications. I said, "It's really important that you show great patience with everyone. You're going to answer the same questions over and over just like your mom and I have had to do. They all love you and are genuinely concerned. Just give thought to what you will say and how you will react." I suspect that Dan was well ahead of me and had already contemplated how he would be received. He had done a good deal of maturing in a very short period of time. I had noticed the ease with which he said "I love you" to each one of us and how he seemed truly happy to see us each day at the hospital. These signs were but a mere hint of the impending transformation.

Dan wouldn't have to wait long to live out our conversation as the next day he announced that he wanted to attend the home basketball game at the high school. While I knew it would tax him physically, I was so pleased to see him get back into his normal routine. About 6:15PM on Friday, December 17, we loaded the van with Dan, Anthony, and Joe and headed for Franklin. I pulled the van near the entrance and let Pam and the boys out and then pulled around to the parking lot to find a space. In truth, I knew it would take them a while to walk to the gym given Dan's condition, but more than that, I was afraid I would become emotional seeing him around people who had not seen him in six weeks. I had quickly learned how to anticipate my weak moments, and this was sure to be one of them. As I finally made my way to the building and entered, I could see the crowd beginning to grow around Dan. There were scores of hugs and handshakes and even a few tears. I could tell they were happy to see him but also devastated with what they could tell he had gone through. As we moved forward toward the gym, one of Dan's friends said, "Hurry, Dan, they want you in the gym."

With Pam on one side and me on the other, we entered the doorway into the gymnasium. Brian Luse (Dan's baseball coach and the PA announcer) came over the loud speaker and said, "Please join Franklin Community High School in welcoming back one of our own...Daniel Mercer!" With that, the crowd jumped to their feet and gave Dan a two minute standing ovation.

He looked at me completely bewildered and said, "Dad what should I do?"

I said, "Walk out onto the floor."

So slowly Dan made his way to center court, taking time to wave to hundreds of well-wishers, friends, and people who may not have known him personally but certainly knew his story. Dan moved to the scorer's bench as they played the National Anthem and was then greeted by the entire basketball team and coaching staff.

Anthony pulled on my shirt and said, "Dad, Mom cried the whole time Dan was out there."

"I know, buddy, I don't think she was alone," as I removed my glasses and wiped my eyes.

I made my way onto the court to help him to his seat. He was completely stunned. He looked at me as if to say, "I know you told me things would be different, but I didn't expect it to be this different."

Before he could speak, I said "How cool was that?"

"Pretty cool" was all he could mutter. We took our seat alongside our good friend Mike Carter, who was hurriedly wiping his eyes too. Throughout the game a constant stream of people made their way down to Daniel to offer their best wishes. He was taken back by the attention, and in reflecting on the moment, I think this was the beginning of an awakening in Dan that was to grow and deepen in him over the next year.

I remember one night after a Franklin High School basketball game that first winter when Daniel was diagnosed. We were taking Daniel home and everyone was coming up to him and shaking his hand or patting him on the back. We got into the truck and Daniel told us he should run for Mayor of Franklin. You know, I think he would have won.

Michele Fox
Family friend

What began as a "Small Victory" in making it to the ballgame, ended up being a huge victory for each of us. The feeling of acceptance for Dan extended beyond what we could have dreamed or he could have imagined. A sense of genuine love and concern was so apparent that even today people fondly recall "the night that Dan received the standing ovation." I think maybe this is what Scott Rolen had in mind, and undoubtedly was something that would fuel Dan as he now had a heightened sense of awareness for what he meant to this community.

"Home for Christmas"
by Sherri Coner (Daily Journal, Franklin, Indiana)

Maybe more than any other young person his age, Daniel Mercer knows the miracles of the holiday season. "Christmas was awesome this year," 17-year-old Mercer said from his rural Bargersville home. "My best Christmas gift was just being home."

In November, a rare brain tumor disrupted life for this Franklin Community High School athlete, his parents, Jeff and Pam Mercer, and his three brothers. Initially, Mercer thought the dull headache he experienced was brought on by a concussion suffered during a September football game. But the headache worsened. Emergency-room tests revealed the presence of a cancerous ependymoma tumor.

Thanksgiving Day was celebrated in a waiting room at Methodist Hospital. An aunt and uncle made the turkey, and more than 20 relatives and friends crowded into the hospital. The following morning, Mercer underwent a risky, four-hour surgery to remove the tumor, located near the crown of his head.

Nineteen-year-old Jeffrey Mercer slept on the cot beside his younger brother's hospital bed. Friends came to the hospital in droves with get-well wishes. More than 20 of those friends shaved their heads to show support for their buddy's challenge. Colored bracelets circulated around the school with Daniel's name printed neatly on each one, a reminder of his fight. And most of the time, Daniel's spirits remained surprisingly high, Jeff Mercer says.

But even the toughest of the tough get weary. Daniel began to tire from the constant excruciating pain of needles being stuck into the back of his head to draw fluid. He stopped eating. He missed being at school to enjoy his junior year. He missed being on the wrestling team. He wasn't sure whether he could play baseball when the season rolled around.

And then one evening, Scott Rolen, third baseman for the St. Louis Cardinals, paid Daniel a visit at the hospital. "Scott got Daniel out of bed, and he walked four times around the ward," Jeff Mercer said. Rolen also gave Daniel a signed jersey that evening, with a simple, inspiring message: "Small Victories." That's when he saw Daniel rally again, Jeff Mercer said.

Daniel began to joke again. He gained back the determination that temporarily faded. A day later, Daniel was in the car with his dad, traveling south. We were on our way home, and he asked if we could stop at Chicago's Pizza in Bargersville. A day earlier, this kid wouldn't eat." Happily, Jeff Mercer stopped at the Bargersville restaurant to share lunch with his son. But complications put Daniel back in the hospital for a few more days.

Ten days before Christmas, Daniel was home again, wearing his own clothes, including baseball caps, sleeping in his own bed and stretching out on the family couch in front of the TV. "I haven't taken my pain medication for three weeks, "Mercer said with a grin.

During the surgery, an optic nerve was moved, so the blurred vision Daniel is struggling with may be an issue for six months or more, Jeff Mercer said. "My balance is really off too," Daniel Mercer said. "But I'm getting stronger." "I was sleeping anywhere I sat down at first."

Beginning today, Mercer plans to attend school for half days until his strength returns. And in two weeks, he will have an answer for whether radiation and chemotherapy will be the next step toward treating what's left of the tumor.

"My faith is the most important thing through all this," Mercer said. "And my family's support; without them, I would have been God knows where."

5. The Heart of a Servant

*"Everyone is born into the world to do something unique and something distinctive
and if he or she does not do it,
it will never be done."*

– Benjamin E. Mays

"All right, Bud, have a good day. Remember, I'll have my cell phone on, so call me if you need anything or if you begin feeling bad. Do you have your medicine? Don't forget to give Mrs. Erick (high school nurse) your note of permission (to take medicine). How do you feel right now?"

"Daaad! I'm OK! I'll be fine! I'll see you this afternoon...I love you."

"I love you too, D."

I felt like I was reliving the day we had put each of the boys on the school bus for the first time. Today was Dan's first day back at Franklin High School in over two months. Obviously, I was much more concerned than he was. Or, at least he didn't allow it to show. Would his head begin to hurt? Would he get sick? Or worse, would the kids make fun of his appearance or his slow lumbering gait? His head nearly devoid of hair told a story of three major brain surgeries and the subsequent scarring. He wore his Boston Red Sox hat into the building but would have to remove it. While I'm sure the school would have allowed an exception to the "no hat" rule, Dan never asked. He would be facing this challenge as he did so many others...head on.

I wanted so badly to be a fly on the wall during Dan's first day back. The urge to protect him was very strong, yet I knew I had to let him fend for himself if he was to return to any sense of normalcy. Just short of 9:00AM, Pam made the first of several calls to me that day. "Did you go in with him?" she asked.

"No, I didn't but I really wanted to."

"Have you heard from anyone at the high school?"

"Not yet," I replied.

"Well, keep me posted on how things go."

"I will, dear." The same conversation took place multiple times throughout that first week.

Pat Hopper, Dan's guidance counselor, had become heavily involved in our lives after he fell sick, and she made it her special mission to keep tabs on Dan, which we appreciated very much. Pat and I had worked together when I was teaching and coaching at Franklin High School. She was a trusted colleague and good friend, and I knew she would take great care of Dan. When he arrived that first day, she had basically set aside her entire day to monitor and assess his progress. She had altered his class schedule to allow two study halls, one to study and one to rest. Dan would trek to the nurse's office nearly every day to lie down and recharge his battery. The long walk between classes took its toll on him, especially early in his return. He would come home each day completely exhausted. His teachers made every available accommodation as they desperately wanted to see Dan succeed. In addition, with Pat's guidance, the teachers crafted plans for permitting Dan extra time on assignments and projects. They also assigned other students to take notes for him and moved him to the front of the room so he could better see the chalkboard.

Dan's surgeries had adversely impacted his vision and to some degree his level of concentration. An unintentional consequence of his situation was the countless students who gladly stepped forward to assist. Any fears we had about how the kids would treat Dan were quickly dispelled. Aside from his good friends Emily, Michael, Ben, Adam and others lending support daily, other students (many of whom didn't even know Daniel prior to his illness) began to serve his needs. Dan later recounted a story about a girl who sat behind him in psychology:

"Some girl handed me her notes after class today."

"She did?" I replied. "That was nice."

Daniel was the most amazing and spiritually inspirational person I have ever met. Although I watched him grow up at the high school events, I really did not know him until he entered my Algebra II class. He looked much different then...no hair; his once athletic body was swollen and weak; he walked slowly with a limp; he had noticeable scars on his head; and he was pale. The mischievous twinkle in his eyes revealed his inner spirit remained unchanged.

— Ruth Heminger
Dan's Algebra II teacher

"Yeah, and she said she would give me a copy every time we have class."

"Is she one of your friends?"

"Nope, I really didn't even know her before." I shared with Dan that he was witnessing what we had observed for some time. The community was rallying to meet his every need.

That first week dragged on for what seemed like an eternity. I would drive past the school each day but always resisted the temptation to stop in. I did break down and call Pat several times. "How's he doing today?"

"He's doing just fine. A little tired, but other than that things are going well. Hey, I have to tell you what happened at lunch today. I happened to be standing near Dan during his lunch period, and one of his special needs buddies [Travis] stopped by to see him. He was so excited to see Dan, and he was equally excited to show off his new shoes. I heard Travis say to Dan, 'Hey, Buddy Boy (his name for Dan), watch this,' and he began to jump up and down to show Dan how high he could jump. 'And watch this,' Travis said as he began to sprint back and forth across the cafeteria. Travis was so intent on showing Dan how fast he could run with his new shoes that he completely ignored Mr. Nevins (Special Ed. teacher), who was in hot pursuit. Mr. Nevins finally caught Travis and led him out of the cafeteria. Travis was smiling widely and waving to Dan, and Dan was waving back and laughing uncontrollably."

Dan's illness seemed to generate in him a new appreciation for others, including his special needs friends. While Dan had a huge cadre of friends, many of whom were fellow athletes, he also found time for the children who were less fortunate. Once he fell ill, I think he viewed them as kindred spirits. Although I never asked him, I believe he now envisioned himself to be challenged. Frequently, Pat would find Dan in the Special Education classroom talking to the kids. I think it made Dan feel useful.

One such friend was a young man with Down's syndrome named Jamie. Jamie wasn't a student at Franklin High School while Dan was there, but he did travel with the football and wrestling teams to each of their games. Each day Jamie would ride his bike to the high school to hang out with Bob Hasseman (wrestling and football coach) and the athletes. He generally stopped by the weight room during the last period of the day while the kids were lifting, and Dan reveled in "pulling his chain." One such day in the spring Jamie stopped in during Dan's class. While Dan wasn't able to lift much, he did what he could and then spent time annoying others...namely Jamie. The weight room was small and lacked air conditioning, so nearly every day Coach Hasseman would have a huge freestanding, circular fan running in order to keep the air moving. Daniel managed to get Jamie positioned in front of the fan, and the fun soon began. Dan would get a mouthful of water, squirt a small amount into the back of the fan, and Jamie would get a blast of cold liquid on his back. He would then spin around looking for the culprit, but of course Dan had already stepped away from the fan and managed to conceal his involvement. Three or four such incidents and Jamie was getting upset. He began to complain to Hasseman, who was oblivious to the whole ordeal. Due to a bit of a lisp, Jamie was a little hard to understand, but upon the next blast of cool water, Jamie's message was crystal clear. "Hatheman, I'm thick of this thit." Hasseman, the entire classroom, and especially Daniel erupted in laughter!

Dan and his buddy Jamie Wilde

In truth, Daniel loved Jamie and looked forward to seeing him at practices and games. During football two years earlier, Jeffrey had begun a tradition of reciting a motivational speech before each game. After Jeff's graduation Dan inherited the responsibility, and each Friday night just prior to taking the field, Dan and Jamie would gather the team in a tight circle, and while standing in the middle, Dan would excitedly shout the message:

Dear Mercer family,

Even though we only had the privilege of knowing Daniel for a little less than a year, he was one of those people that you felt you had known for a long time. Although I didn't have the opportunity to coach Daniel on the field, his contributions to the team were a blessing in so many ways. We know you're all proud of the fine young man that he was and the inspiration he was to others. And as proud as you were of Daniel, we're sure that he's looking down from heaven admiring all of you as well. All that your family has endured this past year and a half, not once was there evidence of self pity or a loss of faith through it all. It's no wonder Daniel coped with his illness the way he did. No matter how poorly he felt he still found ways to make the best of the situation...making people laugh and enjoying the time he had left. We should all learn a lesson from the example that he set about how to overcome adversity in a positive and uplifting way.

— Coach Mike McClure
Franklin Football Coach

We have come together today like one big family sharing one common goal...to fight for victory.

Obstacles have been numerous leading up to this day. Perseverance and one heartbeat combined will show us the way.

So, I ask you Franklin teammates and best friends to fight side by side in this game, so we may be determined in the end.

And, if we don't win in the end.

We'll know we didn't do right, because we'll never give up... we'll never give up.

Because Franklin always fights... Franklin always fights!

When Dan finished, the kids would jump to their feet screaming and shouting and then take the field to cheers and the school song. Even after Daniel fell ill and could no longer play, the new coach Mike McClure allowed him to continue the tradition. So each Friday once Dan finished his speech, the team would charge onto the field, and Dan and Jamie would come lumbering after them.

Now that Dan had gone back to school, he did his best to resume normal activities despite ongoing medical issues. He had by now suffered through five separate diagnoses, so many major and minor surgeries that we nearly lost count, and the heartbreak of knowing that his current diagnosis (ependymoma) was very serious at best and fatal at worst. Nevertheless, I fondly recall a meeting with Dr. Turner. A meeting designed to bring us up-to-speed on the most recent diagnosis, this one occurred at a critical juncture when we still weren't sure of the official prognosis. After our normal lengthy wait, the nurse called us back. Great anticipation always preceded these visits as we felt that Dan's life hung in the balance. Soon, Dr. Turner came blasting through the door. "You're like an old penny, Daniel. You just keep coming back," he said. "I have a copy of your latest biopsy from the doctor here at Methodist. I'm not sure if you've been praying or if you're just lucky, but they've changed your initial pathology from an ependymoma to a central neurocytoma. That's about a 1000 times better than what we had before." Dumbfounded, we listened as he continued. "Generally, this type of tumor just crumbles apart and dissipates and would not require any treatment (radiation or chemotherapy)."

"You have to be kidding," I said.

"No, I'm happy to say I'm not, but just to be safe we are going to send his tissue sample to St. Jude and Johns Hopkins for confirmation." He asked Dan how he'd been feeling and Dan replied, 'Fine.' "Good," he said. "I'd like to see you again in two weeks, and we'll discuss the findings from the other hospitals." Just as quickly as he had entered, he shot back through the door. Dan sat stoically, Pam reached for a tissue, but I pumped my fist in the air.

"Yeeesss! Yeeesss! Yeeesss!" I shouted. "Thank you, God!" Dan just looked at me and laughed.

Unfortunately, we would come crashing back to earth two weeks later when we visited Dr. Turner, and he shared that Johns Hopkins had confirmed the earlier diagnosis...ependymoma. This tumor was a high grade glioma and was malignant. This diagnosis was the sixth but appeared final. Through it all, Dan maintained the Lou Holtz coaching philosophy: "Nothing is ever as good as it seems nor as bad, but somewhere in between reality falls." Dan was much more pragmatic than I; I couldn't resist the temptation to latch onto any bit of potentially good news. The rollercoaster of emotion was almost more than Pam and I were capable of handling. Certainly, this wasn't about us. But our hearts just broke for Daniel.

School and life proceeded for Dan as we prepared for his impending treatment, 30 days of radiation and months of chemotherapy. Dan made it to school each day in January, and although he had to take periodic

Because "D" had so many friends, the whole community of Franklin came together to do whatever they could to help because they knew he would have done the same thing for them. He was just that special. During the whole process, he would try to comfort the ones that were down and keep people thinking he was going to pull out of it. He made sure his friends understood what was going on and [were] not afraid to ask any questions. Dan had a knack for making people very warm and comfortable being around him and what he was going through. I have to be one of the luckiest guys in the world to have had a chance to be one of Daniel's friends.

— Mike Carter
Family friend

breaks to rest, he was doing quite well. That is until Valentine's Day when he stayed home with a headache. By 2:00PM he was violently ill once again. Dan and I made the "mad dash" to Methodist, and once he was admitted, the subsequent CT scans revealed that his tumor was back, bigger than before. This certainly confirmed the pathology report of a malignant tumor, but it was cause for greater concern because not even three months earlier, they had removed all but a small portion of the tumor. It was quickly apparent that we were looking at another major brain surgery to again remove the tumor.

As well as he had been doing just a week before, Daniel took a significant turn for the worse between Valentine's Day and February 19th. He didn't eat anything for three days, slept virtually all the time, and was nearly incoherent. I was scared to death. Not that I wasn't before, but this time he looked as if he might not make it through the surgery, given his condition. Early on Friday, February 19th, Dan was pretty coherent and seemed to be doing a little better. At least we could communicate. Dr. Turner scheduled Dan's surgery for 1:00PM that day in what was supposed to be a 6 hour operation. Quite a range of emotions I felt as we awaited the transport nurses. I was hopeful that this time Dr. Turner might get the entire tumor, but at the same time I was petrified that Dan, in his weakened condition, wouldn't even make it off the operating table. Eventually the nurses came to get Dan, and we accompanied him to the waiting area. As we made our way through the halls and elevators, I kept seeing images of Dan as a little boy full of energy and mischief, and what I wouldn't give to return to those days, without the pain, without the cancer. After I hugged him and told him that I loved him, I stood up to leave. He said, "Don't worry, Dad, I'll be all right."

I thought to myself, "Here goes my kid, whose life hangs in the balance, and he is more worried about me than he is himself. Incredible! My kid is incredible!"

Surgery began at 2:10PM, and as many can attest, those are the longest hours of anyone's life...waiting to hear news about the status of your child. Alone and afraid, the child is forced to travel this path without Mom and Dad. At 4:15PM Dr. Turner emerged. I remember thinking, "Oh, my God, something has gone terribly wrong. This was supposed to last six hours. He must have lost Dan on the surgery table!" Braced for the worst, I waited for Dr. Turner to explain.

"Everything went really well," he said. As I thanked the Lord and breathed a heavy sigh of relief, Dr. Turner went on, "There was very little bleeding. We were able to get most of the tumor, but again a portion of it is wrapped around an artery. If I slice it, Dan probably wouldn't make it." He told us that Dan would be in recovery for a couple hours and then would be transferred back to the Pediatric Critical Care Unit, but I wasn't really listening. I was too busy thanking God for allowing Dan to make it through a second time.

Pam and I anxiously awaited Dan's return to PICU. When they finally brought him back to the 8th floor, we saw a much different young man than after the first surgery. This time his eyes moved together, and he appeared to have good motor skills. He could move his arms and legs on command and seemed to be much more coherent than after the first surgery. He was in great pain, but that was to be expected. They kept him heavily sedated for the first 24 hours and then began to wean him off the morphine little by little. Not quite two days after his surgery, Dan began to feel much better and, in fact, requested a grilled cheese sandwich and French fries...a very good sign. Pam and I felt comfortable enough in leaving him for a bit that we snuck out to see Joe wrestle in the Johnson County Middle School Tournament. Franklin tends to dominate that meet, so other than Joe's matches the eventual outcome was pretty anti-climactic. As we slipped out of the gym for a minute during one of the breaks to grab a sandwich, we noticed a group of five boys selling something from a big jar. As we made our way to our car, we ventured past the boys and saw that they were selling bracelets. Not just any bracelets, they were "Daniel" bracelets. We had heard they were being sold to raise money for Daniel, but this was the first time we had actually seen them. There were blue, red, pink, and green--all with a white "Daniel" printed on them. There were people gathered around purchasing them. We waited our turn, bought five, and thanked the boys for giving their time to do this. It was all Pam and I could do to hold it together. All told, those five boys sold 225 bracelets. They had given their entire day to Daniel and the selling of the bracelets. What great kids and what a great community.

The creation of the bracelets was the brain child of Michele Fox and Ann Gordon. The bracelets were available at all the Franklin schools, as well as other area schools. It seems that the bracelets, which sold for $1.00, kept flying off the proverbial shelves. They ended up on arms from Nova Scotia to California, and as far away as Ecuador. Dan's story crossed all geographic and emotional boundaries. Many people from all walks of life and throughout the world have been impacted by cancer, but when it affects a child, the level of awareness grows exponentially. Coupled with Dan's personality and charisma, the story began to take on a life of its own.

As we were to soon learn, the boys selling the bracelets were not alone in their generosity and love toward Dan and our family. A meal schedule had been prepared and our babysitter, Carla Bechman, along with her husband Tom, provided the collection site. Each day when we picked up Anthony, there was a meal to take home. Our friend Ann Gordon (Ben's mother) established an account at a local bank; people began making donations to assist us with expenses. A concert and silent auction were planned in Dan's honor; a huge dodge ball tournament was scheduled; a trip to the Indianapolis Colts complex complete with chauffeured limousine was offered. Scott Rolen called and invited us to St. Louis as his guest. Franklin resident and "Make a Wish" employee Julie Haney was planning a trip to Boston for our family to spend a

Robbie came home from school yesterday wearing only one of his half-dozen baller, gamer, Nike, Lance Armstrong, etc., etc. bracelets. It was the brand new "Daniel" bracelet he bought at St. Rose. He is very proud of it, and we are equally proud that he chose to support Daniel in his own way. Please assure Daniel that there are little 10-year-olds out there learning important lessons about courage and determination from his example.

— Kerry Prather
Athletic Director and
Men's Basketball Coach —
Franklin College

day with the Red Sox and Dan's favorite player,
David Ortiz.

During the eighteen months of Dan's illness, we
received hundreds of cards and letters, often from parents or others who wished to share their stories of
heartbreak or triumph. In addition, we collected thousands of email messages, notes, and gifts from area
schools and athletic teams, including personalized
gifts from Bobby Bowden (Florida State Football
Coach), John Mellenkamp, the Butler University baseball team, the Indianapolis Colts and Pacers, the St.
Louis Cardinals, the Boston Red Sox, and countless
others.

The call to serve others in times of need appears to be
precipitated by a wide range of influences. Included in
that list is a strong Christian upbringing, positive
parental influence, empathy (due in part to similar life
experiences), or simply a kind and caring heart. As I
shared in my online journal (see Appendix), "Thank
God we chose to raise our family in a place like
Franklin, Indiana." We have subsequently learned
there are hundreds of cities across the United States
just like Franklin that rush to the aid of a friend in
need. Pam and I are very clear on this matter, however; we believe that no community anywhere ever committed themselves more to a young man and his family than Franklin did for us. We are so very grateful.

While such generosity cannot be repaid, the way in
which Daniel carried himself returned dividends to all
who came in contact. Daily, someone who needed to
share how this situation had impacted their lives
approached us .One of the things which makes us
most proud is to know that Dan served as a source of
great inspiration to so many others. His journey and
message also struck close to home, very close.

The profound impact that Dan's illness had on me

*Looking back over the toughest
two months of my life, I would
like to take this opportunity to
thank all who in some way,
shape or form provided help or
comfort to me and my family.
Each one of you has found your
own way to assist. It could have
been a donation, meals for my
family, cards, emails, or just an
offer to help. No matter the type
of contribution, they are all
appreciated more than you
know.*

*I am now on the road to recov-
ery because of the Lord, my
great doctors and nurses, my
family, and the unwavering support of this community. I thank
you all from the bottom of my
heart.*

*— Daniel Mercer
(Daily Journal
"Hearts and Darts")*

This is a note of thanks. I believe that when you started the online updates at the high school's web site about Daniel's condition it was just to let your friends know what was going on, and because you have [...] this was an easy, quick way to keep them informed. But, you have done so much more. I have followed each and every one and have come to feel as if you have opened your front door and invited me to come in, sit down and said, "Let me tell you what is in my heart." What you have shared is so very precious. A couple months back you wrote about hearing a voice that spoke to you. "Worry not my son, for the Lord thy God will bring peace unto you." I too have heard a voice when our first grandchild died the day she was born. Someone said, "God does not give you more than you can handle." I answered, "Oh, yes He does," and in my anger and rage all I could say was "Why, God, why?" The voice came to me and said, "Yes, I hear your prayer; your burden is so great so you must share it. This is why I gave you family and friends." Now the voice has told me, "Let Jeff know what he has done for you." March 14th I felt compelled to write to my four oldest grandchildren (all in high school) about what is important in life and how much they mean to me. Thank you for waking me up to my complacent ways.

— Vivian Kiel
Friend from St. Rose

personally sent me down a number of long, winding roads. Many of those travels I wish never to repeat, but one journey has sent me headlong into my own quest for spiritual fulfillment. Tragedy produces a series of highly complex responses from those close to the situation. It may draw you closer to your family or push you away. It may entice you to display the "Heart of a Servant" or send you into hiding. It may change your personality for eternity. You may become bitter and angry or thankful for every small victory. Most of all, tragedy forces one to reflect on his or her relationship with God. Even those like me who haven't been raised in a strong faith-based environment are forced to explore their inner beliefs. While I don't believe myself any sort of expert on the subject, I would suggest that many turn to God initially out of desperation. "What do I have to lose? Things have not, or are not going well, so maybe God will intercede and help us...help me." I believe this to be a self-indulgent response and make no excuses for feeling the same in a situation out of control.

I didn't attend Church as a child and even into adulthood viewed church almost as a nuisance on Sunday mornings. OK, I knew God was there somewhere, but I hadn't really needed Him yet, so the concept of me as a servant was far from my mind. I expect I am not so very different from others, unfortunately, as we often retreat to God only when we need Him. Some have followed Him all along, but others like me had to have the need. I am ashamed to say that my selfish approach extended into my adult life, but as I used to tell my ballplayers, "You can't control that which is already done, but you owe it to yourself and others to grow from each experience."

I found myself drawn to God from the moment Daniel fell ill. Desperation probably served as the primary motivation. However, that incentive is short-lived; frequently, as soon as the issue is resolved, back to the old ways. Not this time. I believe part of the reason is that I determined there must be an existence beyond what we have here on earth. Oh, I had believed that all along, but now I faced that reality for Daniel. If he doesn't make it, where will he go? Moreover, can I join him at some point?

Another key influence in my journey into God's kingdom was the faith of so many around us. Our friends, our family, our community. Absolute and total conviction that God is at the helm. Wonderful, kind, intelligent people who placed their complete and total faith in God's handling of Dan's situation. They couldn't all be wrong, I surmised, so I began to have daily conversations with God. I talked and He listened. Sometimes it was as if He was returning a message:

(excerpt from my online journal)
On one of my morning walks last week I asked God for strength to guide Daniel and my family through this ordeal. The following message came to my mind, "Worry not my son, for the Lord thy God will bring peace unto you." Maybe I dreamt it, maybe I made it up. I don't know. I do know this, however. God will be with Daniel and our family regardless of the outcome.

God sent his emissaries, too. Mike Mercer (pastor and family friend) supported us every day. Sometimes he would just show up unannounced at the hospital or at our home. He wouldn't say much...didn't need to. He was just there when we needed him. Pam's sister Ann also was an incredible source of faith and hope for all of us, but especially Dan and Pam. Ann was a conduit through which God operated. He charged her up and sent her to serve.

I have had many great memories of Dan, but some of my most treasured moments will be in the time I have spent with him in the last six months. I know that sounds odd. Most may want to forget. But, I have had the most awesome experiences. Dan brought God into my life so I could bring Him into yours. I have no doubts that God is real. I felt His overwhelming joy in my heart, His almighty power as an electric current of energy raced through my body. I felt His presence as His peace swept over my body. I was directed and sent images and words to bring hope during a time that I know I was falling apart. I won't pretend that I had all the messages figured out or that I always understood what was happening. But here is what I do know for sure. God is real. It happened. It happened not because of me, but because of Dan. I know that Dan is very special to our Holy Father. Dan was chosen by Him. He did not give Dan his brain tumor. He did use his illness, however, to reach many people. In this way, Dan carried out God's will.

God sees the big picture. He knew that one day Dan would be ill. I have to think that is why God made Dan the way he was. God did not take anything away from Dan. I choose to think that God gave him a dynamic personality and extraordinary talents to achieve great things in such a short time. Perhaps the Holy Spirit even guided you to give him the name Daniel. Daniel in the Bible was a strong, determined, and courageous person with great faith in God. He trusted God with his life as your Daniel did.

— Ann Dicken
Pam's sister

Benjamin Disraeli, Prime Minister of England in the 1800's, once said, "The greatest good you can do for another is not to just share your riches, but to reveal to him his own." Far and away the most noteworthy emissary for me was a fun-loving, precocious, faith-filled seventeen-year-old boy. Daniel seemed to inherently understand that the real definition of winning is not in finishing first but in achieving victory. He certainly achieved victory through the Lord, and he is helping me to do that as well.

6. *Maintaining a Life and Career in the Face of Crisis*

"Experience is not what happens to you;
it is what you do with what happens to you."

– Aldous Huxley

Early in the morning on Monday, November 8, 2004, my assistant Martha Clark Pfifer called my office. "Jeff, Dr. Moseley is here to see you."

Jay Moseley, the President of Franklin College, made his way in, greeted me with a handshake and sat down. He hesitated as if to compose himself, and then he began to speak. "Jeff, I heard about Daniel's situation over the weekend and I wanted you to know that Candace (his wife) and I have been praying for Daniel and your family. I also want you to know that Franklin College will support you in any way necessary." He went on to share that if I needed some time to address my family needs that he was in full support.

Dr. Moseley's visit eased a good deal of my concern about how I might juggle the many demands of work, Daniel, and family. His kindness and concern were evident, and I appreciated his visit more than he could have known. As I sat and listened to Dr. Moseley, it was difficult to connect myself to the words he was sharing. It was almost as if he were speaking to someone other than me. I guess my new reality had not yet been accepted. I did understand, however, that I had entered a new dimension that included juggling the demands of a son in crisis while maintaining awareness that the stability of my family would be dependent upon continuing my work at Franklin College.

I know my dilemma is born out each and every day across our country-- families wrestling with the chaos of crisis and ill-prepared to respond to their personal and career responsibilities. Clearly, my primary focus was in responding to the needs of Daniel and my family, but something that can be lost on the affected family is that everyone around them is hurting too. So many to consider. So little time to react. So much to handle appropriately with no experience to guide decisions.

During those first few days after Daniel fell ill, it seemed as if our world was spinning out of control. There were countless tasks and duties which needed to be addressed despite my lack of enthusiasm for them. Countless situations would require "global" consideration--global because of the effects on multiple constituents. One of my first realizations was that this new visibility and notoriety was likely to be with us for a while...maybe forever. My coaching background led me to the only reality I had ever known...what's BEST for the team. I had shared the acronym BEST with my players a thousand times. This decision I am about to make: will it make me Better? more Efficient? Stronger? how will it impact my Team? I was facing issues and questions that I never expected to address at age 44. Difficult though the task might be, Pam and I began to tackle a long list of concerns:

Focusing incredible amounts of energy and attention toward Daniel as he literally fought for his life.

Attending to the needs of our other three boys and attempting to maintain some level of normalcy for them in the face of total chaos.

Fielding countless phone messages from concerned family and community members.

Responding to a landslide of email messages from those who were uncomfortable calling directly.

Handling our work realities, absences as well as a very real lack of productivity.

Organizing and orchestrating the myriad people who wished to provide tangible help such as preparing food and snacks for extended hospital stays and infrequent dinners at home, donating money for perceived or real deficiencies, sending flowers or other mementoes.

Addressing the emotional needs of folks (family, friends, classmates, teammates, colleagues, etc.) who were attempting to deal with the tragedy just as we were. (A somewhat invisible but always well-intentioned group, these people can require significant time and energy.)

How, as a family in crisis, should we handle these challenges? While we would not have billed ourselves as experts or even competent participants at the outset, we certainly learned a good many valuable lessons along the way. Foremost, we found essential the communication with our children and one another. Frequently, we would have a "sit down" conversation with everyone present except Daniel. When the time was right, those conversations would include Daniel in order to discuss his role and responsibilities. I'd like to share some of what we did in facing our new reality.

Pam and I felt it was essential to convene our immediately family as soon as feasible to discuss our needs, roles, and responsibilities. In these conversations and decisions, we addressed the following:

Needs

First were the emotional needs of each family member. How would the other children respond to a family in turmoil while continuing to attend school and participate in the daily activities of their very busy lives? A further challenge was how they would respond to questions from other children, such as, "Is your brother dying?" The emotional pounding absorbed by a husband and wife can be staggering, but imagine how that same event impacts a nine-year-old psyche! Fatigue and irritability can and will appear, and no one is immune. Like a swift moving river that constantly cuts a new course, so too does the ever-changing reality of a family in crisis.

Roles

In what ways did we need to work together to minimize the negative impact. Pam and I would alternate the "day shift" and "night shift," as we referred to them. While Daniel was in the hospital, we traded places at or near 5:00PM, depending upon our transportation needs for Joe and Anthony that day. The boys would work to cooperate without too much complaint given the many disruptions we knew would accompany Dan's situation. Jeffrey, for the moment, would continue his education at the University of Dayton so as not to completely disrupt his educational and athletic pursuits.

While focused on Daniel's needs, I felt it was important to discuss with our family the various responsibilities that each of us had to assume:

Joe and Anthony

Pull your weight around the house. Keep your rooms picked up. Don't create additional work for others. Be patient through the many disruptions sure to accompany Dan's illness. Be prepared to sit and wait to be picked up from activities. Understand that you will have to take a rain check on the many events (sleepovers, parties, evening functions at school, etc.) that we simply can not participate in. Finally, maintain your level of effort with your schoolwork – no excuses.

Jeffrey

Support Daniel as best you can. Spend time at home with him when possible, but maintain consistent contact via phone. Additionally, sustain a high level of academic and athletic performance. (Interestingly, Jeff's college experience served as Daniel's as well. Dan lived vicariously through Jeff. When Jeffrey initially asked to drop out of school to stay home and care for Daniel, I explained how his attending Dayton and playing baseball provided Daniel some amount of pleasure and hope. For him to take that away from his brother would not be beneficial at this point.)

Pam

Provide for all of Daniel's needs related to mothering, emotional support, and his daily needs/wants. Try to find time to provide those necessary mothering duties to the other three boys. (Pam and I also recognized the challenges that her responsibilities would present in our own relationship. We were prepared to take "second tier" status with each other and agreed early on to work hard at not taking out our many frustrations on one another. We were convenient targets for each other when the stress grew high, but we really made a concerted effort to never let that happen. And, it rarely did.)

Me

Provide a visible foundation of strength, confidence, and consistency for our entire family, regardless of my ability to do so. Serve as our spokesperson with the media and community. Craft a plan for dealing with any financial challenges presented by the medical expenses, loss of income, etc. Continue to work as much as possible so as not to add financial hardships to the mix. Utilize my coaching experience to work with Daniel to maintain his level of commitment and motivation. Attempt to stay as involved in the other boys' activities as our schedule would allow.

It may be surprising to note that Daniel also had responsibilities. He and I had a lengthy discussion about how people might react to him and his situation and how he could minimize the distress level of his friends and classmates. We discussed how he could make something positive from the obvious negative. People, and especially kids, would take their lead from him. Dan readily accepted that responsibility and was an incredible example of strength, faith, and courage until the end of his life.

Shortly after Dan fell ill, I received a visit from Matt Sprout (Technical Supervisor for Franklin Community School Corporation). Matt and I had worked together for several years when I was with Franklin schools. Measured in what he said, Matt encouraged me to consider maintaining an online journal which would track Daniel's progress. "I don't want you to do something that might upset you, but you might find it helpful in deflecting phone calls and emails if you posted updates daily." Matt could not have been more correct in his assessment. The online journal accomplished exactly what he suggested it would but went far beyond what I could have anticipated. The journal provided our community entry into my heart. I could share my jubilation and despair from behind the screen of my computer. Hidden from the world and yet completely exposed, I poured out my soul through the entries I made each week. Many the day that I would sit in front of the computer screen, deep in the recesses of Methodist Hospital, tears spilling down my cheeks, and pound out the next entry. So difficult, so heartbreaking, and yet I had to press on for myself and for those who made checking the journal part of their everyday routine.

Thousands and thousands of friends both old and new from the four corners of the earth checked in by the day, by the hour, for the latest news on Daniel. Many who had never met or even seen Dan became immersed in the life and death struggle of the kid from a little town in Indiana. Many would share their stories or the story of their child as if to unite us as kindred spirits. The more I wrote, the more I understood how therapeutic it was for me and for others. If I failed to provide an entry for a few days, the gentle nudging would begin. "I've been checking the journal and I noticed you haven't posted anything recently. Would you mind providing an update?" Of course, I would comply promptly as I knew how much it meant to them. They had grown to love the young man who came to life through their personal computers. I had never paid attention to the "better angels of our nature"--so many kind, caring, and compassionate people that I had never noticed. I suppose I was always too busy with life to observe the kindness around me. Now at a time that I really needed them, they were there. Like a battalion of troops sent to protect Daniel, our family, our faith. They were there in spirit, in word, in deed. What began as a convenience for me became a weekly life support. I know not what I would have done without it.

Coach Mercer,
I hope this email finds you, your family, and Daniel in good spirits as I pray for all of you. I apologize for the delay in my response as missions and Internet breakdowns kept me from writing back. I'm doing great and things over here are as best as they could be. When I first heard about Daniel and later read your daily postings on the high school's webpage, a sense of inspiration came over me.

If you could please deliver the following message to Daniel when the time presents itself:

Daniel,
Every time I leave the gate and enter into the dangerous suburbs of Baghdad...filled with roadside bombs and armed insurgents...I try to be as courageous as I can. Not because I want to be a hero, but because my life and the lives of others depend upon it. There are days when I'm in a lousy mood and my courage seems to hide from me. And on days like that, I think about you and the courage and optimism that you have. Once I do that I feel as if nothing can stop me. Your personal courage, your hope, your determination inspires me to do my best and be the best person I can be. Thank you for being an example to me. Thank you for being an inspiration to me. Thank you for your optimism. You are a "hero" to me.

Praying for you,
Kevin O'Neal
1st Cavalry Division
United States Army

My Baseball Hero

Dear Daniel Mercer,

You are my baseball hero. I never liked baseball till I saw you play. My dream is to be like you when I grow up. We are doing awesome in Little League. We are 2-0. Of course, we are the Cubs. Say Hi to your parents for me and to Anthony. I am getting better at shortstop and I tried to catch but, I am not that good at it. But I will try again sometime in the season. You are a person to remember in baseball history. That is why you are my baseball hero.

Sincerely,
Camden MacLennan

I've often wondered what would have happened to our family had our employers not "stepped to the plate." Whiteland High School came to Pam's aid in a thousand practical ways. At some point, virtually every employee pitched in to help her and help us. The Math Department and her dear friend Holly Harlow took care of lesson plans and grading, as well as absorbing many of Pam's other responsibilities, allowing her to focus on Daniel, and for this help we are eternally grateful. Pam would spend any free moment planning and organizing her school work, but without the benevolent nature of her colleagues, the responsibilities of her work would not have been completed. It was much the same in my situation. Aside from Dr. Moseley, my immediate supervisor Dr. David Brailow (VP for Academic Affairs) and my assistant Martha Clark Pfifer were there every step of the way. Whatever I needed to accomplish could wait or they would set about helping me. Several months later I left Franklin College to return to Franklin Community School Corporation as Director of Operations. The same concern occurred there. Dr. William Patterson (Superintendent) and Kay Yoder (my assistant), among others, waited patiently for me to complete my duties, or they simply executed them for me. Blessed we were to have been surrounded by people who truly cared.

Life in the face of crisis forces issues from all directions. They can come at you so fast and so intensely that you feel as if you must just retreat from all things negative and overwhelming. During this time, we developed what some would describe as an almost unrealistic demeanor. Hide the sorrow, minimize the hopelessness, and eliminate the negativity. You see, it's all about attitude. Attitude is frequently the first thing that people notice about you. So what aura do you emit? When bad things happen...and eventually they will--do they make you "bitter or better"? While Daniel's situation could have easily turned us bitter, we worked extraordinarily hard to allow it to make us better. We built our attitude from the inside out. We awoke in the morning with two choices: be positive with those around you or be negative. With so much trouble swirling around us, it made no sense to further complicate things. So, as hard as it was at times, we tried to stay upbeat and positive, always mindful of the "attitude excellent" that we needed to model for Daniel and our community. No martyrs here, simply trying to maintain some level of sanity in the midst of insanity.

I found in myself the very real desire to share this wisdom earned the hard way. Approaching life in any other way for me was to concede complete and total defeat, to say that Daniel's illness had been in vain. While most cannot find the positive in Daniel's plight (and I must admit it is hard), it became important to show them, guide them, convince them that something good could come from this. Along the path were scores of ways to share our lessons. They appeared as brief conversations with a friend struggling to make sense of the senseless, presentations for hundreds interested in hearing the story, or--one of my favorite ways--helping others in their personal challenges. One such occasion occurred for me early in 2007.

As I sat at my desk intently studying the work at hand, Pam Millikan (principal of our local middle school) stopped by my office and said, "Have you heard about Todd Miller?"

"No, I have not," I replied.

"He was on the Bluffton University team bus this morning heading for Florida, and they flew off a bridge, crashing on the interstate below."

"Oh my God! Is he all right?"

"We're not sure at this point," Pam said.

Todd Miller was one of my former baseball players, an incredible young man. Earlier in the year he had stopped in to solicit my advice on a position he had applied for at Bluffton University in Ohio, that of Graduate Assistant for the baseball team. I had helped craft his portfolio prior to his interview, and to his great excitement he was offered and accepted the job. I had spoken to Todd only a time or two over the past couple of months, and Pam's news returned me to Dan's experience. "This is not possible...Pam must be mistaken...surely there is a mix-up?" I jumped up and turned on the TV in my office; on every station it appeared. "Bluffton baseball team crashes on an Atlanta interstate...5 dead, several injured." Thankfully, I learned later that Todd had survived, though he had been thrown through the front windshield and was seriously injured. The individuals both in front of and behind Todd had perished, so he had been amazingly lucky.

On March 15, 2007, Todd phoned me at my office. It was great to hear from him some two weeks after the accident. He said, "Coach, we have decided to resume our baseball season. I will be the acting head coach while ours recovers from his injuries. Would you consider coming to Bluffton the day before our first game to speak with the team?" I was incredibly honored that Todd would invite me, and as I contemplated my answer, I could feel a rush of "Daniel" come over me.

"Todd, I would be honored. If Emmitt Carney (my former assistant coach) and Keith Madison (former University of Kentucky baseball coach) could make it, would you mind if I brought them?"

"That would be great," he said. As I knew they would, Emmitt and Keith cleared their schedules and made the trip with me. These are two really special people who have been a part of my life for several years. There are no two individuals more loyal, more giving, or more full of faith than Emmitt and Keith, and I knew they would assist me in delivering the right message.

The three of us arrived early for practice on March 29th. The Bluffton ballplayers trickled in and were joined by "Coach" Miller. I was so proud of what he had done for the players at Bluffton. I saw a lot of his situation in mine...hold it together...serve the needs of the "team"...be strong. As the ballplayers walked past, I could see remnants of a tragedy not yet one month removed. Players in slings, on crutches, with visible cuts and bruises. Todd took them through a brisk practice. Well orchestrated...highly efficient...upbeat and positive. We stood in awe of the determination and resiliency of the 25 semi-healthy ballplayers who were preparing to take the field of battle in less than 24 hours.

When the team finished practice, Todd gathered them in the third base dugout. He introduced us and each took his turn speaking. Something that Keith Madison said really struck me. "I came with the intent to inspire you before your game tomorrow, and in turn, I have been inspired." It occurred to me that what these young men had done despite the loss of five teammates, their bus driver and his wife, was to show "Daniel" strength. Courage amid the sadness, determination in face of long odds, and a sense of "team" that can never be adequately measured. God had again provided an example of how I must press on--for myself, for my family, for others

7. Defining Moments

"Blessed is the man who perseveres under trial,
because when he has stood the test,
he will receive the crown of life that God promised to those who love Him."

James 1:12

I shot straight up in bed! Bewildered and confused about the meaning of the communication I had just experienced, I glanced around the dark bedroom. Pam lay sleeping silently next to me. The vision which ran through my mind while I was asleep was confusing and frightening. As I tried to regain my senses, I began replaying the message conveyed in a very real nightmare. Now that I was beginning to wake, I felt my eyes welling up with tears. By nature, I am not an overly emotional person, but here I was struggling to "get a grip" on what I had just witnessed in a dream.

There I sat rocking back and forth, alone in a sterile room, lights dimly lit. I was looking through what seemed to be a sliding door separating one room from another. I could see light peeking through the blinds that covered the glass, and I noticed how very quiet it seemed. As my dream began, I experienced the most profound sense of sadness and despair. An emotion-filled nocturnal encounter like none I had ever experienced. I had no idea why I was so despondent but it was very real and very intense.

Nearly instantly, I was transported from my misery to the most overwhelming sense of joy and happiness. I had no more understanding of why I was over-come with elation than why I had been paralyzed with grief. This was a very new experience for me, and one which was so totally disconnected to anything going on in my life at that time.

I sat for the longest time on the edge of my bed struggling to process what I had just experienced. I had no explanation. Although I lay back down, I couldn't go to sleep. I finally got up and went downstairs and turned on the TV. It was not even 2:30AM at this point, but I was wide awake and remained that way until after 4:00AM. I eventually retreated to bed and slept until after 6:00AM. I shared my experience with Pam that next morning, but neither of us had any real understanding of what had just occurred. I somewhat resigned myself to the mysterious nature of this encounter and hurriedly slipped on my clothes and headed out the door on a beautiful May morning for my daily walk.

Symbolic of the emotional rollercoaster we were about to face, this dream so lifelike that it occupied my thoughts for a week or more would come almost full circle some eight months later. I had long since forgotten the dream as I sat in a rocking chair next to Daniel in the Pediatric Critical Care Unit. While he slept peacefully with me by his side, I watched him intently to detect any needs or problems he might be having. He had struggled through a few really tough days after his second surgery to remove the tumor, and I didn't want to be too far away in case of complications. It was now nearly 11:00PM. My bed for the evening happened to be a relatively comfortable rocking chair. As I listened to Daniel breathing deeply, ever mindful of the monitors above his head, my eyes shifted to the sliding door to my left. I was so startled by what I saw that I literally blurted out, "Oh, my God! I have been here before!" I was back in my dream of last May. The same sliding door, the same blinds, the same dim light. My mind spent the next hour racing, trying to understand how this premonition could have occurred and what it might mean.

It was evident that the root cause of the sadness and despair in my earlier dream was Daniel. But what about the incredible sense of elation and joy? Maybe it meant that Dan would soon be healed. Maybe this was a message from God telling us that along with the hopelessness we could eventually expect a measure of euphoria heretofore unknown. At that moment I was in no position to make sense of what had just occurred, but it marked the beginning of a truly significant metamorphosis of my spiritual being. This very surreal experience became a beacon of hope for me. While I didn't control the outcome, there had to be something to this message. How could I possibly have been here before? I had never even been on a critical care ward, much less with one of my children. But here I was reliving the vision in a dream I'd had in May 2004, nearly eight months before Daniel fell ill.

When Dan woke the next morning, I didn't bother him with the events of the previous evening, but they continued to weigh on my mind. When Pam arrived later in the day, I shared with her what had happened. She, like me, had no explanation, but we were both hopeful that the euphoria in the second half of the dream might be a sign that better days were ahead. In the short term, things did continue to improve for Dan. A few mornings later I was confident he was on the upswing when Dan cried out, "Dad, what's going on here?"

"What's the matter, honey?"

"Look at my breakfast!"

"What's the matter with it?"

"Well, they forgot the Rice Krispies and orange
sherbet!"

"I'll bet the sherbet confused them," I said as a smile crossed my face.

Dan's breakfast of champions consisted of a sausage biscuit, 6 pieces of
bacon, and three pieces of toast. He just couldn't imagine how they
might have excluded the cereal and sherbet! He was feeling better, and it
was good to see some of his natural spunk returning. I spent the rest of
the day and most of the next several accommodating his every request. I
calculated he had earned the right.

Minus his short breakfast transgression, I noticed very clearly how much
Daniel had begun to mature. The way he interacted with people changed
incrementally with each surgery, whether a function of effects wrought
by the operations or an awareness of things unsaid that needed saying.
Either way, I was proud of him.

"Dad, be very careful on your way home."

"I will, D."
"I love you, Dad."

"I love you too, honey."

"I'll see you tomorrow, and Dad...be really careful."

"OK, I will!"

I'd lean down into Dan's bed, give him a hug, kiss him on the cheek,
and out the door I would go. Each evening that I went home from the
hospital, the same routine repeated, and invariably before I was out of
the parking garage, Dan would call to tell me he loved me and to be
really, really careful. If I ever felt neglected or unloved, all I needed to
do was spend some time with Dan at the hospital.

Some five days removed from his second major surgery to remove the
brain tumor, Dan returned home. He was exhausted and slept a great

deal of the time, but he was home and his pain was manageable. We ventured out to a Franklin basketball game one evening, and he attended a portion of the wrestling state finals in Indianapolis. While Daniel was settling back into life at home, we were all pitching in to care for his needs. I especially marveled at how well Joe and Anthony responded to Dan's requests. Without complaint they would retrieve his shoes, bring him a drink, help him upstairs--whatever was necessary. At this point Jeff was busy at Dayton preparing for his first college baseball season, but in his own way he helped too. I received an email from him that was indicative of his excitement:

Dear Dad,

Just to let you know I am sending you this from Arizona. We just got in a little bit ago and grabbed some food from Waffle and Steak. Flying out here was an incredible sight. We flew over mountains the entire way.   It was beautiful, just like you said it would be. It's in the 70's here, which is nice because it just snowed 6 inches in Dayton last night; and we are supposed to have a home game on Tuesday. This is all so unbelievable that it's almost surreal. We play Notre Dame tomorrow, and they are so good. There will be so many pro scouts there that it's not even funny. If I get to play I might swing at every pitch they throw (ha ha). All the endless hours I've spent working out and all the sacrifices I've made are starting to pay off. Knock on wood, but I don't think I could ask for much more at this point in my life. Daniel is doing great and came home today; I'm in Arizona playing against Notre Dame on the Cubs spring training field; and I might actually get to play. This is what life is all about.

I wrote in my online journal:

Jeff's email reminded me of a quote by Jorge Luis Borges: "Any life, no matter how long and complex it may be, is made up of a single moment...the moment in which a man

Dear Mercers,

We have lived in Johnson County for 75 years and have never seen anyone bring the county together like Dan this past eighteen months. We have had many movers and shakers in Franklin, Greenwood, and Whiteland but none have been as good, or important, or worthy of praise as Dan Mercer.

— Bill and Carol VanDeman Franklin Residents

finds out, once and for all, who he is." Just like Jeff, I think a lot of us have had that moment in the past 4 months.

Near the end of Jeff's trip to Arizona, his head coach Tony Vittorio called me to say that the Dayton team would be flying into Indianapolis on Saturday. He wondered if it might be possible for the team to surprise Daniel. I said, "Absolutely, what do you have in mind?" He shared that the ball players would have to stop for dinner, so why didn't we meet somewhere. We selected a spot near the Indianapolis airport and agreed on a time.

Saturday at about 1:00PM we announced to Dan, Joe, and Anthony that we were going to Indy for dinner.

"I'm a little tired," Dan said. "Could I just stay home?"

"No, you can rest when we get home. Come on, it will be fun."

So we loaded up the van and took off for Indianapolis. We arrived at the restaurant a little early, and I suggested we sit outside for a minute.

"Dad! It's cold out here. Let's go inside."

"Oh, come on weenie arm. You can hang in there for a minute."

Dan couldn't understand why I would want to sit outside on a chilly February afternoon. I must admit I was running out of reasons when I caught sight of a charter bus entering the parking lot. The bus pulled up right in front of where Dan was seated, and Coach Vittorio was the first person to exit. The look on Daniel's face was priceless.

"Coach, what are you doing here?"

"We came to see you Danny!"

Tony gave Daniel a hug. I could see tears well up in Dan's eyes and spill down onto his cheeks. One by one, every player got off the bus and hugged him. The last guy off the bus was big brother Jeff, who just days earlier had the game winning hit against Notre Dame. We enjoyed two hours with the team, and Dan just soaked it in…eating…telling stories…and laughing. All too soon they were on their way back to Dayton. We were sad to see them go, but as we drove home Dan said, "You know, that was really awesome." It was awesome, and we will never forget how Coach Vittorio always made Dan feel a part of the Dayton experience. As they began their season, Dayton began a new tradition to honor Daniel.

The outstanding player in each Dayton victory would receive a little emblem, "DM." The letters stood for "Defining Moment," but in truth the award was their way to honor Daniel Mercer. In Coach Vittorio's eyes, the two were synonymous. Daniel was a defining moment for a good many people, nearby or afar, in faith, love, or courage.

This past fall my mom informed me that she was going to have Daniel in her Algebra II class. Over the summer she had had a few minor surgeries and was struggling somewhat physically. Knowing that she gets attached to her students and how fragile she was, I didn't know if she could handle the stress of having a student who was battling cancer. I was wrong. Having Daniel in class was probably the best thing that could have happened to her, and I believe it helped her get back on her feet. There were many times at the beginning of the school year that she did not feel well and would not want to go to school. Many times during these conversations we would talk about Daniel. She knew that he felt worse than her and yet he would always manage to go to school. His strength and determination was a great example for her.

After the first few weeks of school she started feeling better and would always share stories about Daniel. It seemed like she was always bragging about him. One weekend she would talk about how he scored a perfect on a test. The next weekend she would talk about something funny he said or did. The story that stays with me the most reveals how Daniel set such an example for his classmates. Her overhead projector blew a light bulb. She asked a boy in the class if he would carry the projector upstairs to the library to get a new bulb. He replied, "No." Before she had a chance to ask another student, Daniel offered to take it up there himself. When my mom told me this story I immediately asked her if she yelled at the student who said no. She said there was no reason to do that because everyone in the class knew how sick he felt and his actions made more of a statement than anything she could have said.

— Allyson Sever
Franklin Middle School Teacher

Two weeks after surgery, Daniel reported to the IU Medical Center in Indianapolis to be fitted for his brain mold. It was actually a mesh apparatus molded to the size and shape of the back and top of Dan's head. The purpose of the "mask," as we called it, was to literally bolt Dan's head to the treatment table so that he couldn't move...at all. Needles, mice, and claustrophobia are virtually the only things which had ever brought Dan to his knees; unfortunately, he would have to experience two of those every time he went for radiation treatment.

March 14th was the scheduled start date for Dan's radiation treatment. Doctors were prepared to deliver massive amounts of radiation to the tumor for six weeks (Monday through Friday). Radiation is a high risk, high reward proposition. It can save your life, but as the rays spill out behind the tumor area, they also damage good brain tissue. Prior to the 14th, however, Daniel received another damaging blow. We received a call on March 10th informing us that Dan's latest MRI revealed tumors up and down his spine. The spinal fluid running from the brain down along the spinal column had carried the cancer almost to his tailbone. Pam and I took Dan to lunch at Chicago's the day he received the news. He was visibly down. We talked about his situation at length, and at one point he paused and said very matter-of-factly, "I don't think I have much longer to live."

I could feel myself getting emotional. While I wanted so badly for him to be wrong, I knew he could be right. What to say? How could I bring him comfort to believe that he still had a fighting chance? As I had done more and more frequently, I told him to place his faith in God.

"He has the answers, D, and He will provide them in His time. There are certain things you can control and certain things you can't. Let's have a positive attitude and show your faith and determination."

He nodded his head in the affirmative, and as he had done so many times before, he chose to spend all of his energy focused on the positive.

Dan would need a new body mold in order to receive the brain and spine radiation treatment. He was scheduled for the fitting on a Monday, but Pam and I thought he needed a distraction before then. So we loaded the boys in our van on Friday and headed for Nashville, Tennessee, to watch Jeff and the University of Dayton play four games. Dan would get to spend some time with Jeff and the team and have a chance to leave his reality at home, if only for a few days. As we had hoped, everyone had a good time. Dayton won all four games, and the boys as well as Coach Vittorio made Dan feel a part of the team. On our way home Sunday afternoon, we stopped at Ryan's Steakhouse in Bowling Green, Kentucky, for dinner. Daniel has always enjoyed eating, but the steroids he had been taking made his appetite even more voracious. Ryan's had long been one of his favorites, especially the unlimited dinner rolls. Pam had become somewhat sensitive to the amount Daniel consumed, and she regularly reminded him that he was going to put on unwanted pounds if he kept up the pace. Near the end of the meal, Dan got up from the table and started across the restaurant. Pam called out to him, "Dan, where are you going?"

"I'm going to ask for more rolls."

"You don't need any more than you've already had!"

Dan wasn't listening, however. I watched him corral a waitress and point to our table. Soon he came back and sat down, only to have Pam chastise him again, "We're ready to leave and you've already had about five rolls...you don't need anymore!"

Dan sat quietly. I noticed a slight smirk on his face, and I became suspicious almost immediately. Before I could ferret out the truth, a pack of waitresses headed our way. With a small birthday cake in hand, they surrounded our table and began belting out "Happy Birthday...to Anthony"! In addition to the fact that it wasn't his birthday, Anthony turned seven shades of red as he glared at a hysterical Daniel. Pam, of course, was mortified, but Joe and I couldn't hold back our laughter. For Dan it was just another opportunity to have fun. The challenges that awaited him at home could wait one more day.

On Monday morning Daniel, Pam and I set out for the IU Medical Center to have his body mold recast. The CT simulation, as it's called, lasted over three hours, most of that time with Daniel bolted to the treatment table. As the session concluded, the radiologist wasn't completely satisfied with the alignment of the radiation to the treatment area, so he determined that the entire process would have to be repeated the next day. Daniel was really frustrated and angry. We hoped the third time would be the charm, but after striking out twice, he was not consoled. Can't say as I blame him.

After the session ended, we headed to Riley Children's Hospital to meet with Dan's oncologist, Dr. Jeffrey Goldman, whom we had only recently met in person even though we had spoken to him several times over the phone in the last 6 to 8 weeks. This was the first time I had been to the oncology ward at Riley, and the experience was agonizing. Lining the walls of the waiting room were families just like ours with children as young as 3 or 4. Some of the boys and girls looked healthy even though I knew a demon lurked deep inside their little bodies. Others were obviously very ill. Pale, thin, and without hair, they looked as though they were refugees from a concentration camp. In a sense I guess they were. So sad, so horrific, almost more than a parent can take.

We had waited for the longest time before a nurse poked her head out of a door and called for Daniel. He was ushered into the vitals room on the right and met by another nurse.

"Hi Dan, how are you?"

"I'm OK," he responded.

"Can you stand up next to the wall so we can measure your height?"

"Yup."

As he moved over to the wall, the nurse asked him to remove his shoes and stand with his back flush against the wall. He complied with her request...well, almost. She peered at the wall, somewhat bewildered. "Six-foot-four? You can't be..."

In Nashville, Tennessee to watch Jeff play for University of Dayton (Luke Trubee, John Baird, Daniel, Anthony, Jeff)

As a smile spread across his face, she noticed he was on his tiptoes. "You little stinker."

As probably the oldest oncology patient at Riley Children's Hospital, Daniel made every day interesting for the nurses and Doctor Goldman. He was always pulling some sort of prank. Standing with one leg off the scale to make it seem that he had lost weight since the last visit, or hiding the blood pressure cuff before the nurses came in. It was Dan's way of lightening the mood, I suppose, because as you stepped out of the vitals room you stepped into a living hell. Children connected by drip tubes to IV bags full of chemotherapy, blood, or platelets. Sounds of whimpering and crying throughout the open room as the stalls were separated only by thin drapes.

On this first visit, we were shuttled into an observation room where in just a few moments a short, frumpy-looking doctor entered. He introduced himself to me, "Hello, I'm Dr. Goldman."

"It's nice to meet you," I replied.

As I would come to learn, Dr. Goldman was a highly competent oncologist who had actually begun his working life as an attorney. Early in his career, his brother fell ill with cancer, and Dr. Goldman felt a calling. He gave up law, went to medical school, and devoted the remainder of his career to fighting cancer in children. Nearing the end of his career, he was now legally blind, shadowed constantly by his assistant Jayne VonBurgen. Jayne was more than his right hand. She served as his eyes and ears while he drew on his years of experience and instinct.

"Dan, can you stand up here and let me take a look at you?"

Each visit to see Dr. Goldman started the same way. He would check Dan's reflexes and strength, beginning with his eyes and muscles in his face.

"OK, Dan. Look up here without moving your head."
"I can't. Since surgery I haven't been able to look up."

"OK. Let me check your facial muscles. Smile for me."

As he complied with Dr. Goldman's request, Dan said, "I'll bet you've never seen anyone so good looking!"

Dr. Goldman was perhaps the most stoic, emotionless individual I have ever met. However, even he couldn't help but laugh. "No, I guess I never have," he replied with a chuckle.

I always marveled at the ease with which Daniel established relationships. After several visits to Riley, I expected to hear the nurses call out to Dan as he moved down the hallways. "Hey, Dan, how you doing?" He brightened everyone's day, but none more than Dr. Goldman's. A kind and caring soul but lacking in charisma, Dr. Goldman's smile shone through his normally sullen demeanor when he was around Daniel. I continue to be so thankful that Dan experienced Dr. Goldman and vice versa as not even one year after our initial meeting, Jeff Goldman himself succumbed to colon cancer. While the hundreds of children Dr. Goldman saved during his career serve as a living legacy, none enjoyed him more than Daniel.

8. Friends Forever

As we walk our path of life,
We meet people everyday.
Most are simply met by chance.
But, some are sent our way.

These become special friends
Whose bond we can't explain;
The ones who understand us
And share our joy and pain.

Their love contains no boundaries.
So, even when we are apart.
Their presence enhances us
With a warmth felt in the heart.

This love becomes a passageway,
When even the miles disappear.
And so, these friends, God sends our way,
Remain forever near.

– Lisa Pelzer Vetter

I had the chance to take Daniel on his first successful turkey hunt in the spring of 2005. Due to surgery, Dan had difficulty with his vision, so I set the decoy about 20 yards in front of us. I had him propped up against a big ash tree. He asked me how far the decoy was and I responded about 20 yards. He said it looked more like 60. We managed to call three jakes into the decoy, and they stood there for several minutes. I watched him take aim for what seemed like an eternity. They were beginning to get nervous, and I finally said, "Shoot one," and he did. I took off after the turkey and brought it back to Dan. He was all smiles. It was one of the best days of my life!

Bob Kieffer
Dan's uncle

Dan and Uncle Tim
"competing in the backyard"

As a small child, I heard the story of Brian Piccolo, who played for my favorite football team, the Chicago Bears. Piccolo contracted a rare form of cancer which eventually took his life. A few years ago I watched a documentary which included excerpts from his wife Joy. She said that prior to his illness Brian would never tell her he loved her. He said, "You should know that I love you without me saying it." Joy indicated that once Brian fell ill he began to tell her that he loved her virtually every day, and interestingly enough, she shared how much that scared her. Joy Piccolo's fear was all too familiar to me as once Dan fell ill, he behaved as if he had only so many days to say "I love you." It was such a break from the norm that it gave rise to great concern about how Daniel viewed his situation.

Daniel also became much more aware of time spent with his family. Nearly every week he would request to invite family over for dinner or suggest that we travel to visit Grandma and Grandpa. He just seemed to glow in the presence of the Mercer and Kieffer clans. As I reflect now, I understand the fear that Joy Piccolo felt. Dan had come to the realization that the old saying "There's always tomorrow" might not apply to him. As usual, he seized the moment and set the tempo for all. His newly found dedication to saying "I love you" has remained with us all and continues to be part of our daily lives.

Daniel's deep and everlasting devotion to family was obvious, but so too were the incredible ties that bound him to his large circle of friends. From childhood he was compelled to be surrounded by as many people as possible. I, ever the loner, feel little need for crowds, but for Daniel...the more the merrier. This approach served him well after he became ill as there was a steady stream of visitors to Methodist or to our home. Incredible indeed the persistence his friends displayed over the course of eighteen months. Day after day they called, they visited, they sent cards, letters, and emails. They were in it for the long haul.

For Emily Fox and Michael Reese, the stakes were even higher than for the others. As long as I can remember, they seemed joined at the hip with Daniel. Now that he was sick, they drew together even more closely. Rare was the day that Emily or Michael or both didn't visit the hospital or the house. Given their long list of activities and a forty-five minute one-way drive to the hospital from Franklin, I found it incredible for them to be so committed to Daniel.

Emily and her younger sister Hilary come from an extraordinary family. Their parents, Joe and Michele, run a very successful business in Indianapolis, and though they are always busy with work and the girls, they managed to find time for kids like Dan and Michael. Their home, located not five minutes from ours, was a natural haven for kids. The own a hundred acres or more in Bargersville, and the property contains several fishing ponds, prime deer hunting ground, and enough four wheelers and other "toys" to keep all the kids busy. The land is a kid's dream, and Daniel took full advantage. In fact, before meeting Joe and Michele, I was concerned with the amount of time Daniel spent at Emily's house. I couldn't imagine that he wasn't wearing out his welcome. In addition, fairly regularly Dan would come toting home some new hunting gear that Joe had purchased for him or our other boys. Their generosity seemed so unusual, but once Pam and I got to know them, we came to realize that they were quite possibly the kindest, most generous people we had ever met. When Dan fell ill, Joe or Michele or both would bring him lunch nearly every day...all the way to Methodist. Also, at the root of almost every event held in Franklin on Dan's behalf, the Foxes were heavily involved. They are the embodiment of the Heart of a Servant.

When Daniel was in the hospital, he always had so many visitors. Not just at the beginning. Oftentimes visits and visitors taper off, but not for Daniel. I knew that had to show how amazing he was as a person. But then, when he became so sick, I continued to see his room full of teenagers, talking to him like normal and just wanting to be a part of what was left of his life. I thought what an impact the last eighteen months must have had on them. Sure, they did not want to lose their friend. But mostly, I think through his illness he showed them who they want to be, and they were just so grateful to be a part of his journey and around someone so strong. I was grateful as well.

Erica Short
Methodist Hospital,
Social Worker

"Hanging out" at the Fox's
(Michael Reese, Hilary Fox, Emily Fox, Daniel, Kayla Dickey)

Michael and Daniel were always hanging out at our barn. They both loved to ride four wheelers and shoot snakes. They would always get me to let them ride when Joe was gone. I could never say no to them, especially Daniel. I don't know how many times they would come get me from the house and show me some snake or something they killed. One night I remember coming home and going down to the barn to put the dogs up and there were Michael and Daniel sitting in lawn chairs in front of the barn in the dark with guns in their laps. I said, "What are you guys doing?" They said they were hunting opossums. I just laughed and thought to myself, "Is there even a season for opossums?"

Michele Fox

Hilary and Emily Fox

"Hey, Dan! How are you feeling tonight?"

"OK, I guess."

"I brought you some White Castles."

"Awesome!"

This scene replayed itself day after day. Emily would appear in Dan's PICU room with some gift, food, or both. After soccer practice or a game, she would make her way to Methodist to visit Dan. Depending upon her arrival time, she might stay only 20-30 minutes. No matter. She always felt better for having stopped in, and so did Dan. She didn't limit her dedication to just Dan; frequently she would swing by the house and collect Joe and Anthony for a trip to Chicago's. A momentary distraction for the boys as well as for Pam and me. Emily seemed to have an impeccable sense of timing, knowing just when to give us a break. Although Pam and I weren't blessed with any daughters, Emily and Hilary are as close as it gets. We will always feel a special bond regardless of where life may take them.

Michael and his parents, Jim and Cindy, were equally involved in Dan's life. I'm certain there were times when they must have thought they had been awarded custody, especially when the boys would frequent their house for lunch, complete with their favorite Three Cheese Hamburger Helper. The two boys were so connected that they even developed their own language. Michael would come crashing through our front door and greet Daniel.

"Hey, Dizzle!"

"What's up, Fizzlet?" Daniel would respond.

And on they would go with a conversation cloaked in

mystery--maybe even to themselves. It mattered not.

I once laughed myself silly when they had five Eastbay catalogs sent to our home, all arriving on the same day. They were addressed to the following: I.P. Freely, Wehadababyitsaboy, and Huge Pizzle, among others. I'll let the young folks translate the last one as it took me the longest time to figure out why Daniel called his Uncle Tim "H-Pizz."

Be it football, wrestling, fishing or hunting, Michael and Daniel were always off to the next great adventure, and where you found one you found the other. With Jeffrey now away in Dayton, the Tom Sawyer / Huck Finn adventures were recounted every few evenings by Daniel and Michael, like the time the boys were at a Pizza Hut buffet with their wrestling buddies. Daniel, fighting over the last piece of pizza on the buffet line, slapped an elderly lady's hand with a spatula, thinking it was Michael. He had some explaining to do. Or maybe the two week period when Dan spotted a beautiful 10 point buck within bow range three separate times but failed to get off even one shot. One time Michael climbed down out of his tree thirty minutes early and spooked the deer; the next time Dan dropped the arrow; and finally as he drew a bead on the beauty, a tree behind Daniel's platform stand decided it was time to come crashing down. Whatever the circumstance, the true enjoyment rested in hearing the two of them tell the story.

Kayla, Daniel, Emily

One thing was certain: neither Michael nor Emily left Daniel's side. If ever there is a Hall of Fame for great friends, those two deserve to be the first inductees. I'm sure they know, but it's worth repeating. Daniel loved them both with all his heart, and we do as well.

On March 21, 2005, Daniel began his treatment odyssey: radiation to the spine and brain over the course of thirty days and oral chemotherapy until the body rejected it or he was cured. A race to live...winner takes all.

With the onset of treatment looming, the demands of caring for Daniel became too great, and we decided that Pam should take off the rest of the school year to attend to his needs. Her ability to do her job as a teacher had been greatly compromised, and we knew she would have her hands full concentrating on Daniel's care. It was a decision in the best interests of everyone involved, one we would never regret. So every day at about 7:30AM, her regimen would begin again as she set about readying Dan for the day's activities. They would load up the van mid-morning and make the trek to the IU Medical Center in Indianapolis for Dan's radiation treatment. Monday through Friday for six weeks, the process began anew each morning. Then every night there would be the routine of chemotherapy and a host of other medications. Sorting out the various medications and doses nearly required a medical background. Yet Pam tackled the challenge of learning the intricacies of Dan's at-home medical needs.

While juggling the demands of treatment, Daniel and Pam met with Pat Hopper (Dan's guidance counselor at Franklin) and crafted a plan to move Dan's graduation back from 2006 to 2007. Even though he wanted desperately to graduate with his class, he understood that missing 60% of his junior year would drop him too far behind to catch up. Treatment would prevent him from attending school until August, but he so looked forward to the opportunity to get started again. He slowly resumed some of his normal activities, and it was nice to see him once again exert some independence.

"Hey, Dad, do you think I could drive my truck to Emily's house?"

"Dan, I know you want to get out on your own again, but do you think you're ready to drive?"

"I'll be fine!"

"Well, I know you think you're fine, but why don't we take a test drive one evening after dinner just to see how you do?"

"That's fine. How about tonight after dinner?"

I could feel myself on the losing end of this conversation, just as when he was little. So I gave in, and shortly after dinner Dan and I piled into the truck for a test drive. Anthony begged to go, but I figured that if we ended up in a ditch, I didn't want to have to worry about more than Dan and myself. With much trepidation, we headed out of our driveway and down the many country roads which encircle our house. Dan's vision was of primary concern on the road, and I wanted to make sure his depth perception was suitable for being behind the wheel. Since surgery, Dan had described his eyes as being permanently crossed. His sight was fine if he closed one eye; it was just when his eyes tried to work together that things went awry. Anyway, we spent twenty minutes traveling in and around Bargersville, and he actually did quite well.

"All right, D, you've done pretty well so I don't mind your getting out, but let's take it slow for awhile. You can drive to Emily's and around here for a few days, and then we'll see how things go."
Dan did begin to venture out further and further over the next couple of weeks, and he eventually began attending baseball practice in the afternoons. He would take swings off the batting tee, throw the ball into the sock nets in the indoor field house, and in general, just hang around the guys. He would then make his way home and collapse into his chair downstairs. What can be taken for granted by the rest of the kids, such as attending practice, was truly a blessing for Dan and our family. He was thrilled to be "one of the guys" again, and we were so thankful that he could return to being a somewhat normal seventeen-year-old.

During the last week of March, the high school baseball team took off for the annual trip to Kentucky. Heading straight to Bowling Green, they would be about 3.5 hours south of Franklin. This would be the first time in nearly ten years that Dan wouldn't be able to go. The trip fell right in the middle of the radiation treatments; that timing, coupled with pain in his back, would prevent the long ride. I could tell by his demeanor that he was really upset by his inability to participate. I understood, as I was disappointed for him. Mike Carter and Coach Luse kept him updated with periodic phone calls, but it wasn't the same.

During Dan's initial treatment phase, the days ran together. We kept track of each day on the calendar hanging on the refrigerator. Ten days down, then 15, 20, and 25. Dan absolutely hated the radiation treatments as he had to be bolted to the treatment table and perfectly aligned for the short flash of rays. The treatment itself lasted only a few seconds, but the preparation process was agonizing. I told Dan that each day completed was one day closer to feeling better, and initially Dan responded pretty well. Eventually, he became less and less tolerant and couldn't wait until it was over. In one sense Dan was very fortunate because for the first month he exhibited very few side effects. Aside from fatigue, he seemed to be dodging many of the harsher realities of radiation and chemotherapy.

Unfortunately, his luck eventually ran out. After the first month of treatment, we witnessed some of the effects of treatment taking a toll on his body. He fatigued more easily. His hair began to fall out. He had sores in his mouth. And probably worst of all, his lower back hurt. He couldn't sit in a chair for any length of time. He'd have to lie down to alleviate the pain; in the strangest of places, Daniel would be lying on the floor or across chairs. Restaurants, the license branch, the hospital, the airport--Daniel would be stretched out somewhere in a corner. But this was the only way he could cope with the pain caused by the radiation treatment to the spine.

Despite not feeling well, Dan continued to venture out, if only for short periods of time. It was as if part of his treatment regimen included being among his friends and the community. The reception he received from the Franklin kids and families was guarded at first. We knew we could count on family and close friends through the initial months of illness as they continued to visit and call. But for some others, this was a very new and difficult reality. How would they be able to engage Daniel? Should they call or visit? Should they just send a card? How was one to appropriately respond to a friend in need without becoming a nuisance? It was almost as if the reality surrounding Daniel was so terrifying and/or confusing that some hoped if they didn't acknowledge the problem, it might go away. However, once Dan went back out into the community, all the walls came down. People couldn't see him or talk to him enough. Perhaps his appearance was different, but his personality was still there and eased any discomfort they might have had.

The emotional metamorphosis that Daniel underwent from the onset of his illness seemed to be matched by our community and beyond. We continued to receive emails, cards, gifts, and invitations to all sorts of events. The constant attention and activity helped to redirect Dan's energy. He spent less and less time focused on how he felt and more and more time on what he had to look forward to. Oh, lest one think the physical challenges disappeared, they did not. Over the next few months, we made several more "midnight runs" with issues related to fever, low white blood cells, head pain, etc. Fortunately, however, the trips were brief in duration, and Dan was able to persevere.

"Anthony, look at this!"

With a smile on his face, Daniel walked into the kitchen, clutching a clump of his hair.

"What did you do?" Pam shrieked.

"I pulled it out."

"WHY?"

"It was coming out anyway. Do you think you can shave my head?"

"Well, I guess I'm going to have to now!"

Nearing the end of his treatment and with his hair falling out in clumps, Dan had decided to speed up the process by yanking out a whole handful—a decision he would later regret as that spot never grew back, but alas, hair was a minor detail at this point. Daniel had successfully made it through thirty days of radiation. Although his ANC count (infection fighting measure) fell really low toward the end, he was able to get it back to an acceptable level through blood and platelet transfusions.

Dan's initial treatment concluded at the end of April 2005; then the waiting game began. An MRI was scheduled for the end of May to determine the impact of the radiation and chemotherapy--undoubtedly, one of the longest months of our collective lives. We tried very hard to keep him as active as possible and wasted little time as the Franklin Prom fell on the last day of Dan's treatment. The moment he arrived

Prom night 2004
(Jeff's Senior year and
Dan's Sophomore year)

home from the IU Medical Center, he went straight to bed in order to rest up for the long night ahead. Although he was terribly fatigued, he had no intention of missing this big event. Just before 6:00PM, Daniel emerged from his room in his white tux with a grin from ear to ear.

"You look great, D!"

"Thanks," he said.

"Hey, how about a little demonstration of how you intend to 'slice the rug' tonight?"

"Well, only a little." And he broke into a dance that only he could have developed. It reminded me of the dance made famous by Elaine on Seinfeld. We laughed hysterically at both the dance and the fact that he could be such a good sport.

Soon, Pam loaded Daniel into the van and headed for Joe and Michelle Fox's house for a round of pictures. Dan was terribly excited because Joe and Michelle had rented a stretch Hummer to transport twenty kids to the Stone Creek restaurant. Dan loved Stone Creek, but I'm sure it was more the feeling that he was "one of the gang" again. Dan's appearance on this night was in stark contrast to the prom a year before. A year earlier he had been lean and handsome with a sparkle in his eye that revealed the mischievous spirit housed within. On this day, his body was heavy due to the steroids, he was virtually devoid of hair, and his sunken eyes harbored the nightmare that had become his physical existence. It mattered not to Emily, Michael, and the rest of his friends. The lens through which they viewed Daniel had remained crystal clear from the day he fell ill. Selfless, dedicated, and devout in their love for Daniel. They were transparent from the start.

Later in the evening, Pam drove over to the dance to
take additional pictures and be present for the crown-
ing of the king and queen. Dan had been nominated as
had Emily. I would love to have been there as well,
but Anthony had a ball game, so for this night I drew
the short straw. At about 10:00PM, Pam called to tell
me that Daniel AND Emily had won. It made my heart
smile as I knew the ballot box had been stuffed in
Dan's favor.

Over the next couple of weeks, events planned by
friends and the community kept Daniel and us on the
go--a good thing at this point. I wanted his mind on
anything but the impending MRI. On a Friday in early
May, the community hosted a silent auction and concert to benefit Daniel. Items had been donated by
countless organizations and individuals, from the
Pacers, to the Colts, to his Uncle Tim, who donated a
custom set of golf clubs. Hundreds of people attended
in support of Daniel and our family, and well over
$10,000 went into Dan's fund. A band comprised of
Franklin students played, followed by the Blind Side
Band featuring Mark Pieper (Daniel's baseball coach).
It is always a pleasure to listen to "Coach Peeps" sing,
but even more so on this night. Near the end of the
evening, Coach Pieper asked Dan if he would like to
join them on stage. Slowly, and with Jeffrey at his
side to steady him, Dan made it up on the stage and
played tambourine for one song. Then he asked if he
could have the microphone to say a few words to the
crowd.

"Thank you to everyone who made this evening possible. You have no idea how much I appreciate all you
are doing for me and my family. I feel so lucky to live
in this community."

At this point Daniel paused to collect himself. I could
see him getting emotional. Jeff stepped forward and
asked if he wanted him to finish up. I could see

Prom night 2005 –
Dan's Junior year –
Post chemo, radiation, and steriods
(Daniel, Emily, Michael)

"King Daniel" –
Prom 2005 with Emily

Dan and Michael at the
Indianapolis Colts complex

Next to Peyton Manning's locker
(Daniel, Michael, Anthony, Joe)

Daniel shake his head no. After a moment he regrouped and continued.

"I can promise you this...I won't be down for long!"

At that point the entire gymnasium stood and cheered this courageous young man. I was so proud of who and what he had become. Jeff helped him off the stage and back to his seat. You know, at that moment I really wouldn't have bet against him.

Later in the week the Indianapolis Colts--through Tom Zupancic, Kevin Kirkhoff, and Bob Potter--sent a limousine to collect our family, along with Michael, and transported us to their practice complex. Tom, the community relations representative, took us behind the scenes where Dan met players Cato June, David Thornton, and Jason David among others. They were all incredibly kind to Dan while we toured every inch of the complex. Before we left, Tom presented Dan with Colts hats and an autographed football, and he promised field passes to a game during the upcoming season.

The following weekend, we loaded the family into the van and took off for St. Louis to spend some time with Scott Rolen. Scott and Dave Taylor had planned the entire weekend, complete with hotel accommodations, meals, tickets to a game, and a pregame visit to the clubhouse, dugout, and field. We arrived in St. Louis at about 2:00PM, Daniel took a short nap, and then we headed across the street to Busch Stadium, home of the Cardinals. Dave met us at the park and led us to the clubhouse. Scott came out of the clubhouse to greet us, and then took all of us into the players' inner sanctum. The boys, especially Dan, were enthralled with the magnitude of the opportunity they had been given. The Cardinals' young catcher, Yadier Molina, came over, and Scott introduced him. Daniel had watched Molina catch many times on TV and loved the way that he played. To actually meet him was quite a thrill.

Scott led us down a tunnel and up into the dugout. We were met there by one of their public relations folks who had a full box of Cardinals hats for the boys. They each quickly located one which fit and wore them proudly the entire weekend. In fact, Jeffrey, Joe, and Anthony--nearly three years later--continue to wear theirs. Scott took us out on the field for pictures and then called out, "Hey, Skip, got a minute?" Tony LaRussa (Cardinals Manager) made his way over to meet Dan. He couldn't have been more gracious as he spent a good five minutes speaking to us. As game time neared, we said our goodbye's and thank you's to Scott and retreated to our box seats. Throughout the game, Scott made sure the kids were able to order anything they wanted from the roving concessionaire hostess. Hot dogs, bratwurst, cotton candy, popcorn...they wore it out.

I remember looking around midway through the game and thinking just how lucky we were to be there, how much we appreciated all that Scott had done for us, and how I wished this night would never end. Daniel was on top of the world, and I wished he could stay there forever.

When the life and wellbeing of your child hinges on the outcome of a single conversation, the emotions are indescribable. But on May 27, 2006, shortly after our trip to St. Louis, Daniel, Pam and I traveled to Riley Hospital to see Dr. Goldman and receive the results of the MRI. Thirty days of radiation and the accompanying chemotherapy had taken a visible toll on Dan's body. Hopefully, it had taken a toll on the tumors on his spine and in his head as well! If prayer in the month leading to this meeting helped determine the outcome, then he should be completely healed, but we all sat quietly waiting for Dr. Goldman to make his

"The family" with Scott Rolen at Busch Stadium in St. Louis

entrance. His assistant Jayne, sensing the tension, stopped in and joked briefly with Daniel. Dan smiled but I could discern the fear that gripped him as he awaited his fate. Soon Dr. Goldman opened the door and eased his way in. True to form, he would not allow the news he possessed to dissuade his protocol.

"Stand up here, Dan. How are you feeling?"

"Really well, but that may depend on what you are about to tell me."

Dr. Goldman cracked a small smile and continued with his series of observations. "Follow my finger with your eyes. OK, I'm going to hold down your arms. Now attempt to raise them. Lift your leg." On and on it went for what seemed an eternity.

I could hardly stand it anymore when he quietly said, "The cancer in the spine is gone...completely. The tumor in the brain is tough to read because the spot is actually larger than before, but often when radiation is recently completed the area swells. It appears that there are cysts in the mass, and often they accompany the tumor dying."

When Dr. Goldman left the room, I was at it once again. "YESSS! YESSS! YESSS! D, that is great news!" He sat motionless except for the smile which crept across his face. Pam looked completely spent. Thrilled but spent.

Dr. Goldman prescribed a new dosage of Temodar (chemotherapy) to continue fighting the tumor. The dosage level was nearly double what Dan had done before, but the duration was cut in half. I knew Dr. Goldman was preparing for an all-out assault. This news had been the first ray of sunshine we had received in quite some time, so the new dosage was small potatoes to us. We left Riley on an incredible high and couldn't wait to call and tell the other boys as we knew they were on pins and needles, too.

Nearly a month passed, and Dr. Goldman ordered another MRI. Dan had been feeling pretty good except for the occasional bout with nausea. We hoped for good news. The results this time were very good again. The size of the tumor had decreased, and there were three or four black spots, which often mean the tumor is dying. We were so excited! Two good reports in a row. We seemed to have the cancer on the run!

From June until the end of July, we actually lived life pretty normally. Aside from surgery to remove Dan's pic line and insert a port just under the skin in his chest, we really didn't have too much contact with the hospitals and/or doctors. The port would prove to be a godsend as it eliminated any visible tubes and allowed easy access for blood draws, IV, medications, etc.

Late in July we were notified by the Make a Wish Foundation that Dan had been awarded a trip to Boston to visit with the Red Sox and his favorite player, David Ortiz. The rest of us were allowed to travel with him, so on Saturday, August 6, we flew out of Indianapolis, headed for Boston. Such a tremendous gift to Dan, and we were all so thrilled that he would have this opportunity.

I had known of the Make a Wish Foundation for some time but had never had the occasion for first hand knowledge. I must say that the efficiency and preparation displayed by this wonderful organization is impressive to even the most seasoned businessman. Every detail had been attended to, and even though a family from tiny Bargersville, Indiana, had been dropped into the middle of downtown Boston, we were able to navigate the city with relative ease. Sunday was our day to explore the city, and we managed to take in quite a bit before Daniel wore out completely. The highlight for Dan was the time spent on the "Duck Tour." The Ducks are WWII amphibious vehicles that run on land and water, so we took the land tour and then splashed into Boston Harbor. Our guide was a delightful fellow who went by the moniker Captain Foghorn. Daniel took an instant liking to him and vice versa. Captain Foghorn asked Daniel and then Anthony to come up and drive the vehicle once we were out in Boston Harbor. It was a great highlight for Dan, who must have recounted that experience to every person in Franklin three times upon his return.

Dan was up early on Monday to get himself ready for his big day. About 1:30PM a limousine arrived at the Marriott to begin our excursion. We were first shuttled to a Hard Rock Café where we were informed that we could order anything we wanted, completely on the house. As our meal wound down, the manager collected Dan and escorted him to the gift shop where he allowed him to select several articles of clothing for him-

"The family" at
Fenway Park in Boston

The boys with Captain Foghorn on
the "Make a Wish" trip to Boston

self and his brothers. At 3:30PM the limousine picked us up again and transported us to Fenway Park. Two young ladies, Julie from Make a Wish and Jennifer from the Red Sox, were there to take us on a tour of Fenway. They brought a wheelchair for Dan, which really allowed him to enjoy the sightseeing without getting terribly fatigued. The tour ended near the Red Sox dugout where another young lady named Vanessa escorted all four boys into seats they had reserved inside the dugout. Over the next hour, one after another, the Red Sox players stopped by to say hi to Dan and the boys. John Olerud, Jason Varitek, Trot Nixon, Johnny Damon, (Anthony's personal favorite), and even Peter Gammons from ESPN. They all signed baseballs and shirts and in general made Dan feel really special. Soon Vanessa took our entire family further into the dugout, and out walked David Ortiz. A huge man with a great smile. He made his way to each of us and introduced himself. He shook Dan's hand and put his arm around him, then spent a good five minutes asking Daniel questions and answering the questions the boys had for him. "Who's the toughest pitcher you've faced? How many years have you been in the United States? Where did you grow up?" He answered their questions thoroughly and patiently. Such a nice man. It's no wonder the city of Boston has fallen in love with him.

As game time grew near, we said our goodbye's to David and were escorted to our seats. I remember as a little boy hearing a story about Babe Ruth, who visited a sick child in the hospital and promised to hit the boy a home run in the game that day. As it turned out, Babe hit not just one but two, and the legend was born. As David Ortiz stepped to the plate in the first inning, the thought of a home run did not even enter my mind or Daniel's, I'm sure. But on the first swing in his first at bat, this mountain of a man hit a towering blow deep into the right field bleachers. I had just turned on our video camera. I guess something inside told me this at bat would be worth recording. I leaned over to Dan and said, "I think he hit that one for D." He just smiled.

Amid all the sadness, it had been a special year in many ways. So many wonderful friends, both old and new, had come into our lives to rally around Daniel. They provided a beacon of hope and love. For their daily visits, their acts of kindness, and the myriad opportunities provided to Dan and our family, they have become our "friends forever."

Hey D,

Michael and I are sitting here just reading all of your online messages. We want you to know we love you so much and the three of us will always be best friends! We can't wait until you get to spend the weekends fishing and tearing up the four wheelers! But I know somehow Michael and you will blame it on me. We miss you and love you so much, and you know we have your back.

Love always and forever, Michael and Emily (Best friends forever)

9. I am my Brother's Keeper

*"Dealing with our challenges on a daily basis
is no different than climbing the highest mountain...one step at a time.
You can handle any circumstance that becomes an obstacle
by being completely committed to incremental success."*

– Jeff Mercer

"JEFFREY! I THINK I GOT THE DEER!" Daniel's voice screeched through his walkie talkie.

"Are you sure?" Jeffrey asked.

"I think so," Daniel said.

"Well, hold on, D, and I'll be right there."

Of the many adventures the boys enjoyed, none were more pleasurable than spending time at Grandma and Grandpa Kieffer's farm in southeastern Indiana. Daniel and Jeffrey loved to hunt, and on this cold day in December they were off on a deer hunt with muzzle loader and 12 gauge shotgun in hand. Dismiss the fact that had they ever shot a deer; neither one would have a clue how to field dress or clean it. But when you're on an adventure, you shouldn't let small details get in the way! Besides, Grandpa would always be there to "bail them out."

The boys in the fall of 2005 at Grandma and Grandpa Kieffer's

Jeffrey had decided that because they had seen some deer bedded down in a thicket the day before that it might be wise to push the deer to Daniel for a shot. So off they went, Jeffrey ? mile to the west, and Daniel due north toward a large, round hay bale where he would wait for a shot. As Daniel waited on the action, he studied his muzzleloader. The particular type he was using operated with a set trigger and a regular trigger. When the set trigger is pulled, the regular trigger becomes cocked and sensitive to touch. Thus one does not risk pulling too hard and possibly altering the shot. Daniel waited quietly while Jeffrey made his way toward the spot he had last seen the deer.

"DANIEL?"

"Yeah?"

"I just jumped two deer, and they're heading right for you!"

"OK, I'm ready," Daniel blurted through his walkie talkie.

He could see the two deer moving quickly toward him. They appeared to be young does. As one moved into position for a shot, Daniel excitedly shifted his gun onto the hay bale and attempted to pull the set trigger, but in his excitement, he pulled the wrong trigger. BOOM! The muzzle ball whistled over the back of the startled doe. For a few seconds, Daniel could see little because of the smoke from the gunpowder. However, as the smoke cleared, he could see the doe standing in the same spot, but now she was pawing the ground with her hoof.

"JEFFREY! I THINK I GOT HER!"

"Is she down?" Jeffrey asked.

"Well, no, not exactly."

"Where is she?"

"Well, she's standing right here in front of me, pawing the ground."

"PAWING THE GROUND?" Jeffrey chuckled.

"I think I shot her in the hoof," Daniel said.
Disappointed, but fully prepared to explain their near miss, Jeffrey and Daniel spent the next half hour at Grandma's kitchen table, recounting the deer hunting adventure. Jeffrey doubled over in laughter recalling how Daniel pulled the wrong trigger and declared that he had shot the deer in the hoof. Daniel, of course, spent his time explaining how it all made sense and how a hoof shot could in some instances actually put venison on the dinner table. Of course, no one was buying the story, but it mattered not. He was already on to his next tall tale.

As mentioned before, Pam and I have been blessed with four fine sons, but given their proximity in age, Jeffrey and Daniel were always thrust together--occasionally much to their chagrin, I might add. Through school, bantam football, and little league baseball, where you saw one, you saw the other. Eighteen months separated the two, but light-years divided their personalities. Jeffrey...rock steady and mature, ever aware and insightful. Daniel...flighty and inconsistent, live for today and worry about tomorrow when it arrives.

At times their differences gave rise to disagreements, especially in their early teens. Jeffrey struggled with Daniel's carefree attitude, and Daniel rebelled against Jeffrey's fatherly instinct and approach. As they moved through their early teens and into high school, however, the boys grew closer and closer--to the point that Pam and I marveled at how they seemed to enjoy their time together. Apparently Daniel and his friends had matured to the point that Jeffrey could tolerate being around them. They even began riding to school together after Jeffrey received his driver's license. For Pam and me, this became a watershed event.

It may be true that absence makes brothers grow fonder. When Jeff left for college in the fall of 2004, the two really seemed to connect.

August 2004, letter written by Daniel and given to Jeffrey

Dear Jay,

It's that time, big guy, the time I have been dreading for the past seventeen years of my life. The time when my older brother leaves and moves on to bigger and better things. It seems like just yesterday we were out there in our A's uniforms playing catch at Scott Park. It's hard to believe that was almost ten years ago. It's hard to believe you and I will never play a football game together again. It's hard to believe you and I will never chalk it up and step between the white lines at Franklin Community High School again. I never really noticed it, but I now notice how much I am going to miss you. Having no one like you to talk to any more. No one to stand up for me any more, even though I don't need it now. It's just more comforting with an older

Daniel and Jeffrey ages 6 and 8

brother there by your side. I don't know if you notice it, but I look up to you more than any other person. I really don't know where I would be without you. I would probably be nothing if you hadn't been there pushing me the whole way. You are the best big brother anyone could ever have. I wish I was just like you, so honest and so kind. You have the chance to be something big some day.

I think about all the times we spent together and how much I am going to miss them, though I take so many memories with me. Our squirrel hunting adventures at Grandma and Grandpa Kieffer's. Our crawdad hunting in the creek. Our backyard baseball and football games. There are so many good times we have had together. I just want you to remember everything we have ever had together and all that we have gone through. I don't know if I have ever really told you before, Jeffrey, but I love you. I mean that too. I don't know what I am going to do without you here. I hope you have a great time beginning the rest of your life at Dayton. I wish you only the best in school, but also in the most important thing, baseball. Love and best wishes for everything.

Your younger brother,
Dan

They spoke by phone several times a week, and Dan was looking forward to spending time discovering the mysteries of college life, untethered from Pam's apron strings. Unfortunately for both, Daniel never really had the opportunity to spend time at the University of Dayton with Jeff. However, Jeff and the University of Dayton baseball team brought their experience to Dan. The following article written during Jeff's freshman year at Dayton serves as an accurate depiction of the relationship among Jeff, the Dayton baseball team, and Dan:

Brothers redefine 'extraordinary'
By Tom Archdeacon
(Dayton Daily News — April 11, 2005)

It was a conversation a frightened Daniel Mercer shared with only one person. "I'd come home from school and we were sitting in his bedroom," University of Dayton baseball player Jeff Mercer said. "He goes, 'J...I'm not gonna make it. I'm not gonna live through this second surgery. I want you to take care of our family. Help them get through it...when I'm gone.' "

Daniel — Jeff's 17-year-old brother and one of the top high school athletes in Indiana — had just found out the brain tumor he'd had removed some 45 days earlier had returned with a vengeance, jumping to his spine and prompting one doctor to say it was the fastest spreading cancer he had ever seen.

"I told my brother, 'D, don't talk like that. Not making it — that's not an option,'" said Mercer, his voice now barely a whisper. "But I was saying it almost more for selfish reasons than for him. I need my brother around."

Now, seven weeks since that second surgery, Daniel Mercer certainly is "around." When it comes to University of Dayton baseball, he's everywhere you look. If everything goes as expected today, he'll be in the stands at Time Warner Cable Stadium when the Flyers host Temple at noon.

He was there in the UDM award coach Tony Vittorio handed out Saturday after his Flyers swept a doubleheader from Temple 8-2 and 11-4. Unofficially, the DM stands for Daniel Mercer, but where the NCAA is concerned — since technically the Franklin (Ind.) Community High School junior is a recruitable athlete — the DM stands for "Defining Moment." The award — a magnetic decal players put on their lockers — goes to someone who does something extraordinary.

But if you want the real defining moment of this 19-11 season, it's the way Daniel Mercer has become a special presence for the UD team and especially his brother, Jeff, a 19-year-old Flyers' freshman, who is hitting .250 as a pinch-hitter including a pair of game winning hits against nationally ranked Notre Dame.

Jeff calls his brother two or three times a day: "We talk about everything, especially the team. He loves hearing about the guys and coming over here. It's kind of what he lives for."

And there's no denying that Daniel Mercer is a college-caliber athlete. "He was an all-state athlete in three sports," Jeff said. "In baseball, he's a solid 6'2" or 6'3", 210 pound catcher. He was being recruited by every school in the Midwest."

But then came the night when the headaches became unbearable and Daniel began to vomit. Pam rushed him to the hospital where tests revealed a mass on his brain and he quickly got the brutal truth. "He was asleep from all the medication," Jeff said, "and the doctor just woke him up and told him real bluntly,

'You've got a tumor in the middle of your brain.' That's the first time in my life I ever saw Daniel cry. He automatically assumed his life was over."

"He had the world at his fingertips and then almost everything was taken away and still he's cracking jokes and fighting back. I used to always look up to pro baseball players, but now I look up to him. He's not just my brother — he's my hero."

In August 2005, not quite two weeks after our return from the "Make a Wish" trip to Boston, Daniel underwent another MRI of his head and spine. Again, the spine appeared clear, but rather than dying, the tumor in his brain had grown. "I'd like to try a different regimen." Dr. Goldman's news cut us like a razor-sharp knife. He added that he and Dr. Turner agreed that the brain could not handle another procedure like his earlier surgery. Such disturbance of the brain could produce profound physical side effects. In fact, Daniel could be paralyzed as a result of another surgery. Dr. Turner was not going to take that risk.

The news of the recurring tumor did little to dampen Dan's resolve surrounding his return to school. When the doors swung open for the start of the 2005-06 school year, Daniel was in attendance. Mrs. Hopper had rearranged his schedule to allow him to have lunch and study hall back to back. This schedule allowed him to eat lunch and then lie down for a nap in the nurse's office so that he could make it through the full day. From the start, Daniel seemed committed to succeeding in the classroom. I suppose such success was one of the few ways he could continue to be competitive, but also I think he was out to prove to himself and others that he could still achieve excellence. From the outset he studied harder than he ever had, he joined study groups, and he took great pleasure in sharing his high marks with us.

On August 30th, 2005, Dan began a new round of chemotherapy. Dr. Goldman informed us that they were bringing out the "Big Guns." Truthfully, I wished they had rolled out the big guns earlier, but I understand they follow a certain protocol. The new treatment involved three different medications: 2 intravenous and 1 oral. The warning on the packet for one of the intravenous medicines indicated that it would burn skin if spilled. Can you imagine what that medication was doing on the inside? Pam and I held lengthy conversations about what other options we might have. Obviously, Dr. Goldman was doing all he could with chemotherapy. Dr. Turner was now out of the mix. So where should we turn? Did we have anywhere to turn?

I had done much investigation many months earlier on a variety of cancer treatments, all the way from organic enemas to Mangosteen supplements to treatment centers in Mexico. I even watched cancer treatment infomercials at 5:00AM. You name it and we looked at it. There was one, however, which seemed to hold some promise. Months earlier, Pam's cousin Mike Kieffer had told us about the Proton Therapy Center in Bloomington, Indiana, which had opened within the past couple of years. We resurrected that conversation and actually scheduled an appointment to meet with the director of the center. His claim was that the Proton Therapy was an alternative to traditional radiation with far fewer side effects. The proton beam can be delivered in massive amounts directly to the tumor but does not spill out beyond the tumor as radiation does. The only downside to the program from our perspective was the lengthy waiting list. It might become a race to treatment if Dan's tumor continued to grow. We added Dan to the list and resigned ourselves to the fact that it could be months before they could get him started.

With a myriad of family activities in the month of August, nearly lost in the shuffle was Jeff's return to Dayton for his sophomore year. It was a day that Daniel dreaded, but to his credit he encouraged Jeff's return.

"D, are you sure you are OK with me going back to school?"

"Of course I am. You need to get back and get started with your baseball again."

"You know I will stay home if you want me to."

I still have the image of Daniel dragging that pillow around [because it hurt too much to sit] and his napping in the nurse's office because he was so tired. And this image is especially vivid when I see kids who just don't seem to care about school, others, or even themselves.

Pat Hopper
Dan's Guidance Counselor

"I know you would, but that's not what I want or what's good for you."

I could tell that Jeff was really struggling with having to leave Daniel after spending all summer at home with him. But Dan seemed to be doing pretty well, and as long as they could connect by phone each day and see one another every few weekends, he seemed to be OK with his decision. The last voice Daniel heard each night was Jeff's across the airways. We would each tell Dan goodnight, and then he would pick up the cell phone and call Jeffrey. We could set a watch on the two of them, and Pam and I were happy that Dan had that outlet. I know he confided his deepest thoughts and fears to Jeffrey, and to this day I have never asked Jeff to breech that trust by sharing the contents of those conversations.

Dan's life moved forward fairly normally through September and October. He suffered the usual bouts of nausea and fatigue that accompany chemotherapy, but other than that, he was off to class, football games, and dances. Monday through Friday without fail, Dan made it to class. He might have had to excuse himself to the restroom to get sick or to the nurse's office to collapse on the cot, but he always made it back to class. We received his grades in October: 5 A's and 1 B+. It was the best grade card he had ever received in high school. He was so proud, and so were we.

On Friday nights Daniel always delivered the pre-game speech to the football team, and of course, Jamie would be by his side. They would then retreat to the sideline where Daniel would be perched in his folding chair. The players would frequently come down to speak to him. He would periodically get after someone or provide some advice on how to handle a particularly tough opponent. These games allowed him to stay involved and really served as Daniel's

Daniel never used his illness as an excuse. He worked extremely hard in Algebra II. He excelled in class. He told me that the surgeons must have done something during brain surgery to make him smarter in math. Toward the end of the first semester, he was unable to sit the entire block so he would have to lie down in front of the room. His study group would come down to him on the floor to complete their class work. He had only one eye that was working properly, so a fellow student would take notes for him, but he still helped his group do the problems. Many times he would have to leave class to throw up but he would always return.

Ruth Heminger
Dan's Algebra II teacher

Friday night football –
Daniel and Michael

lifeblood from week to week.

I recall one Friday night when a couple of the opponent's student fans were yelling from the stands and making fun of Daniel's appearance. I was close enough to hear them. While I was boiling inside, I didn't even have time to get down to them before several other students from their school told them to leave him alone. "Don't you know who that is?" they said. "That's the kid with cancer...so shut up!" Not a single word was uttered toward Daniel from that moment forward. You know, there are a lot of great kids out there.

Dan also tried valiantly to continue his outdoor pursuits. He was so driven to take his first deer that despite not feeling well he continued to pull himself from bed in the wee hours of the morning to be in his tree stand before the light of day.

Early in November, Jim and Michael Reese had stopped by the house at 3:45AM to collect Daniel and take him deer hunting near Terre Haute, Indiana. Dan had harvested his first turkey back in the spring, but he so badly wanted that first deer. Jim had placed him in a prime spot and moved off to his own tree stand. Shortly after daylight, using the new crossbow that Joe Fox had recently purchased for him, Daniel sent an arrow whistling through a startled doe.

"Michael! I just shot a doe!" In a high pitched whisper, Daniel excitedly screeched the news over his walkie talkie to his good friend.

"OK, I'll be right there!"

The deer leapt straight into the air and shot off through the underbrush. As Daniel rose to look for blood, he heard a twig snap to his right. He stopped dead in his tracks when he saw an 8 point buck approaching. Some twenty feet from his crossbow, which lay behind him on the ground, he quickly surveyed his options. Outfitted in his camouflage gear, he determined that the best course of action was to hug a nearby tree. Maybe the deer would consider him to be a part of the tree? As he and Michael recounted the story to me later that day, I couldn't get past the vision of Dan wrapped tightly around the tree, attempting to hide himself. Needless to say, he didn't get a shot off at the buck, and unfortunately, despite locating the blood-covered arrow, they were never able to find the doe. It certainly wasn't for lack of effort as Jim and Michael spent the better part of two hours searching. I think they were more disappointed than Daniel as they apologized over and over about not being able to track her down.

Sandwiched amid plans for hunting trips, we received a phone call from Dave Taylor in October that Scott and Nikki Rolen would like for our family to attend their annual Enis Furley Foundation Gala in Indianapolis in November. Dave indicated that the Rolens were interested in doing something special for Daniel and would really like for us to have him there. We were certainly honored and set about making plans to attend. Not only would the six of us attend, but we would be joined by my dad, as well as Tim and Karen. At this formal event in Indianapolis, we would be joined by about 300 hundred others for an evening designed to grow the Foundation while honoring one very special young person. In 2004, the Rolens had honored Tyler Frenzel, a very special young man. Tyler had contracted leukemia and valiantly struggled for survival. Scott and Nikki had created the Scott Rolen Hero Award to recognize children like Tyler, and this year's award would go to Daniel. Thrilled that Dan would be recognized in such a way, and Pam and I chose not to tell him in order to keep it a surprise.

We arrived shortly before the start of dinner, spent a moment with Scott and Nikki, and then entered the hall which had been decorated in a Hawaiian theme. Flown in straight from Hawaii were native musicians and hula dancers extraordinaire. Daniel was entranced with their performance, which lasted for quite some time. I think the beautiful girls on stage had something to do with his interest. The meal was served in six courses, allowing us time to thoroughly enjoy the experience. Soon after, the program began and Scott took the stage to recognize all those that helped plan the evening. He also recognized Tyler Frenzel's

Michael and Daniel at the Fox's

Senior night 2005

Dan receiving framed Bulls jersey
along side Scott Rolen
(Enis Furley Foundation
dinner 2005)

Dan and his Scott Rolen
"Hero Award"
(Pam, Joe, my Dad – Roger, Dan,
Me, Anthony, Jeff, Aunt Karen,
Uncle Tim)

family. Unfortunately, Tyler had lost his battle with cancer several months before. My heart ached for his parents as they struggled through the evening. It wasn't long until the program advanced to Scott's Hero Award. I think by this time Dan suspected he would be the recipient, but he was visibly moved when Scott called his name. As he made his way to the stage, Dan received a lengthy standing ovation, and we had yet another incredible moment to remember. The wooden trophy which Scott presented to him included one of Scott's game gloves and read:

Scott Rolen's
Enis Furley Foundation, Inc.
2005 Hero Award
Daniel Mercer
Thanks for your
Strength * Courage * Integrity

Later in the evening as we prepared to depart, Eric and Pam Frenzel made their way to our group. With tears in their eyes, they each hugged Daniel and wished him well. I had surmised all along that they were wonderful people, and they certainly confirmed my instinct. I only hoped that should I be confronted eventually with their reality that I would respond with such strength and kindness. On our way out we stopped to thank Scott, Nikki, and Scott's brother Todd. Such a magnificent evening and yet another in a long line of "small victories."

Near the end of November, Daniel was scheduled for another MRI. Given the results of the August test, we were apprehensive to say the least. Had the "Big Guns" done their job over the past three months? Two days later we reported to Riley to meet with Dr. Goldman. Though little explanation was provided, Dr. Goldman wasn't available to meet with us. In fact, we never again met with Dr. Goldman as he had begun his own fight for life with colon cancer. The young doctor now assigned to Daniel was soft spoken, very kind, and highly competent, but it wasn't the same. He related as gently as he could that while the tumor appeared somewhat cystic (less dense), there was a new growth which appeared to be emanating from the side of the existing tumor. It was not good news and we knew it. Words were not exchanged on the entire forty-five minute drive home.

On December 6th Daniel, Pam and I made another "midnight run" to Methodist. The culprit again was severe head pain. Dr. Turner happened to be on duty that night, and they eventually called him to the emergency room to take a look at Dan. He asked Dan a series of questions, poked and prodded the shunt area, and headed out of the room without saying much. I chased after him, somewhat frustrated by his lack of communication and direction. I caught up to him halfway down the hall.

"Dr. Turner, can you give us any idea of what's going on?"

"Yes, unfortunately I think I can."

I looked at him somewhat puzzled.

He continued, "This tumor is going to take Daniel's life within the next six months, and there is nothing we can do about it."

"There is no type of surgery we can do?"

"We're out of options. I'm sorry," he said, and he turned and walked down the long hallway.

I was completely stunned. Like the accomplished surgeon that he was, he had, without malice, skillfully cut the very life out of me. Dr. Turner had always been very honest with us. Although I knew his heart was breaking, he was again telling me the truth. I paused for the longest time, staring off into space. The tears flowed off my cheeks onto the floor below. I knew Pam would come looking for me soon, and I needed to get myself together. I ventured off to the restroom, cleaned myself up, and headed back to Dan's cubicle. He was sleeping when I returned, but Pam could tell something was wrong.

"What's the matter?"

"Nothing," I said.

"Are you sure?"

"Yes."

She knew I wasn't being honest, but she didn't press the issue. I don't think she wanted to know what I had heard, and I didn't have the heart to tell her. I can't adequately describe the feeling of knowing that my son was dying. Oh, I had probably known for a long time that this is the way it would end up. I had done enough research to know that only 5% of all anaplastic astrocytoma patients were alive after 5 years. The odds had been stacked against us from the start, but you hope against all odds that you can be one of the 5%. From this point forward, every time I looked at Dan, Dr. Turner's words would come ringing through: "This tumor is going to take Daniel's life within the next six months." The awareness that we had only a few months left with Dan ate at me every minute of every day. I couldn't get away from it at home, at work, any-where. It ate me alive from the inside out. Every time I looked at our other boys, I was reminded that they too were about to lose their brother. Every time I saw a father with his son or daughter, I wondered what it would be like for him if he knew his child would be dead in a few short months. Should I tell Dan? Should I tell Pam? What about the other boys? How was I going to concentrate on my responsibilities at work or at home? How could I think of anything else? A few sleepless nights later I harkened back to something I had written in my online journal months before: "There's no song in my heart; sing anyway." There was no time to feel sorry for myself or for Dan for that matter. We might have only a few months left, but we needed to make the most of them. The memories would have to last me a lifetime.

Dan was in and out of the hospital from the first week of December until Christmas Eve. Buoyed by a new combination of pain medication and Jeff's arrival home from Dayton, Daniel did everything in his power to get home for Christmas. At about 8:15AM on December 24th, the doctor on duty on the 7th floor announced that Dan would be headed home for Christmas. While excited, Dan was really apprehensive. He didn't feel well, and if he got sick at home, could we get him back out there quickly?

"D, you can't live every minute of every day worrying about the next time you're going to get sick."

"That's easy for you to say! How many times have we done this?"

"A bunch," I said. "If we have to go back, we'll go back. In the meantime, let's go home and enjoy Christmas Eve."

Daniel, Jeff, and I loaded our belongings into the car and headed for home. At 12:30PM we pulled into our driveway, and Pam came out to greet Dan. We helped him inside and ushered him downstairs into his chair. At about 3:30PM my family began arriving, and Dan, though weak and weary, was so happy to see them all. Everyone made sure that all activities took place downstairs so that Daniel could participate. Danielle's little boy Jackson sat in Dan's lap for the longest time. Jackson and his sister Savannah brought so much joy to Dan. He was crazy about them, so having them there made the evening that much better. At about 5:30PM Carolyn, the Hospice Coordinator from Methodist, knocked on our door. She had given up a part of her Christmas Eve to make sure we were prepared to care for Daniel and his many medications. As Pam and I sat at the kitchen table listening to her instructions, she added, "Now that Daniel is considered terminal, we will be available to stop in every few days to assist." This was the first time Pam had been confronted with the finality of this news, and I could tell it really upset her. Once Carolyn concluded our session, she headed out the door and to her own family celebration. Pam gazed at me across the table.

"Why did she have to say that?"

"Well, honey, maybe it was her way of helping us come to grips with his illness."

"I don't care," she said. "I don't need someone else telling me my son is terminal."

"I understand. Why don't we join everyone else downstairs? We can talk about this later."

As I watched the remainder of the Christmas Eve celebration with the kids opening their presents, laughing, and playing with their toys, my mind took me back to Christmases past when there was no illness and cancer was someone else's concern. Not tonight. Not ever again.

Jeffrey spent Christmas Eve unusually quiet, and I could tell something was on his mind. After everyone had left and Dan had retreated to bed, Jeff came downstairs and sat down on the couch.

"Hey, Dad, I'd like to talk with you a minute."

"Sure, Jeffrey, what's up?"

"Before you say anything, I want you to hear me out."

"OK."

"It's pretty obvious that Dan isn't doing well, and let's be honest. I don't know how much longer he has. I am going to sit out the next semester at Dayton to stay home with Dan and help you and Mom. If something happens to Dan and I'm away at Dayton, I will never forgive myself. You can be upset with me if you like, but I've made up my mind."

"I'm not upset with you. I'm proud of you for thinking of your brother and family. You need to call Coach Vittorio and let him know, and then I'll call him to sort out the details."

In truth, I had expected that this conversation was coming. Jeffrey had dropped a few hints that this news might be imminent. A year earlier I didn't think his staying home was in Daniel's best interest. This time was different. I was the only one who knew for sure that Dan's time was short, but Jeff was smart enough to see what was approaching. Daniel was pleased to hear that Jeffrey would be staying home, but I always wondered if Dan made the logical connection between Jeff's staying home and the severity of his illness. Surely he must have known, but even if he did, I knew he would be thrilled to have his big brother with him every day.

From Christmas to the middle of January, I watched Daniel's body begin to fail him. His legs went from unsteady to almost non-functioning in a

three week period. His once chiseled frame had deteriorated to the point
that I'll bet he didn't weigh 150 lbs. He spent most of his time downstairs in his reclining chair, watching TV. Because he was constantly
freezing, we kept him covered with the many blankets that had been
made for him. Due to his lack of mobility, he required almost constant
attention. Everyone pitched in, but Joe and Anthony went out of their
way to provide help to their brother. Whether it was getting him a drink,
another blanket, his cell phone, etc.-- without complaint they fulfilled
every request.

After dinner one evening, Dan announced that he needed to use the restroom, so Joe and I took our place on either side of him, literally lifting
one leg at a time and inching our way toward the restroom. Once we
got him inside, we closed the door and waited for him to let us know
when he was finished. We waited and waited and waited. Nearly 30 minutes later Pam and I were getting worried. We continued to check on
him, and he assured us he was fine. Now 45 minutes into his restroom
break, Pam called in.

"Are you done yet?"

"No. Why do you keep asking me?"

"Well, I thought you might be ready to quit."

"MOM! This is Daniel...and I NEVER quit!"

Dan had captured in a few short words what we had all come to know
over the past year. The word quit was not in his vocabulary. Never was,
never would be.

With Daniel nearly incapacitated, we considered full-time hospice care,
either in our home or in the Yellow Rose Unit at Methodist Hospital.
While Jeff and I could handle moving him from one place to the next,
additional medical issues began to present themselves. His blood counts
were now so low that all chemotherapy had to be stopped. We had not
yet been able to get him to the Proton Therapy Center, and we had rapidly run out of options. The oncologist decided to order one last MRI to
see if something might be going on aside from the tumor. Truthfully, I
thought it to be a waste of time. Nonetheless, we loaded Daniel up on a

Sunday evening and took him in for his test.

On Tuesday, not quite two days later, I was in the middle of an important meeting at work when my cell phone vibrated. I pulled it from its holder, and the phone read "DANIEL." I had long since determined to answer any and all calls from Daniel's phone, so I excused myself from the meeting and took the call.

"Dad?"

"Yeah, D?"

"You're not going to believe this."

"WHAT?"

"The MRI said my tumor is significantly smaller."

Feeling the tears beginning to well in my eyes, I said, "Are you serious?"

"Yup!"

"That's great news, D! Do they have any idea how that could happen? I mean, you haven't even been on your chemo for weeks."

"The doctor said he couldn't understand it either. He also said that it looked like when the tumor decreased in size, that the open space had collapsed on my shunt, and that could be causing my legs to not work. He thinks we need to speak with Dr. Turner about surgery to 'inflate my brain.'"

"OK, honey. We can talk about it tonight when you get home. I'll see you in a little bit."

"I love you, Dad."

"I love you too, D."

I stood in the waiting room at our office for a few minutes. I was completely stunned. The rollercoaster continued. At that moment I didn't care. Any bit of good news was a cause for celebration. Finally, I went back into the meeting. I just wanted to scream out loud and tell the world that my son's tumor had begun to shrink. I maintained my composure, but I must admit I didn't hear another word during the meeting.

The following Monday found us back at Methodist for another surgery with Dr. Turner. This time he was to drill "burr" holes in the frontal area of Dan's skull and to install a new shunt. The surgery was very painful, and Dan didn't feel good at all, but we began to see almost instant improvement. His legs began to work again, and although he was very weak, we began rehabilitation almost immediately. Not quite one week after surgery, Daniel was walking again with the aid of a walker. What a blessing!

After his arrival home from Dayton, Jeffrey became Dan's constant companion. He made it his personal mission to get Dan back in shape. I might add that "shape" is a relative term. We were just hoping that Daniel could once again move about freely. The goal was to get up and down the stairs and out to the vehicle and back. The prolonged steroid use had caused Dan's body to assume the frailty of an 80-year-old woman, according to his oncologist. So the process would not be a short nor an easy one, but Jeff was determined to help Dan overcome this latest physical challenge.

Through the end of January and the first week or two of February, Dan continued to make good progress. We were able to take him to the wrestling regionals and out to a basketball game or two. However, just as things began to look up, I received the following phone call at work:

Jeffrey,

I could not pass up the opportunity to tell you how proud I am of you. You have matured into a gracious, well-spoken, caring man (no longer a young man). I need to share a story about Daniel. It was toward the end of first semester in 2005. Daniel was busy gathering his stuff to go to the next class. He told me you had decided to take the semester off of college to be with him. Then he said, "You know he is my best friend!" How true that statement was! Daniel was blessed to have a brother like you. You are an inspiration to me and others. I'll continue to pray for you and your family.

Ruth Heminger

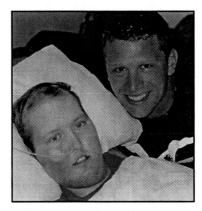

Jeffrey and Dan in April 2006

"Dad?"

"Yeah, D?"

"I'm out in the parking lot with Jeffrey, and my stomach is killing me."

"OK. Come on inside, and we'll see what's going on."

I could tell the moment Jeffrey helped him inside that something wasn't right. He was in an incredible amount of pain, and there was no point in postponing the inevitable. I called Kay into my office and said, "We are taking Dan to the hospital. Can you cancel the rest of my appointments for today?" Jeff and I then helped Dan to my car, and we began the race to Methodist. I called Pam along the way to let her know what was going on and to have her pick up the other boys. Forty-five minutes later we arrived at the Emergency Room at Methodist. Things moved quickly for a change, and we were called back after about a half-hour. Pain medication was administered, and Daniel began to relax a bit. The ER doctor ordered a CT scan of Dan's stomach. It didn't take long for the culprit to be identified. Dan's low blood counts had resulted in internal bleeding. A pocket of blood had formed on his left side, just beneath his lung. Soon, they moved Dan to the 7th floor and into a room.

As Jeff and I moved our belongings into the 7th floor room, it occurred to me that this was the third time we had been in this same room during the past year. In fact, we had been assigned at one time or another to nearly every 7th and 8th floor room. We knew every nurse, every receptionist, many of the cleaning folks, and a huge number of doctors. Over a hundred days so far, and the count was sure to climb.

Two days after our arrival back at Methodist, four of our wrestlers were scheduled to compete in the

Michael carrying Dan's picture into the Wrestling State Finals 2006 (Coach Lynch, Coach Hasseman, Cody Johnson, Michael, Philip Glasser, Brad Gallagher)

Individual State Finals, not even five minutes from Dan's hospital room. He had missed last year's State Finals while in the hospital, and here we were again. From the time Dan was in 7th grade, he had attended the High School State Finals and he so looked forward to that two-day event. When Dr. Turner made his rounds on Friday morning, Dan asked if there was any way we could get an ambulance to take him to Conseco Fieldhouse (site of the finals). Dr. Turner said to do that would be to risk his life. Jeffrey and Joe did attend as we received word that there would be a tribute to Dan during the Parade of Champions. Jeffrey filmed the event, and as Franklin's four boys and coaches walked into the arena, it was easy to locate them. Michael Reese carried a poster-size placard with Daniel's picture. The public address announcer called attention to the contingent from Franklin and the warrior that could not be present with them. When he finished a two-minute tribute to Daniel, the entire fieldhouse, 10,000 plus, rose to their feet and gave Daniel a prolonged standing ovation. Hundreds, and I mean literally hundreds of wrestlers and their families had followed Dan's story through a message board maintained by Dan's assistant coach, Chris Lynch. From the northern most portion of Indiana to the tip of southwestern Indiana, they paid tribute to the heretofore faceless kid from Franklin. Dan and I watched the video the next day. I couldn't even bear to look at him. When it finished, I turned it off and left the room to compose myself.

Dan managed to stay in a holding pattern for about five days until February 23rd. I was alone with him in his room when he began to act strangely. His eyes rolled as if he were struggling to focus.

I said, "Dan, are you all right?" But he didn't answer. I moved up into his face and I said, "Dan, you're scaring me...are you all right?"

He responded, "I'm scaring myself. Something is wrong!"

I rushed into the hallway and nearly ran headlong into Dr. Lyle Fettig.

"Dr. Fettig! You need to come in here. Something is wrong with Daniel!"

Dr. Fettig took one look at Daniel, stepped out into the hallway, and called for a Code Blue. I had heard this request come over the loud-speaker scores of times during our various stays at Methodist, but this time was different. It was for my son. Dan's blood pressure had dipped to 60/33. He was barely alive! Petrified, I stood helplessly by as nurses and doctors sprinted into his room from all directions. They leapt into action, stripping his hospital gown away from his chest. IV medications were ordered and delivered almost immediately. After about 30 minutes, his heart began working properly again and his color returned almost to normal. One by one the doctors and nurses left his room as the danger had for the moment subsided. Dr. Fettig ordered several tests. While they were drawing blood samples, I stepped into the hall to call Pam. I was still shaking, and Pam could tell I was completely unnerved. She and all the boys jumped in our van and flew to Methodist.

Less than 24 hours later, the doctor on call asked to meet privately with Pam and me. I knew instantly that this wasn't good. He outlined our predicament.

"Daniel is in very critical condition. He has contracted sepsis, which is a very serious blood infection. The only way to treat this is with antibiotics and massive amounts of fluids. The challenge is that the fluids cause the lungs to fill up, and the only remedy is to place Dan on a ventilator. I must tell you that many times when someone goes on the ventilator, they do not come off."

I could feel my heart sink. I expect Pam and Jeffrey felt the same way. What a choice we had. Either do nothing and watch Dan die or put him on a ventilator and risk causing his lungs to become so dependent that he would never come off the artificial breathing apparatus. It was like the old show *Let's Make a Deal*. Select what is behind one of the curtains and see what you get. Unfortunately, all of our choices were awful. Nevertheless, the doctor left the room with his answer: put him on the ventilator.

For the next six days, Daniel was strapped to his bed, heavily sedated with various tubes running down his nose and throat. He made steady if not incredible progress, and by Saturday morning they removed him from the ventilator. One minor miracle down! They eased Dan out of his sedation, and he began to wake. The tubes had irritated his throat, and he could barely speak, but late that evening he mustered enough strength to ask Pam and Jeff if he was going to die. Cowardly I may be, but I am thankful I didn't have to answer him.

The more ill Daniel became, the more Jeffrey refused to leave his side. He was there for Dan when they hooked him to the ventilator. He was there when the insulin shots were administered to combat Dan's next new illness...diabetes. He was there when they drew blood off Daniel's lung. He was with Dan seven days a week from early morning until late afternoon. Joe and Anthony came out every other day or so. I could sense the internal struggle that both were engaged in. While they loved their brother, to see him in such bad shape was very difficult. Jeffrey, however, was immersed in the greatest battle of his young life. He was determined to fight this affliction with his brother until he could fight no more.

Dan continued to persevere, glimpses of the true warrior shining through. Early one morning as I sat half asleep next to him, I heard one of the nurses say to him, "Now, Dan, I'm going to give you your antibiotics and your insulin shot. Then I'm going to draw some blood for cultures, and then we'll get you cleaned up. Do you have any questions?"

In a voice barely audible and broken into short bursts, he replied, "Yeah...Why...am I...so...big and studly?"

While she burst out laughing, I just shook my head. Staring death in the face, he did not intend to concede. Not now. Not ever.

10. *Gone and Not Forgotten*

"What an extraordinary situation is that of us mortals!
Each of us is here for a brief sojourn; for what purpose he knows not,
though sometimes he thinks he feels it.
But from the point of view of daily life, without going deeper,
we exist for our fellow men...
in the first place for those on whose smiles and welfare
all our happiness depends, and next for all those unknown to us personally
with whose destinies we are bound up by the tie of sympathy."

– Albert Einstein

"Jeff, you need to get to the hospital now!" I could hear Pam's voice breaking over the phone. "Daniel stopped breathing. The nurses were able to get him started again, but I'm not sure for how long," she said.

"I'm on my way," I replied. As I had been doing for months, I worked as much as I could. With the myriad of challenges we faced, we didn't need financial woes in the mix. Pam had taken the last few months off from school, and Jeffrey had been spending mornings and afternoons with Daniel. I would come out each evening to sit with Daniel, though I must admit that the visits became more and more difficult.

Dan's birthday May 21, 2006
at Methodist Hospital

From March to May of 2006, Daniel had undergone a steady decline. He had grown increasingly weak, but in March he lost all use of his legs and his left arm. In addition, he became diabetic from the massive amounts of steroids used to decrease swelling in his brain. However, the real culprit of his eventual demise was a pocket of blood and fluid which gathered in his abdomen. What many people do not realize is that the death of a cancer patient is frequently a result of the treatment as much as the disease. The radiation and chemotherapy had destroyed Daniel's ability to manufacture red blood cells that give a body the ability to prevent/stop internal bleeding through clotting.

From the internal bleeding and pooling of blood, sepsis became a constant worry. Our concern proved to be well founded. Daniel's care for nearly a month had been entrusted to a rotation of doctors that populate the Pediatric Critical Care Unit. Dr. Michael Turner had served as Daniel's surgeon, but given the reality that surgery was not an option, Daniel was in medical limbo. The matter-of-fact nature of some of the doctors conflicted with Pam's emotional state in the early going. They would start, "Because Daniel is terminal, we plan..." The first few times they used those shocking words, Pam was reduced to tears. The tears eventually morphed into anger, and she grew increasingly less tolerant of the doctors.

I found myself unable to adequately respond to Pam's inability to recognize the reality of Dan's condition. She continued to display optimism that something miraculous would occur and that Dan would somehow improve to the point that he could get to Bloomington for Proton therapy. It had become clear to me that our hope was gone and that the doctors were merely verbalizing what I already knew to be true. I think everyone recognizes the "truth" on a different timeline, and Pam wasn't there yet.

Pam's sister Ann had played an intimate role in Dan's journey from the outset and I think was responsible for providing Pam a spirit of strength, courage, and hope based exclusively in faith. Ann spent inordinate amounts of time supporting Pam, Dan and our family. She was our "spiritual advisor" and truly felt that she had been called by God to support our journey. It was her encouragement and positive attitude that helped buoy Daniel and, in turn, Pam. I will be eternally grateful for all she did to keep us positive, but this approach did little to enhance Pam's relationship with the various doctors.

The longer Dan's illness progressed the more reflective I became. I found myself constantly analyzing and evaluating the happenings around us. From the hospital, nurses and doctors, to our family and community, I noticed all the little things which might impact Daniel's eventual outcome or our response to it. I had watched one particular doctor, Dr. Lyle Fettig, grow through his relationship with Dan. Initially, he had been abrupt and somewhat pragmatic in his dealings with our family. Of course, this approach flew in the face of what Pam wanted as she was grasping for anything which resembled good news. Not only did he not deliver good news, he delivered the bad news very directly.

As the days went by, Dr. Fettig stopped in more and more frequently. He softened his approach. His voice lightened, and he grew cautious about what he said in front of Pam and Dan. I watched him become a "doctor" during that month, and I'm sure he will be a wonderful caregiver for years to come. He had joined the legion of folks who learned countless valuable lessons from a 19-year-old from Bargersville, Indiana.

On Sunday May 28, 2006, as the evening grew late and Dan's visitors headed for home, I paused to reflect on our situation. This was so surreal. I had spent 100+ consecutive days in this hospital room, watching my son gradually fade from our lives, and now he was undoubtedly less than two hours away from taking his last breath. How could I capture his last few moments that would have to last a lifetime? In reality, I was torn. I wanted to remember, but at the same time, I wanted to forget all of this.

I scanned the room. Jeffrey sat on Dan's right, holding his hand while remaining silent. Pam sat at Dan's left and gently rubbed his arm. Joe and Anthony sat quietly waiting for someone to tell them what to do or feel. We were joined by our good friend, Emmitt Carney, who had driven straight through from Florida once he heard the end was near. Erica Short, the hospital social worker who had become our good friend, was there as well. Our many nursing friends were in and out of the room, making sure that Daniel was as comfortable as possible and that we had some uninterrupted time to say our good-byes. It was obvious to me that while their hearts were breaking just like ours, they had lived out this scene many times before. They were professionals to the end. In fact, several chose to stay through their shift change at 7:00PM. Recognizing that Daniel was nearing the end, they wanted to be there for him and for us.

The doctor on call came in about 9:00PM and spent a few minutes outlining how the last few hours would go. She said, "Dan's heart rate will eventually begin to slow down as will his breathing, and then he will just go to sleep for eternity." I listened to what she said, and although I knew she was right, I hoped with all my heart that something inexplicable might happen. "Dan! Get up! Keep fighting sweetheart. Don't leave! Who will be here to make me laugh? Who will tell me he loves me ten times a day? Who will call my cell phone just to make sure I'm OK? What about your mom and brothers? They will be so heartbroken. All your friends will be devastated. What will I say to them?"
I looked down at Dan and his shattered body, and I knew that despite my selfish desire to keep him here with us, it was time for him to go. God was calling him. No one should have to endure the pain and heartbreak that he had lived with for the past eighteen months. In my heart I knew it was time, but there I stood with tears running down my face. A broken man. I had been reduced to a little boy who longed for a long, loving hug from his own mom who would say that everything would be fine. It

wasn't fine for me, but it would be for Dan because I'm sure that my mom (Dan's Grandma Mercer, who passed in 2000) would be waiting to wrap him in her arms. "Welcome to your new home, sweetheart. I've been waiting for you," she would say.

I could just hear him now, "Hi G-Ma! Where's the food? I haven't eaten a good meal in two months, and I've been dreaming of your chicken and dumplings!"

"No need to dream anymore, D. Eat as much as you want."

I watched as the monitors started to grade downward. Shortly after midnight his heart rate began its downward spiral: 157...133...110...82...56...23...0. Jeff's head fell onto Dan's chest and he sobbed. It was the first time I had seen Jeff drop his guard. Though I had cried countless times, I hadn't witnessed him lose control until now. Jeff whispered something into Dan's ear and hugged him one last time. Anthony sat to Dan's right with Pam, and the tears rolled down his little cheeks. Joe stood to my right. Ever quiet and guarded, he turned to me and cried on my shoulder. Pam, almost incredulous, sat motionless, holding Dan's left hand and rubbing his arm. As the minutes passed and the blood ceased to flow through Daniel's tattered frame, he turned nearly ghost white. He fit my image of what an angel must look like. I waited until everyone had said their good-bye's, and then I made my way to his bedside. I took his hand and said, "I love you, sweetheart, and I always will. I'm so sorry for all you've had to endure. God will take care of you now. I will see you again some day, but until I do just know that there won't be a day that goes by that I won't think of you. Good-bye D-man."

All the nurses in the room dabbed their moist, red eyes. They had come to be part of the family over the past year-and-a-half. While Dan loved them all, Emily Parkinson had become his favorite. Her perky, upbeat attitude was instantly engaging, and she and Daniel had an ongoing banter. In fact, there were times that Emily would negotiate a different work schedule or trade her patient(s) with other nurses just to have Daniel. Emily, ever the professional, went about her work while taking brief respites to wipe away her tears. She was joined by several other nurses as they set about preparing Dan to be moved downstairs. The doctor on call entered the room and ran Dan's vitals one last time to confirm his passing. Just as she rose from her position next to Daniel, Dr. Fettig dressed in jeans and a t-shirt rushed through the doorway. Although not scheduled to work, Dr. Fettig had been informed that Daniel was near death, and he left his home at 11:30PM to be with us. The look of utter despair upon his face told the story of this young doctor's metamorphosis over the past month. "I am so sorry," he said to me.

"I know you are, and thank you so much for all you have done," I said. His heart, like ours, was broken.

Being a nurse can be a very rewarding experience. With rewards come the difficulties too. Difficulties I was prepared to face, or so I thought. Dan Mercer changed my heart forever. Soon after Dan passed I realized why my heart felt so heavy; it was Dan's footprint. Dan left an impression that I know will never fade. His journey has taught me to appreciate and love my family more than I ever did before. I am saddened by the fact that we couldn't fix Dan's illness; we could not make him better to send him home with his family and play baseball or wrestle again. I question God every day for why He had to take Dan away from his family. It is with faith I have come to realize that Dan would not want to come back to life here on earth. He is in a place of peace he would never choose to leave. Some people around Methodist Hospital say that I was Dan's favorite nurse (an honor I hesitate to really accept), but the truth is, Dan is and always will be my favorite young man. A young man that has made me a better nurse and person.

Emily Parkinson
Methodist Hospital Critical Care Nurse

Emmitt took Jeffrey out into the hallway. Em had been close to the boys for many years, and especially so with Jeffrey and Daniel. He had coached with me for years and took great pleasure in watching the boys grow up. I knew he would find the right words to share with Jeffrey, much as he had done so many

On that late May night in the dark 8th floor room at Methodist Hospital, I held Daniel's right hand with my right hand and intertwined them with a rosary and watched as he passed away, and at that moment...in that second, a part of me like his tired body was no more.

Jeffrey Mercer

times with the teams we coached. Jeffrey soon returned to the room and announced that he had to leave. I suspect that he, like his father, needed time alone to attempt to make sense of the senseless. Pam, bless her heart, was busy collecting all our belongings--a considerable collection given the duration of our stay. Ever the mother, she was organizing our departure. In reflection, I understand that walking away was so much harder, knowing that I was leaving my son completely alone for the first time in his life. Soon we had gathered our belongings, and I turned one last time to see Daniel. A glance that will need to last a lifetime.

During the months leading up to Daniel's death, I had organized our affairs. As much as I dreaded this reality, I did know it was real. I had put together a "call list" of those that we needed to notify so that they, in turn, would spread the news of Daniel's death. In the preceding two days, I had penned my last online journal entry as well as Daniel's obituary. I suppose that might sound morbid to some; however, one would have to know how our community hung on every word written about Daniel. It was so very important that the right message be shared because we had a responsibility to think of the "team." Our team would be waiting for my message. This is what I wrote:

May 29

Shortly after midnight on this 29th day of May 2006, Daniel Patrick Mercer touched the face of God. He drifted off peacefully while surrounded by family, friends, and his caring nurses and doctors. The past few days have been vintage Daniel. Knowledge that the end was near has brought scores of friends and family members. As I observed the scene around us, I thought how much Daniel must be enjoying the stories being told about him...the baseball games on TV...and Kenny Chesney in the CD player. After some initial sadness, the conversation inevitably turned to something off the wall that Daniel had said or done during his short life here on earth. He was a "piece of work." Like the time when he was 4 or 5 and said "Dad" 86 times in an hour and fifteen minutes on the ride home from Grandma and Grandpa's. Gaining 16 lbs. in one day after nearly starving himself to make weight in wrestling...probably at Chicago's Pizza while being served by his favorite lady, Petunia Daylily (a name that of course he had given her). Or, the time that he got his truck stuck in a ditch backwards, at midnight (after curfew), while trying to shine his truck lights on several deer standing out in a field. I still remember standing in a pitch black kitchen waiting for him and what was sure to be a creative excuse.

As a good friend reminded me recently, amid all the sadness how very lucky we have been to have had Daniel for 19 years. Conversely, how lucky he is to have been so loved by so many. Some people, in a full life, never experience one-tenth of the joy and happiness that Daniel did.

As a family, we have been so fortunate to have been surrounded this past 18 months by so many wonderful friends and family members. They have given and given and continue to offer help in any way necessary. Even though we haven't been able to thank each one of you personally... please know that we love you for all you have done. Our friend Mike Carter once said, "You are the richest man in the world if you have five friends you can truly count on." Mike is probably right, but it occurs to me that his assessment must make us the richest family ever. I cannot count the number of people whom I know we could have depended upon at any time...day or night.

I encourage each and every one of you who reads this note to always remember Daniel. Not for him, or for us, but for what the journey had meant to each person it touched. We have been reminded of what is truly important in life, and it's not winning or losing, making money, or even getting a car on your 16th birthday. It's about enjoying every day you have with family and friends. It's about telling those you care about that you love them every chance you get. It's about giving life everything you have during the time you are here. Daniel taught us that and more every day for the past year and a half. Daniel, you were one of a kind, you are one of my four best buddies, and I will forever love and miss you.

11. There's no Song in my Heart...
Sing Anyway

*"This is the one time we couldn't make things better,
but we believe that Daniel is in a place where the big picture is clear...
he doesn't hate us for not being able to make it all better...
he loves us for doing everything we could."*

– Jeff and Pam Mercer

We arrived home from Methodist Hospital a little after 2:00AM and all headed to bed exhausted. I woke at about 7:00AM as I had much to take care of. I made a few of my calls. Tim (my brother), Mike Carter, Mike Mercer, and Paul Sylvester. Pam made a few of her own. She had called her sister Ann from the hospital in the wee hours of the morning so that was done, but she wanted to call her parents personally. She also called her good friend Holly Harlow, who herself had been battling breast cancer for nearly 11 years. Holly, a math teacher and department chair at Whiteland High School, had provided great hope to Pam and Daniel throughout his journey. She would frequently prepare Pam's lesson plans, copy and grade tests, and do whatever else that might lighten her load. This, in spite of her ongoing chemotherapy treatments every Friday. Unfortunately, Holly would lose her battle to cancer in February 2007. Pam and I agree that God surrounds you with people who are destined to be your support structure. Holly was one of those people, and I'm sure Daniel was there to greet her when she entered the gates of heaven.

Shortly after 8:00AM I could hear Jeffrey's alarm sounding downstairs, and soon he came bounding upstairs. "Where are you headed?" I asked.

"I've got to go throw batting practice to the high school team and tell them about Daniel."

I had nearly forgotten that the Franklin baseball team was scheduled to play Southport in the sectional tournament that day. Ironically, the last high school game that Daniel had played in was two years earlier against Southport, in the sectional, with Jeff on the mound and him behind the plate. I was pleased that Jeff would be meeting with the boys on this very difficult day. Jeff had spent the entire season volunteering with the team. He would join Dan at the hospital early in the morning each day, and then at 2:30 he would take off for Franklin High School and baseball practice. This provided him an outlet as well as a way to stay around the game he loved so dearly. Shortly, Jeff went out the door on his way to the high school, and I said to Pam, "I think we ought to go to the game today. I think it will do everyone, including us, some good." She immediately agreed and announced to Joe and Anthony that they needed to shower and get ready to go to the game.

We arrived at the ballpark about fifteen minutes before the start of the game. I expect everyone was as uncertain and uncomfortable as I about the reaction we might receive. The first few familiar faces belonged to good friends John Carpenter, Mike Carter, and Mike Mercer. Daniel's best friend, Emily Fox, came down out of the bleachers and gave each of us a long and loving embrace. I wiped the tears from her angelic little face and told her things would be OK. The reception put Pam and me at ease and allowed us to interact at our own pace. Jeff, of course, was on the field with the team, and Joe and Anthony melded into the crowd, reappearing only when they needed money for the concession stand. My trepidation in attending the game was instantly erased, and it actually became quite therapeutic. Not social by nature, I welcomed the warm reception and hugs that enveloped me in the loving embrace of our community, an embrace that I desperately needed and appreciated.

The game proceeded rapidly, our Grizzly Cubs quickly dispatching Southport 12-2. While pleased with the win, our players were guarded in their show of enthusiasm. They had some twelve hours earlier lost a member of their baseball family, though the team had played with tremendous precision and effort and seemingly had given their all to insure great honor would be placed at the feet of Daniel's memory. They were spent, and so were we. One by one the boys made their way to Pam and me. We hugged each and offered our congratulations, stopping for an extended greeting with Daniel's good friend Bart Carter. Now in tears, Bart had pitched the complete game and was certainly pleased to have paid homage to Daniel in the only way he could. I told him how proud I was of him and that Daniel would be really pleased...except for the two runs he allowed. He laughed and moved on to join his teammates.

We stopped by Tim and Karen's house for dinner on our way home. My niece, Danielle, her family, and my nephew Brian were there. It was actually nice to sit and relax for a little while. This was the first day in many months that would not be spent shuttling back and forth to Methodist. We almost didn't know how to react. We arrived home late in the afternoon, and each of us retreated to a separate area. Worn down by months of running and the emotional turmoil surrounding our loss, we all collapsed early in the evening.

Early the next day, Pam and I went to Flinn and Maguire Funeral Home to make arrangements. Jerry Maguire had been a friend for many years, and I had asked Mike Carter to contact him about three weeks before Daniel's death. So Jerry and his staff were well prepared for our visit. His son Austin and assistant Gay led us through the process with kindness, compassion, and many helpful ideas. We selected his casket, which, you will be happy to know, came complete with decorative baseball gloves and deer statuettes on each corner. (You might be a redneck if...) We then traversed to Greenlawn Cemetery to select his gravesite. We went ahead and purchased his plot along with our own so that we will always be together, one of us on each side of him. Mike Mercer, our good friend and Hospice Chaplain, called and set a time for his visit to our home. We had asked Mike nearly a week before Dan's death to speak at his memorial service. Mike has a gift for saying and doing the right things at the right time, and we knew this occasion would be no different. Maria Coudret, a friend and the boys' Religious Education teacher, stopped by with Father Tom Schleissman to discuss Dan's memorial service and funeral. We all agreed that the funeral home was ill-equipped to handle the volume of people we expected at the memorial service, and Father Tom was gracious enough to allow us the use of the Parish Life Center. Once the details were finalized, everyone left and we were able to wind down a bit. I sat downstairs and stared at the TV. Pam, as usual, set about doing laundry and making sure the boys had "good" clothes that fit for the memorial service and funeral. The boys, with the exception of Jeffrey, resumed their normal activities, which included tormenting one another and eating. Jeffrey took off for a while and I suspect ended up at his friend Levi Smythe's house or maybe Kristen's (his girlfriend).

Naturally, the calls, cards, and emails began pouring in. Jeffrey was kind enough to intercept most of the phone calls, which was probably unfair, but I was grateful as I wasn't prepared to talk on the phone just yet. Both of the area newspapers (Daily Journal and Indianapolis Star) called. We did speak with them. They had been most gracious over the past eighteen months, and we knew they wanted to bring this story to closure. Pam and I discussed what the memorial service should look like. We wanted Mike Mercer to speak along with Pat Hopper (Daniel's guidance counselor at school). In addition, we wanted Danielle Taylor (my niece) to speak just as she had at both my sister Connie's and brother Roger's funerals. She always did such a nice job of sharing the story from our family's perspective. Finally, Jeffrey asked if he could speak at the service. I was taken aback as I didn't know how he would be able to hold it together. I knew that I would not be able to do so, and I surmised, incorrectly, that he wouldn't either. I must admit that Pam and I were very proud of him that he felt so strongly about making the attempt. Two days later he would quell our concerns with an absolutely amazing remembrance of Daniel. Soon we retreated to bed, needing the rest but not looking forward to what the next day would bring.

Teenager loses battle with brain tumor
By Misty D. Wick (Daily Journal)

Franklin Community High School athlete whose off-field medical struggle inspired teammates and other students lost his year-and-a-half-long battle with brain cancer. Daniel Patrick Mercer, 19, died at 12:05 a.m. Monday at Methodist Hospital in Indianapolis.

As Daniel's condition weakened him, small, everyday activities became major milestones. They included returning to school for a few days, sitting on the bench with the baseball team and joking with his friends. Then this spring, the tumor got larger and eventually moved into his brain stem, Pam Mercer said.

Daniel went into the hospital for the final time the day after Mother's Day. He celebrated his 19th birthday in the hospital May 21. The nurses decorated his room, and his friends made a video for him. His father wrote in the blog Thursday: "I realize that it may appear like sour grapes, but I feel so sorry for all that he has missed and will miss. As strong and determined as he has been, I still long for him to return to the activities of a normal teenager, despite the fact that I know it will never happen."

Daniel was a three-sport athlete: football, wrestling and baseball. His older brother said he could have played pro baseball. Since December, Jeffrey Mercer, 20, has been at home taking care of his brother so that their parents could work. He also was with his brother while he was in the hospital. Jeffrey Mercer is a student at the University of Dayton and is going to school on a baseball scholarship. He gave that up this spring so that he could spend time with his brother. I love that I could stay at home and make more memories with him," Jeffrey Mercer said. The two played a lot of cards while they stayed home together Mercer said.

"I was always so amazed at how he could continue to fight even when he didn't have use of the left side of his body or his legs," Pam Mercer said. His father wrote May 17: "Through it all Daniel doesn't complain about his plight other than to tell us that something hurts. God love him."

The baseball team lost a great friend rather than a player, said Mark Pieper, former baseball coach. The team will carry him in their hearts forever, he said.

The Cubs' players learned of Mercer's death Monday morning. His family attended the Grizzly Cubs' first round sectional win against Southport in Indianapolis. "The boys know Daniel will always be with us in spirit," Franklin coach Brian Luse said. "I'm sure it helped that the family was here because they've battled. The family overcame adversity. The team can overcome adversity."

The alarm startled me at 7:30AM. I made sure Pam was awake and headed to the shower to prepare for what I knew would be a long and difficult day. Friends and family had agreed to help us set up the Life Center at St. Rose. Shortly after 9:00AM, we arrived with a van full of Daniel memorabilia. Chairs sat in straight rows, and bleachers lined the wall as we made our way into the large room. Floral arrangements had begun arriving, and we set about decorating the room. We discussed how we wanted the room to be interactive, full of life, just like Daniel would want it.

There was a collection of Daniel remembrances to unload and set up. Hs framed Scott Rolen "Small Victories" jersey; the Indiana Bulls framed jersey and hat; the American flag flown in Baghdad and sent to him by former Franklin baseball player Kevin O'Neal; photos, trophies, and a host of other items dotted the walls. Pam's friends at Whiteland High School had created a video collage of Daniel photos, complete with Kenny Chesney music (his favorite artist).

We made the decision to keep the casket closed during the memorial and funeral. Daniel's body had undergone a massive transformation over the final three months of his life, and we didn't want to upset those who hadn't seen him recently. Pam and I felt that since there would be no body to view that we would have the ability to move throughout the room and greet those who attended. We finished setting up by about 10:30AM and headed home to change clothes. Visitation was scheduled to begin at 1:00 and conclude at 7:00, with a memorial service from 7:00 to 8:00. In the last 48 hours, I had given a lot of thought to what I was about to experience. How would I hold up? What about Pam and the boys? Daniel's friends? We were running on empty, but I hoped that our strong belief that we would once again join Daniel in the kingdom of heaven would carry us through. We had held up reasonably well thus far; however, we were preparing to enter a new dimension.

Dan's Memorial Service in the Parish Life Center at St. Rose of Lima Church

We arrived back at St. Rose at 12:40PM and quietly entered the Parish Life Center. Daniel's casket had been placed at the far end of the building, surrounded by large bouquets of flowers and greenery. We had not seen him since the night he passed away, and I must admit I was unsure how I would react. Most of Pam's family was already there. Her mom and dad stood near the back of the large room and waited for us to make our way to them. Pam's sisters, their husbands, and children sat huddled in the center of the room, crying and consoling one another. I was yet unprepared to be of much comfort to them. My brother and his family were there as well, making their way around to the various displays. Austin and Gay from the funeral home stepped forward to greet us and review the arrangement of the room as well as the agenda. Austin said, "I hope the room is what you envisioned." I replied that it looked wonderful. He continued, "Can we go over the agenda quickly before things get hectic?" I nodded. "We have arranged the room so that people can disperse, view the various displays, and have time to reminisce. I know you both want to avoid the traditional receiving line, and we have done our best to accommodate that wish." I let him know that the set-up was exactly what we had asked for. "We would like to open the casket in about five minutes to allow your family to view Daniel before the visitors arrive." Pam indicated that would be fine.

Once Austin concluded, my nephew Brian was the first to greet me. I could see that he had been crying, and he gave me a hug without speaking. I searched for Pam as I wanted to make sure she was going to be OK. I noticed her standing with her sisters and parents. She seemed to be holding together. I continued toward the front of the room and was met by my dad, who gave me a long embrace. There was a large screen on the north wall; the video collage of Daniel was playing. I glanced at it but had to look away quickly. It was too much for me to handle at that moment, and in fact, over a year later I still can't watch live video of Daniel and struggle when looking at pictures of him. I hope some day soon I can resume that activity. Soon I had greeted everyone, and Austin signaled that he was ready to open the casket. The crowd would be arriving in a few minutes. We would need time to collect ourselves.

Pam's family went first. The kids were distraught and remained close by their parents. I think the single hardest thing for me through all of this was in watching the kids: Daniel's friends and the children in our family. It just broke my heart to see them hurting. I should be able to handle almost anything at this point in my life, but the kids? This just made no sense to them. My family went next. I could see how visibly upset my brother was. He is a quiet almost stoic person by nature, except when it came to Daniel. When Dan was little, he drove Tim to distraction; but with age, maturity, and his incredible sense of humor, Dan had become good pals with him. While everyone was heartbroken, I think Tim hurt worse than most and continues to do so. Next it was our turn. Truthfully, I'm not sure I wanted my turn. This would be so final, and even though I would see him again tomorrow before the funeral, this verified that Dan was really gone. Somehow I had hoped, and even prayed, that some miracle would occur and Dan would come bursting into the Parish Life Center. But there he lay, decked out in his Boston Red Sox shirt and hat and khaki shorts. Jeffrey stayed back as he had made the decision that he would remember Dan as he was prior to his growing ill. He never approached the casket that day or the next, and we respected his decision. There was no questioning his loyalty to his brother now or ever. Joe, who has always struggled with his emotions, looked bewildered and disconsolate. Little Anthony rested his head on Pam's shoulder and cried softly. He had been Dan's buddy since birth. The two of them were far enough removed in age (eight years) that Dan had enthusiastically assumed the role of big brother.

While basically undemonstrative with the rest of our immediate family prior to his illness, Dan would smother Anthony with kisses, even until the day he grew too ill to continue.

As I stood there looking at the shell of a son who had eighteen months earlier so easily wrestled Jeffrey to the floor in our front room, I thought, "How is it possible that this could have happened? This is so totally unfair to him, to his friends, to us." As I fought with my feelings, I heard rain beginning to pelt the roof of the Life Center. The skies absolutely opened up for the better part of a half-hour. I thought, "Even God is crying over this one." Although it was only a few minutes, it felt like an eternity that I gazed at Daniel's body. Not many opportunities left, so I needed to soak them in. I cannot put into words just how proud I am to have been his dad. He was truly one of a kind, and we were about to find out just how special he had become to others.

No sooner had Austin closed the casket than Gay propped the doors open to the Life Center. The procession began. For more than six solid hours, one by one, they came to pay their respects. Teachers, teammates past and present, coaches, opposing teams, umpires, nurses, doctors, friends and family from one end of the state of Indiana to the other. They came from Ohio, Kentucky, Michigan and other points. At about 5:30 I took a 5 minute break then made my way back to a solid wall of people. Our plans for dispersing the crowd with displays was scrapped before things even got started. The line wrapped around the room and out the door. They came to honor; they came to grieve; they came to let us know they loved Dan. More than a thousand made their way to the Parish Life Center that first day of June 2006. The first registry book filled quickly, and they scrambled for a second. So many hugs I received that day that my pressed white shirt was stained with make-up and mascara. My right hand ached for a week afterward from shaking hands with literally hundreds and hundreds of well wishers.

Pam and the boys held up well. There was so much activity that it was nearly impossible to dwell upon the finality of this day, and that was, I'm sure, a good thing. At nearly 7:00PM and close to the conclusion of the visiting hours, I saw Erica Short (Methodist Hospital Social Worker) and Dr. Michael Turner (Dan's surgeon) making their way to the front. While Erica had become a trusted friend and I knew she

I would have loved to change the ending of Dan's life story. I even thought I knew what was best. I thought I knew how God could turn hundreds of people to Him through Dan's healing. Then last Thursday night (June 1, 2006) I looked around the room for seven hours, and even though I was sad, mad, and hurt, I thought to myself, God is amazing! There were not hundreds of lives that Dan had touched, but a thousand or more. He so impacted this world with who he was, not what he could do.

Ann Dicken (Daniel's Aunt)

would be there, I was astounded that Dr. Turner would attend. Michael Turner is widely regarded as one of the finest pediatric neurosurgeons in the world; his many speaking engagements all over the globe attest to that fact. His schedule alone should have made it nearly impossible for him to be with us, but here he was, to pay his respects to a young man he had grown to enjoy and admire. I hugged him tightly and thanked him for all he had done and had tried to do for Daniel. Pam asked Erica if she wished to speak at the memorial service. She indicated that she would be honored. Austin broke in and said, "We probably need to wrap up the receiving line so that you all can have a minute to relax before the memorial service." With a line of visitors still winding around the room, we reluctantly agreed to retreat to a side room to catch our breath.

Ten minutes later we made our way back into the Life Center for the service. We made our way toward the five chairs set aside for us in the front row. I paused to look around the room. Chairs and bleachers were filled with friends and family dabbing their eyes with tissues. I had discussed this scene with Pam in the days leading up to the service. I told her I felt it was important for us to remain strong, lean on one another, and stay attuned to the needs of others. After all, we had eighteen months to prepare ourselves, but many of these folks were coming to grips with this moment for the first time.

Mike Mercer greeted the audience, led the group in prayer, and outlined the agenda. Our good friends Mark and Sherry Pieper played and sang the Lord's Prayer. Then began the speakers. Danielle Taylor (our niece) went first, and as she had at my sister's and brother's funerals, delivered a heartfelt remembrance of Daniel, pausing frequently to collect herself. Pat Hopper (Dan's guidance counselor at Franklin High School) stepped forward next. I would like to share a few of her comments. Pat began:

Daniel's Dad called me before [Daniel] started his freshman year and asked if he could serve in our office as a guidance aide. In my mind I was thinking, "Oh, I bet Daniel is just like older brother Jeff: a nice kid, kind of quiet." WELL............He certainly was a nice kid, but anything but quiet. In fact, he would talk nonstop for the whole block he was with us. He was always telling funny stories or making Katrina Phillips crack up or asking Mrs. Fiddler about herself or conversing with anyone who walked in. That is, IF we could find him. You see, Daniel liked to wander. We had a saying in the Guidance Department: "Where's Daniel?" kind of like the Where's Waldo game. Most times he would find his way back to us, but on occasion I had to go hunt for him. Invariably, he was visiting with a teacher or coach or was chatting with the special needs kids in Mrs. Bishop's room. Sometimes I would scold him and he would just smile and say, "Oh, Mrs. Hopper, are you mad?" and of course how could I be? Now I understand what he was doing: he was going about his business, and Daniel's business was "people." He never met a stranger, he was genuinely happiest when he was with others, and he gave the gift of himself to everyone without hesitation or discrimination. I imagine him now chatting with his fellow angels in heaven and quizzing them on baseball statistics!

Pat went on to say:

During the past year in the many talks we had about life, about his profound love for his family, about his faith in God, about his choice to live each precious moment as best he could, I came to know that Daniel was not just another great kid. He was also a great teacher. He taught all of us how to live each moment because he understood that every moment mattered; every second is another opportunity to experience this precious present, this here and now that IS life. He didn't want to miss a thing! He wanted to be part of it. So he would drag his pillow to classes so he could lie on the floor because it was too painful to sit; he would go to games to support the teams even though it was a struggle; and he would still laugh and tell stories and try to put others at ease. You see, he was going about his business, and he was a master at it.

The last time Daniel came to my office was this past December. He had not been able to come to school for a long while. He had to be helped in by his brother Jeff, but he wanted to bring me a gift. He gave me a picture of himself and his brother Joe. They were dressed up in suits and had Hawaiian leis around their necks. It seems Daniel had received the Scott Rolen 'Hero' award and this picture had been taken at the banquet. He told me a funny story about the banquet and how there were hula dancers and that someone had taken his steak away while he was, of course, visiting another group of people! So we laughed about that. Then he told me that he had prayed every day to have his tumor go away, but now there were more of them, and he said he knew that God had other plans for him. And I cried because I could not help it. Daniel told me that no matter what happened, he knew he would be all right. Imagine that, he was facing death and yet was trying to comfort me! But that was so like Daniel. I struggled to find words of comfort, how he had shown us all how important courage and determination were in life. He thought for a moment, then smiled a little and said, "I'd just rather play baseball."

Naturally, we were so proud of what Pat had to say but the last line made it hard to keep my composure. What I wouldn't have given to make Daniel's wish a reality. Dan's best friends, Emily Fox and Michael Reese, followed Pat and shared a number of funny stories. I must admit they were well timed, given Pat's tribute. Emily and Michael had stood by Dan's side from the start. I knew they were distraught, but they pulled off their portion of the memorial brilliantly. Erica Short approached the podium next and even brought Dr. Turner along with her. I looked at Pam in disbelief. "Did you know he was going to speak?" I said. She said that she had had no idea. Erica related a number of stories about her time with Daniel in the hospital, about how she had appreciated getting to know our family over the past eighteen months. Then she turned it over to Dr. Turner. Sometimes it's hard to get a read on doctors, and we should know given our involvement with scores throughout Daniel's illness. Stoic, reserved, guarded and always in control, Dr. Turner couldn't even get started before the tears began to flow. In thirty plus years of practice Michael Turner had, I'm sure, lost hundreds of children to various ailments of the head

June 6, 2006

Jeff and Pam,

There is not much we can say that you haven't already heard. That Daniel was so special, an inspiration, a fighter, funny, loving, etc. The only thing that comes to our minds when we think of Daniel is that we just loved him; we truly loved him.

Joe, Michele, Emily, and Hilary Fox

and brain, but here he was with his emotions on display. He recounted his many memories of Daniel including an episode at the hospital weeks before:

Daniel wanted to return home after months in the hospital. He used his cell phone and dialed 9-1-1 from his ICU bed to get help to get him out. Naturally, it didn't work, but just like many other things with Daniel...that was a first for us.

Jeffrey followed and did a masterful job while maintaining his composure. A feat that Pam and I couldn't have replicated. He shared that "longevity was Dan's only shortcoming in his time on earth." I'm not sure that was totally true, but we'll leave it that way. He also recalled, "Many times Dan told me he would play baseball again, and even to his last breath, I didn't doubt him." I was concerned with how Jeffrey would perform because he was delivering the eulogy the next day. As is frequently the case, he exceeded our expectation. He is quite a big brother...even to the end. Finally, Mike Mercer concluded the evening with a beautiful celebration of Daniel's life. Though not related to us, Mike has become a cherished member of our family and someone who is there for us at a moment's notice. It was essential to us that he open and close this evening. While painful to endure, I found myself not wanting the evening to come to an end. But alas, it must, and soon we were headed for home.

Early the next morning, we rose to prepare for the funeral. Pam had ordered thirty helium-filled balloons to release after the ceremony at the cemetery, and she called to make sure they would be delivered. The boys got themselves ready without complaint. They looked so handsome in their suits and ties. Pam was running a bit late, as she often does, and I thought how nice she looked on this solemn day. Soon we were out the door and on our way to the funeral home. The last ones to arrive, we were again

I never met the son...never shook his hand, never saw his smile. So many nevers that will not be undone...

It wasn't until that final tribute that I realized how well I had actually come to know this Daniel of my prayers. He had been right before me all along. I had felt the warmth of his gentle strength every time I shook his father's hand. I had seen his smile shining brightly through the light of his father's eyes. Just as the father had shaped and nurtured the son, so had the son served as an indelible source of inspiration and transformation for the father. Where one walked, so did the other.

Tim Garner (Franklin College, Associate Dean)

greeted by Austin and Gay, who shuttled us into the viewing room where Dan's casket had been placed. This would be the final opportunity to view him before he was laid to rest. Several of our family members had written letters or brought mementoes that they wished to place into the casket. Many tears were shed as, one by one, they said their final goodbyes to Dan.

Pam, Anthony, Joe and I were the last ones to approach the casket. Pam's muffled sobs alerted me to hold her tight as we stood before him the final time. While there is no way that anyone could love their children more than I do, the bond between mother and child is deep-seated beyond comprehension. The closeness secured during the time in the womb is evident, at least to me. Pam and Dan had become inseparable through the final eighteen months. He mirrored her stubbornness while growing up, and they frequently would spat about everything from his room to his clothes to his attitude. But, when push came to shove, he retreated to her loving nature and compassion--to the degree that I sometimes felt left out. However, I knew that this closeness was precious to them both; I would find my niche in other ways. Though not recited out loud, because I had not the ability to speak at that moment, I let Daniel know how much I loved him and would miss him, how very proud of him I was, and how I would do all in my power to assure that his life would not be lived in vain. Truth be known, there is no one more stubborn than I, and I will not rest until Dan's memory has been adequately honored. He earned it. So let it be written; so let it be done.

We made our way out of the funeral home as the casket was loaded into the hearse for the trip to St. Rose. When we arrived, the church was full, people standing along every wall. The pallbearers--Jeffrey, Joe, Anthony, Bart Carter, Michael Reese, Ben Gordon, Adam Miller, Philip Glasser, and Joe Fox--brought Dan into the Church and set the casket on a rolling cart. We fell in line behind and followed Father Tom and Father Paul Shikany (our former Priest) to the front of the Church. There we took our seats to the left of the main aisle. Anthony leaned over and said, "Dad, Scott Rolen is sitting behind us." It wouldn't be until after the service that I would have a chance to thank Scott, his wife Nikki, his brother Todd, and Dave Taylor for chartering a flight on a St. Louis Cardinals game day to be with us. The Rolen family, along with Dave, had been an incredible support structure for Dan and our entire family. To this day they continue to be involved.

The customary formalities of a Catholic mass were attended to with readings by Ann Dicken and my brother Tim. Tim struggled, barely able to finish. Father Tom and Father Paul shared many of the responsibilities, and soon it was time for Jeffrey to deliver his eulogy. At twenty years of age and completely on his own, he delivered the following address without so much as breaking stride:

"Even if I knew that tomorrow the world would go to pieces, I would still plant my apple tree." (Martin Luther King, Jr.)

Daniel Mercer knew many times over that tomorrow was no guarantee and that the only given was that nothing in his life was a constant. He knew that every breath he took could be his last, and yet he still planted his apple tree. He planted his apple tree of hope, love and courage and prayed mightily that the roots would take deep hold in all of those who knew him. He knew that tomorrow may never come and still he went about his work.

I have won national championships, had game winning hits, received more awards than I can recall. But nothing in my life sends a rush of pride through my body as when I claim Daniel Mercer as my younger brother, my blood, my best friend. My kid brother started his battle with cancer nearly 2 years ago as a good man, not a great man, but good...he had not had time to become great. Very few individuals are born great. My father is one of the few who I believe was born into greatness. For most, a lifetime of learning and shaping must take place before the label "great" can be applied.

Daniel was the most fun and endlessly hilarious individual I have ever known. I guess that is what bonded us and always will...our ability to laugh together. A mere look and we could have each other in tears from the intensity of our laughter. His personality was such that he could keep an audience captive with the slightest effort. As I look back at all of our time together, I realize that he would nearly glow at times. I do not know why or how this occurred. I know that this is improbable, probably impossible, but if you have ever been around a person like this, you know what I am describing. For those who live life in its entirety and never meet such a person, I pity you and consider this a travesty. Daniel helped all to realize that life is made of millions of miniature moments. The way the light comes through your window can affect your entire day or have no effect at all depending upon what we choose to do with it. Our lives are not comprised of breath-taking event after breath-taking event. It is dinner with our family, on those rare occasions; it is basketball in the front yard with our brothers; it is Easter Sunday at Grandma and Grandpa's. These are the memories we take with us for all of time...the small moments spent with those we love.

By my junior year of high school, Daniel had become my best friend. Many siblings claim to be best friends, but Daniel truly was more than my friend and more than my blood. He was the one person I could lean upon with any problem, as he did with me. We played high school football and baseball together for 2 years. My most fond memories come from our time spent together on the varsity baseball team. I took the game so extremely seriously and he took it as he took everything in his life...as a game...a game meant to be fun. Throughout our 2 years of high school baseball, I found myself becoming less serious and him becoming more serious. As we spent more time together, we learned to appreciate the qualities that the other possessed. Many times, I would become frustrated with the ease at which Daniel glided through life. As I look back, I realize this was to offset the difficulties he would soon face in life. Once he became ill, we drew closer still. Even though I was at college we would speak daily...it was as though we had each been separated from our other half. He took on his illness with such a courageous vigor. He never lost faith that he would some day be healed. No matter how severe, and at times terrible, the news he would receive...he would be fine by the next day.

Throughout his fight, I watched him transform from a good man to a great man. Great men never relinquish their ideals for those of lesser significance. They never look for others to fight their battles and they always put others' needs in front of their own. Daniel did all three daily. When his body began to crumble and falter, we would have discussions on the true meaning of beating cancer. We decided that cancer may cause his step to falter and his hand to shake, but cancer had never won until it stole your personality. Cancer never won.

I watched him fight for one last breath before his body would allow him to fight no more. As Daniel was lifted to eternal joy, I saw a tear swell in the corner of his right eye. As simply and peacefully as I wiped it away he was freed from the remnants of his mortal shell and the toils of life. I knew at this moment that he was gone, but he had given me the greatest gift he had left to offer...a tear. A tear to confirm that although he was in the presence of the Lord, our bond would cross eternities and that he too was sad to part, if only for an instant.

Daniel Patrick Mercer...you came to us as a burst of energy dressed in cowboy boots and a coonskin cap, and you left us with a zest for life like nothing this

*world has ever seen. You epitomized life and the reasons
we wake each morning. From your first smile as an infant to
the last witty comment you made as a man, you filled the
lives of all those around you with nothing less than exuber-
ance. In this age when inspiration is lacking and the youth
of our world are left with few models of true consequence in
their lives...you were a hero. In this day when adults look at
the state of society with dismay and disdain and wonder
where the discipline and character have gone...you were a
shining beacon of hope of what is possible and what could
be good once more. In this time of conflict and turmoil when
the world seems to at times balance on the edge of a
blade...you taught us to laugh and take life for what it is...a
joyous ride. And, although not every day may be perfect,
you made it clear that rare is the occasion to be disheart-
ened and discouraged. So let Daniel's roots grow deep in all
of us, breed hope...live with love...and never ever give up.
Daniel I miss you BIG DAWG and love you so very much.*

— Jeffrey Daniel Mercer

June 3, 2006

*Thank you for sharing Daniel's
story in your online journal...a
lesson in love, family, strength,
determination, character, and
attitude. It reminded us of all
that is important and good.
Jeffrey was so right when he
said, "Daniel became a great
man." We feel blessed to have
known him and will always
remember Daniel.*

Paul and Julie Hass and family

12. Leaving a Legacy

*"I cry not only for Daniel and the pain he endured,
but I cry for all of us who have been deprived of his
personality, his energy, and his enthusiasm for life.
Although he suffered mightily, I think in the end
we are the ones who suffered the greatest loss."*

– Jeff Mercer

The hearse pulled out ahead of our family and headed for Greenlawn Cemetery. By the time we arrived, scores of car were parked alongside the road inside the cemetery. Our driver made his way around them and pulled up behind the vehicle which held Dan's body. Standing just behind the hearse, waiting for his buddy to arrive, was Jamie, Dan's special friend from football Fridays. He had ridden his bicycle to the cemetery to pay his respects. The poignancy of the moment drew our hearts even closer to the small victories which we continued to experience. While it was there before us all along, the full impact of Daniel's life was only beginning to be felt. As I stood facing Jamie in thoughtful contemplation, I realized that the final chapter to this life so tragically lost had not yet been written.

If I truly believed that Dan's death was the end
of this story, it would be even more tragic than it already is. But I don't believe that death is the end of his story. In fact, I'd like to share some of the
rest of the story.

Some six months after Daniel's burial, I received a call from a colleague in a neighboring school district. New to his district, this gentleman had called for advice on a project they were preparing to undertake. He indicated that if I would agree to assist him that he would gladly buy my lunch. I was happy to be of assistance and agreed to meet him. I arrived a bit early, took my seat, and waited for him. Although I had never met him before, it wasn't long before a man in a suit and tie made his way into the restaurant and headed my direction. I greeted him. He introduced himself and sat down across the table from me. After a few minutes of pleasantries, he looked at me with great seriousness.

"Are you the father of the boy who died from the brain tumor?"
"Yes, I am. Are you familiar with Daniel?"

"Well, for some reason, even though I didn't know Daniel or your family, I felt drawn to his story. I read all the newspaper articles, and I read through your online journal. In fact, about two months after Daniel passed away, I drove to the Greenlawn Cemetery in Franklin to look for his gravesite. I looked for quite some time, and then I found it. When I arrived, there was another man standing in front of the headstone. When he turned to see who was standing behind him, I recognized that he had a notable handicap."

I smiled and asked if he had inquired about the man's name. He said that he had, and he was surprised when in unison we both said, "Jamie."

"How did you know?"

"Just a guess," I said.

Two months, six months, one year later, Daniel's legacy continues to flourish here in Franklin. Not a day goes by that his name isn't spoken by friends or colleagues. And I have come to realize that I have been forever redefined as a father, a husband, a man. From this point forward, I will be known as Daniel Mercer's dad, and I must say that I can't think of a better way to be remembered.

I've frequently wondered how other families like ours not only deal with the tragedy of the death of their child but also insure that the memory of that child is not lost to the ages. In Daniel's case, his story was worth remembering and maybe even telling. I could write the story of his life. We could create programs and events which honor his existence. We could tell his story over and over so that those who didn't know him could benefit from the many blessings he left behind. We have done many of those things, but maybe the single most important way to remember Dan is in the simplest way of all. It took Scott Rolen and his emissary to remind me.

As the completion of this book drew near, Jeffrey and I traveled to St. Louis to meet Scott and Nikki Rolen and Dave Taylor. We were there to discuss Scott's writing of the Afterword to the book. It was a delightful discussion, spanning a broad spectrum of

Daniel has not only been an inspiration of courage, faith and hope, he has made me notice what is truly important in life. I had always said the minute I met him...there is something unique about that boy. I just never knew how special.

Michele Fox
Family friend

topics, but soon we focused on why Scott and Nikki feel so compelled to immerse themselves in the lives of so many sick children. Scott recounted his initial visit to Temple Hospital in Philadelphia and his concern that though he had visited, he would never have a personal relationship with those children. He related that the most special part for him was in getting to know the kids and their parents and allowing them to know him. His one minute, two minute, five minute visits fell far short of fulfilling his desired objective. As often happens, however, it takes a child to make us aware of what's *really* important.

Scott, on one of his many visits to a children's hospital, happened through the open door of a room and stumbled onto a disturbing sight-- a young boy wired into an apparatus unlike any he had ever seen. Wires extended from above the boy's head down to a helmet which was bolted to the boy's skull. Standing upright, this boy had some sort of spinal problem, and the apparatus forced him to be completely immobile except for his arms. Unable to speak, the boy slowly opened his eyes and caught sight of Scott and Nikki. Instantly, the boy raised both arms to the sky, and while pumping his fists into the air, his grin spread from ear to ear. Scott said at that moment he understood that while there is a value in getting to know the kids personally, the true value rests in a much simpler concept. He realized that the most precious gift is simply "showing up." The willingness to take time to visit and to let someone, in this case a child, know that you care enough to "show up" is truly what matters.

As I sat with them and considered what Scott had just said, it occurred to me that he had absolutely captured the essence of what's important in everyone's life, not just a child's. Show up when people need you. Show up when they don't. Show up to listen. Show up to talk. It matters not...just show up.

Jeff and Pam,

Wow, it is amazing to think it has already been a year since we lost Daniel. I have thought of all of you so often in this past year. Sometimes, it will be here at the hospital, in the oddest moments, that he comes to mind. While admitting a patient back from surgery and thinking of the unbelievable bravery with which that child endured so much struggle. And all of it without complaint. Sometimes, it will be when we are asking a patient a question about their pain, and it will be remembering an answer only Daniel could give. Like the time we asked if his abdominal pain felt like a stabbing pain, and with utter sincerity he said, "I don't know, I've never been stabbed before." Other times it is remembering the time we snuck the baby in for him to hold, and he just wanted to smell her first. And finding those pictures later in the memory of my cell phone. What a precious young man. Oh, or the "Be careful when you look into my eyes, you might be mesmerized," when doing a pupil check. Of course, I have never had a kid call 911 from their bed before Dan or since. Or when I watched the NCAA tournament this year and thought of how we picked brackets together last year. In some ways it is hard to believe that was just last March. To me it seems much longer than that. I can't imagine what it must seem like to you.

Of course, my time with him was often when he felt his worst. I missed out on the times when he was at his best. But what a blessing that you have those precious memories of such an amazing child. He was truly a one in a million kind of kid. I have done this job joyfully for 17 years. There have been many times when we lose a child that the utter despair is very difficult for me to overcome. Daniel was one of those kids. It is difficult to reconcile my faith with the taking of such a special kid who had so much to offer this world. But I know it is not mine to question. And I absolutely know that while he was on this earth, the lives he touched were all made better for his place in them. I just wanted to let you both know that you will always hold a very special place in my heart. Your son will never be forgotten. He was truly one of the most special, unique individuals I have ever had the honor of caring for as a nurse.

Tracy Davis
Methodist Hospital Nursing Supervisor

Dan's legacy was in many ways already beginning to take shape even before he passed. I think of the dogged determination shown by Pam's cousin Linda, her sister Ann, and our friend Maria Coudret in

Please forgive my selfishness and the ways in which I have taken my children for granted. Help me to truly understand and cherish how much I have been given through my children.

Our teenage daughter came home the other evening and regaled us with a non-stop replay of the highlights of a recently viewed movie. Of course, we set aside what we were doing and did our best to listen attentively. However, I eventually found my patience growing thin and I grew weary of listening. It was then that I thought of another father and his teenage son. I tried to imagine what that father would give to once again have the opportunity for this kind of inane, babbling conversation with his child. Chastened by this awareness, I re-tuned my heart and mind to my daughter, determined to enjoy the precious gift I had been neglecting just moments before.

Tim Garner
Franklin College Assistant Dean

tracking down the Archbishop (Daniel Buechlein) on Daniel's birthday, just one week prior to his death, and their unrelenting quest to have him visit Dan and conduct the "Anointing of the Sick." Such a great honor, and so highly unusual for the Archbishop to have time to make a personal visit. It was as if his role was to bring the journey full circle: from November 3, 2004, when Daniel was confirmed into the Catholic Church by the Archbishop, to May 21, 2006, when the Archbishop would issue Dan last rites. He was there in the beginning, and he "showed up" at the end.

June 10, 2006
The Daily Journal

Family's loss offers lessons on love, faith

When Daniel Mercer died May 29, his family lost a son and a brother. Franklin Community High School students lost a classmate and teammate. And the community of Franklin lost a young man whom many people had come to care about, even if they never met him.

Mercer was diagnosed with a brain tumor in November 2004. A football player, he thought his headaches were the aftermath of a concussion. Shortly after the diagnosis, Mercer's father, Jeff, began writing an online journal to chronicle his son's illness. Over the next year and a half, Jeff Mercer wrote about the ups and down of Daniel's treatments. He told of hopeful signs but didn't shy away from the bad turns.

More importantly, he wrote about the emotions that wracked the family. On November 7, 2004, Jeff Mercer wrote: "We intend to go to battle like we never have before. It will take much faith, strength and determination, but we are full of all of that and more." A few months later, he wrote: "Daniel continues to be a source of great strength for...our entire family."

In June he shared one of many lessons he felt he learned during his son's ordeal: "I have learned through all of this that you never take anything for granted, you never assume, that nothing is ever as good as it seems, nor as bad, but somewhere in between reality falls."

He wrote one of his most poignant entries January 17, 2006: "The worst part is the feeling of helplessness that accompanies our reality. When Dan asks, 'Dad, can you help me?' what can I say?"

It wasn't just the father's public mourning that people can draw lessons from. The entire family showed impressive strength. For example, Daniel's brother Jeff left college so he could spend more time with his brother and relieve his parents of some of the care-giving responsibility. Jeff wasn't sad about this. In fact, quite the opposite. He considered it a gift. "I love that I could stay at home and make more memories with him," Jeff said.

After Daniel died, his father thanked the community for its support and offered some final thoughts: "In a community like Franklin, it seems, at least for us, there was help around every corner. Frequently, we as parents forget that therein lies the value of living in a community such as Franklin."

While we mourn a life cut short, the grace that the Mercer family showed and their willingness to share their lives with the community is something everyone can learn from. Jeff Mercer wrote: "We drew our strength in large part from [a caring community], and for that we can't possibly thank you enough."

But it is we who should thank the Mercers. Their strength can be our inspiration.

Over the course of Dan's illness, people "showed up" in so many practical ways. One of the most tangible ways was in the contributions and donations which flowed into Dan's fund, set up at Mutual Savings Bank in Franklin. Upon his passing there was a significant amount of money in the account, and even more poured in at his memorial service. Pam and I decided that it would bring great comfort to our family and others to establish a memorial fund at the Johnson County Community Foundation. I met with Sandy Daniels (Executive Director of JCCF), and she quickly helped us launch the Daniel P. Mercer Family Fund. With an initial investment of $25,000, the mission of the fund was to accomplish the following:

Whereas Daniel Mercer drew great strength, courage, and character from his participation in athletics, it is the mission of the Daniel Mercer Family Fund to provide financial support to Franklin, Indiana, youth athletics and the Indiana Bulls Baseball organization.

The fund provides a scholarship annually to an Indiana Bulls player who exemplifies the following characteristics:

Ability

Academic Standing

Character

Courage

Determination

Mental Toughness

Unselfishness

We were so pleased to present our first Bulls award in February 2007 to a young man from northern Indiana. Coincidentally, he too was a catcher just like Dan. Our first Franklin awards are scheduled for distribution in December 2007.

We have established an Advisory Board which governs the distribution of the Foundation Funds, and it is the goal of that board to grow the fund to $100,000 over the next 5 years. In doing so, we will provide annual awards totaling at least $5,000. In fact, the yeoman's share of the proceeds from the sale of this book will assist in growing the fund. In the event that Pam and I are unable to administrate the fund in the future, then Jeffrey, Joe, and Anthony have the responsibility for honoring the legacy of their late brother. It is a responsibility which they will gladly assume when the time comes.

Franklin Community High School has done their part as well. In September 2006, the Daniel Mercer "Set a Good Example" (SAGE) award was established. The intent of the program is to honor students who consistently model the expectations of Franklin Community High School and their community and also exhibit daily personal choices that make a difference for others. These students, sometimes quietly and without expectation of recognition, truly Set a Good Example for fellow students, faculty and staff. The SAGE winners inspire through example every day.

The written criteria for the SAGE award honor Daniel in the following way:

Through his physical battle he was a living definition of our SAGE criteria. Although the honor each year will be for our students, we believe the example Daniel set for the Grizzly Cub community deserves a place of ongoing recognition. His name and face on this award will serve as a constant reminder to all of us to Set a Good Example every day
and a reminder that we need to treat every day as a day
of opportunity.

Each month throughout the school year, 2 seniors (1 male and 1 female) are selected to receive the award and are honored with a medallion presented by the principal. In May 2007, another 40 Franklin students were honored in addition to the monthly winners at the year-end SAGE banquet. Our family was deeply honored to have the opportunity to attend and participate in the first recognition program. Pam and I were moved nearly to tears when one father approached us after the ceremony, tears streaming down his face, and asked if we would have our picture taken with his daughter (one of the award winners) because this award meant so much to their family.

Shortly after Dan's passing and through the efforts of Buzz Bay (Hospice Coordinator) and Mona Heck (Franklin High School teacher), a Franklin High School Hospice Group (first of its kind in Indiana) was established. This was done in large part as a response to Daniel's struggle. The organization subsequently raised over $500 to place a memorial tree and commemorative plaque honoring Daniel near the new Franklin High School baseball and football fields. Nearly three hundred family members, friends, teachers and coaches were on hand for the dedication in August 2007.

So honored and humbled by this show of love and compassion, we feel a very strong responsibility to do our part to honor Dan's memory. People frequently ask how our family has remained so strong in the face of such adversity. The answer, while simple to provide, is actually far more complex. First, there must be an underlying faith that insures the notion that we will once again be united with Daniel. Second, there must be a measure of teamwork that allows each of our family members to be buoyed by the determination of the other four. Third, there

Daniel had an incredible wit. He could make any situation hilarious, but Joe and I both saw a different side to Daniel, too. I saw a respect from Daniel for his parents that you don't often see in a 17 or 18 year old. I swear if you didn't know better, our daughter Emily and Daniel were the only two kids at Franklin High School that didn't get to do anything their freshman year. But even at that you could see that Daniel wouldn't have wanted it any other way. He loved and respected Jeff and Pam in so many ways. Daniel's love continued so deeply for his family when he became ill. There was not a day that went by when we saw Daniel that he wouldn't mention how much he loved his family and how lucky he was to have them.

Our family was also blessed by Daniel's unconditional love that he gave. I miss all the wonderful hugs he used to give me. I have never witnessed such a strong and amazing young man through incredibly trying times. His faith and love for life were overwhelming. Daniel renewed my faith in God and appreciation for life in so many ways.

Michele Fox
Family friend

must be the strength we draw from our community, a strength that provides an indelible source of inspiration.

With each passing day I feel an energy growing inside of me. The obligation that I have to honor Dan's legacy is compelling, but it's more than a sense of responsibility. It's as if I am now accountable for insuring that the courage, love, determination, and selflessness exhibited by Daniel be remembered until I am no more. It's a message that must emanate from every fiber of my being. It's who I am and what I must do.

So let it be written...so let it be done.

I sit here thinking about what I could say to you that could make any sense of the events in the last year and a half, but again, I've come up short.

I know there are many people in your life that surely are more comforting and helpful than these simple words could ever be. I just want you to know how deeply sorry I am for your loss. You are loved more than you know.
If ever a family has exemplified faithfulness and continued obedience, it has been yours. Daniel's perseverance has prevailed throughout all the trials and tribulations this world has placed before him. He showed great strength in life as do each and every one of you. Through you and your family, God has been brought into the lives of MANY people. Sermons can be preached and scriptures can be studied, but to see God live in you displays priceless lessons of love and obedience.

I think about all the lives that have been affected by this tragedy. Even though it is difficult to understand God's will, it is what it is. God is forever etched into the hearts of Daniel's circle of friends and family. I for one am eternally grateful for the examples you have set for us.

God be with you and comfort you. I wish you peace.

Love,
Sherrie and Jim Jones, Brad, Brian,
and Bonnie Gallagher, Brent Scott

Starfish
Two men met on a beach.
"Good evening pal. What are you doing?"
"I'm throwing these starfish back in the ocean. If I don't, they'll die."
"There must be thousands of starfish on this beach.
You can't possibly get to them all.
You can't possibly make a difference."
He smiled, picked up yet another starfish and threw it into the sea.
"I made a difference to that one."

(Daniel made a difference.)

13. The Next Place

Two months after Daniel's passing, our family took a trip to Colorado. It took that long, for me at least, to be able to enjoy an activity without being consumed by the vision of Daniel participating. Of course, I continue to imagine how much fun he would be having and how we would enjoy being with him, but I'm able to work through it.

The home we rented in Estes Park, Colorado, backed up to the Big Thompson River. The river is mountain-fed and ice cold; I could easily get used to sitting on my back porch, watching the water move swiftly past. The patio extended to within five feet of the river, and each time I went down to enjoy the soothing ripple of the water, I was joined by a hummingbird. His little green tail feathers shone brightly in the sunlight as he consistently hovered right over the middle of the river, watching my every move. I imagined to myself that it might be Daniel stopping by to keep an eye on me.

I find myself watching for any indication that Daniel might be trying to send a message that he is still around, if only in spirit. I long to go to sleep and see a vision of Daniel in which he tells me, "Dad...I'm OK...don't be sad...I'm in a wonderful place, and you'll be joining me some day." To date, my faith has had to satisfy me...well, maybe. Daniel's journey was, from the start, a series of interesting coincidences. His being confirmed on the evening of November 3rd and falling ill less than eight hours later and the many experiences his Aunt Ann and others had related to messages and visions they received. No experience, however, has rivaled the one I wish to share now. It should be noted that neither I nor Daniel ever met the person who wrote the following; in fact, this woman had never even seen a picture of Daniel until nearly a week after this experience occurred:

Nine years ago my dad died from a brain tumor. It was so devastating. I was always "Daddy's Little Girl" and there wasn't anything he wouldn't do for me, so to say the least my life hasn't been the same.

I tried for a long time to have my dad come to me and tell me he was OK. The harder I prayed and talked to my dad about this the more upset I became because I didn't get any kind of response. That was not like him at all. He hated to see me cry so I couldn't believe that he wouldn't try to comfort me. Although I had certain things happen to me in regards to my dad, I knew it was God telling me that my dad was with Him and he was well. But for me that was not enough...I wanted to see and talk to my daddy.

I finally gave up on the idea about my dad coming to me and I was so hurt over it. I even questioned what I had done to make my dad mad at me. A couple of months later I had a really bad day and while I was in bed I saw my dad standing over me smiling. It was the first time in years that we were together and I couldn't even speak.

Although I talk to my daddy every day I don't always see or hear him. As a matter of fact, I have only had about four encounters like that. Each time he was alone and always smiling, and when he left my heart always felt so big and happy and full of love.

When I heard that Ann Dicken's nephew Daniel was in the hospital with the same thing my dad died from I immediately began talking to my dad about him. I prayed every night for my dad to help Daniel in any way he could. I even started asking my dad to go to Jesus and see what else could be done for Daniel. I knew that Jesus was with Daniel but I thought that if my dad would just keep reminding Jesus that Daniel is needed here and he is so young, and if my dad could keep going to Jesus and telling him how horribly it affects the family maybe he would get well. Anything is better than doing nothing. For several months it was my mission and just about the only thing that I talked to my dad about. I kept asking him to let me know if he could hear me and if he was helping. I wanted my dad to go to Daniel and sit with him because I knew first hand about what everyone was going through.

When I heard that Daniel had died I was at a complete loss. I was shocked because I just knew that my dad would help this young boy. In a weird sort of way, since I had never met Daniel, it was as if some of the pain and anger came back to me just like when my dad died. I even cried and yelled at my dad because I couldn't believe that he didn't help Daniel.

About a month later I was going through a rough time and questioning some decisions I had made with my life. I was talking to my dad and said that I didn't understand why God took him because I leaned on him so much and I needed his approval and support and now he wasn't here for me anymore. That same night I was going to sleep still feeling sad and confused when all of a sudden my dad was beside me smiling and standing shoulder to shoulder with a young guy. He was handsome with a big smile on his face, he had a great build, and I will never forget how pretty his eyes were. My dad encouraged me about what I was doing with my life and then he said that he wanted me to know that he did help. As he said that he looked at the young guy and put his hand on his shoulder. That is when the young man said that although he wasn't ready to leave, if he had a choice to come back he wouldn't. He went on to say that some day a long time from now we would all know why. He said that it may not make sense now but some day it would. When they left I didn't see them walk or float away; they were moving slowly and then they were gone. My heart was so full of joy and it was like a heavy weight was lifted from my shoulders. Although I had never met this person it was like my dad had taken him under "his wing." They didn't say his name but something immediately told me that it was Daniel.

When I told Ann about the encounter she said she had a picture of Daniel and wanted me to see it. As she handed me the picture with a small glimpse of that big smile and beautiful eyes, I knew it was him. My heart sank and I could even hear him say, "I wasn't ready to leave but if I had a choice to come back...I wouldn't." Tears filled my eyes and strangely my heart had the same wonderful feeling as it did the same night Daniel was with my dad talking to me. When I looked closely at the picture there was no doubt that it was Daniel that was with my daddy that night. He was a little thinner than in the picture and his hair was lighter and combed but without gel, but it was the eyes and smile that I will never forget. He was truly happy...not scared or sad, but relaxed and carefree.

Colleague of Ann Dicken

When Ann shared this story with us, I had a hard time believing that something like this could be based in truth. Wishful thinking maybe? Trying one's best to bring comfort? Any number of things crossed my mind. I asked Ann to have her friend provide her encounter in writing so that it would not be lost to time and so that I could analyze what she had experienced. I suppose one could discount the story as an overactive imagination, and while trying to be objective, I must admit to that thought. However, there are three pieces of this story that lend some credibility.

First, the photograph Ann shared with this young lady was Daniel's school picture taken during his junior year and in early fall. This was the time when he was at his heaviest due to the significant amount of weight lifting he did in preparation for football. That fall Dan had checked in at about 210 lbs. while his typical weight would have been 195-200, even less during wrestling.

Second, she also mentioned that Dan's hair was lighter than in the picture. His picture that year was taken in the period immediately after Weights class. Dan had taken a shower and put gel in his hair, making the color of his hair look much darker than normal. Generally, he liked to keep it blonde, even using "Sun In" to artificially lighten it.

Finally, she mentioned his eyes. Daniel had sky blue eyes that instantly captured attention. Pam and I often wondered where he might have come up with those beautiful eyes considering that her eyes are brown and mine are green. (I suppose the milkman is out since we don't have one.)

As I have learned since Dan's passing, dealing with the loss of one's child is a very personal journey. While friends and family do all they can to comfort and console you, for some like me, it is a private passage which must be traveled, in large part, alone.

Shortly after his death I spent time thinking of Daniel and how I missed him. A little later, I began the process of writing this book. I categorized the many emails, letters, and cards which we had received. I also began the outline for what would become Small Victories. Eventually, I took a much more aggressive approach to remembering Daniel. I read several books related to life after death and connecting with the departed.

During this period of exploration, I tried so hard to reconnect with Daniel. A song, a vision, a dream? Anything that would allow me to know that Dan is OK, that he is happy and watching over us. Try as I might...nothing. I eventually put away my attempts to connect with Dan, assuming that if it was to occur it would happen in God's time.

Daniel in the fall of 2004

Less than a month after my sabbatical from searching for Daniel, it happened. Like most other nights, I had quickly drifted off to sleep. This night would be different, however, as I experienced my first dream about Daniel in nearly a year since his passing. Realizing that dreams are only visions of what was or what has never been, any dream would give me a chance to see and interact with Daniel. This much-anticipated dream took me to, of all places, a baseball diamond. There was Dan, on the pitcher's mound, preparing to start the game. As Pam sat next to me on the bleachers, we agonizingly watched as Dan struggled through the first inning. It was obvious he was in a weakened state, much the same as he had been early in his illness. He was gaunt and pale yet ever prepared to give it his all. Several hitters and 4 runs later, he was still competing. Always the coach, I couldn't help myself. I jumped down off the bleachers and headed to the mound. When I arrived, I noticed that he was sweating profusely. I looked at him and said, "That's enough, D...you did your best." He just looked at me, and without speaking, he let me know he wasn't coming off the mound. At that point I started to wake. I was coherent enough to realize I was seeing Daniel for the first time since he had left us, and I didn't want to wake. I had things I wanted to say. I needed to tell him that I love him and I think about him every day. I needed to make sure he's doing OK. Too late...I was already fully awake. I looked at the clock; it read 1:48AM.

The numbers 1:48 hold little significance for anyone but me. You see, since 1988 my baseball uniform number had been 14, or some iteration of 14 if that uniform was too small for me to wear. Daniel's number in his last season at Franklin High School was 8. In fact, after he fell ill, all the boys wore the number 8 on their helmets as a way to remember Dan. I was so overcome with the irony of the dream and the time that I woke Pam. I was nearly shaking by the time she was lucid enough to understand what I was saying. Pam held me close as for the next 10 minutes I could not hold my emotion.

Unable to suppress the feelings which the dream elicited, I left the bed and made my way downstairs where I sat in the dark for what seemed an eternity. I just couldn't get the vision of Daniel out of my mind or the mystery of the message it carried. After a time, the dream became clearer to me. I was thoroughly convinced that Daniel was sending me two very distinct messages. First, he is watching over us, as evidenced by the timing of the dream…1:48; and second, giving up…giving in, is not an option. It was his way of saying, "All right, Dad…snap out of it! I'm OK and I'll be waiting for you, but your time left on earth should be spent in more productive pursuits." From the day that Daniel passed away until now, well over a year later, that dream remains my only such nocturnal vision of Daniel, which to me is further validation of the experience.

Regardless of the coincidence of these events, they provide great encouragement and hope that Dan is happy and content while he awaits our arrival. And therein may lie the greatest irony of all. Dan's death may have resulted in saving countless others; scores of people impacted by his story have now moved much closer to a personal relationship with the Lord. My personal journey began shortly after Daniel fell ill. I found myself searching for something that was not present in my life. I felt a void, a vague emptiness. I am now convinced, as others are, that God is real and that one day, if I do my part, I will be reunited with Daniel.

I suppose in the final analysis we must all ask ourselves the question, "What has my life contributed of lasting value?" While the chapter and verse on Daniel's life have been written and recorded, my story and the stories of millions of others are still being crafted. On Judgment Day I hope that God will look at me, as he has Daniel, and say, "Well done, Jeff. Your time on earth has left it a better place." In the meantime, let us be thankful for the many blessings, both large and small, that enrich our lives each day. Because, in the end I realize that I have *been given* more than I gave, I have *been loved* more than I loved, and I have *been inspired* more than I inspired.

Number "8" in the spring of 2004

May your lives be filled with happiness, love, family, friends—and countless "small victories"—until the day when each of us will join Daniel and touch the face of God.

Afterword — Scott Rolen

I will start this at 2 a.m., alone on my basement computer, long after my wife and daughter have gone to bed. I am reading an email version of "Small Victories" Jeff had previously forwarded to me, and fretting about the invitation to pen the Afterword. I am shaken emotionally as I scroll the text reading humorous, harrowing, and heart wrenching stories of Daniel and his struggles. I need a night like this to reflect on my own life. I ask myself if things are going too fast or if I am taking myself too seriously…back to the matter at hand, the Afterword. I must admit I have spent much time thinking of greatness on this project. I feel compelled to match the importance of this book and astound the reader with a moving explanation of the concept of small victories. However, I realize Daniel has already done this. The notion of small victories is not mine – it is ours. It is gaining self-confidence piece by piece. It is losing one pound when faced with a hundred. It is writing your son's story when you are filled with grief. It is finding the strength to walk four laps around a hospital floor when you are an all-state athlete. These appear to be small victories, but in our hearts we know they are monumental triumphs. The truth is that there is no greatness in these words. It is simply a long winded way to say that I care. If I may speak for my wife, brother, and countless other friends and family members—we all care and are thankful to have been a part of Daniel's life. I hope the reader concurs. I don't have the words to tell you how much I have enjoyed this book, though I will say that my heart aches every time I read or think about Jeffrey's farewell to his little brother. I am in hopes the reader is able to both laugh and cry with these pages. This book does not have a happy ending, but I do not believe it is written to be sad. It is real. It is a father opening his heart to honor his son, and that is true love.

Thank you to the Mercer family and friends,
Thank you to Jeff,
Thank you to Daniel,

We are proud of you – you have made us smile.

Friends,
Scott Rolen

Appendix

Journal Entries

The entries which follow comprise the complete collection of recorded text from my online journal. The emotions which accompanied each entry are beyond description. Many a late night spent in the small 6th floor medical library at Methodist crafting the next message. While extremely painful to comprise many of the entries, I am so thankful that I have this documented history of Dan's journey. I hope you will be too.

November 4, 2004

Last Thursday my son, Daniel, was diagnosed with a brain tumor. Quite a shock given that we thought he had been fighting a concussion from playing football. He was operated on on Friday to relieve pressure in his brain and to take a biopsy.

Thanks to you and the entire high school for your support through all of this. We are still waiting for the results of his MRI and biopsy. To be honest, I am braced for the worst. However, cancer has seen few opponents as tough as the one it will face with Daniel our family, and this entire community. Dan made great strides yesterday. Jeff and I drug him out of bed, made him walk up and down the hallway, and by last night he was sitting in the waiting room with all his friends - eating White Castle. We think he will come home probably tomorrow. You know, it's times like this that I thank God we live in a place like Franklin. You have all been incredibly supportive.

Please do me one favor.....tell the students who have made the trek to Methodist over the last several days "thank you"!!! Daniel lights up when he sees them, and they will be his best medicine over the next several months.

November 7, 2004

Daniel spent the better part of Saturday and Sunday virtually incoherent. Medicine and the stress of surgery had been more than he could physically handle. He was so weak from lying around that he was moving backward in his recovery process. So, yesterday morning I determined it was time to get him moving. His older brother Jeff and I got him out of bed, sat him up, dragged him down the hallway and back.

By last night, he walked to the waiting room in critical care, sat with his many visiting friends, and ate White Castle - typical teenager. We anticipate that he will come home tomorrow or Thursday. As of this morning we are waiting on results of an extensive MRI and his biopsy. While we are braced for the worst, but are hoping for the best.

Regardless, we intend to go to battle like we never have before. It will take much faith, strength, and determination, but we are full of all of that and more. We truly appreciate all of the cards, emails, and calls wishing us well. It's times like this when you understand why you live in a community like Franklin. Keep Daniel in your prayers.

November 9, 2004
Newest update: We received word yesterday from Daniel's surgeon that his upper torso MRI came back clear. That is a minor miracle in itself given that the type of tumor they believe he has tends to spread quickly to the spinal column. So, for now we are only dealing with a tumor in one spot...which is a blessing. We meet next Wednesday with his surgeon to get his pathology report and to begin to chart a course of action. Until then, we are working to get Daniel back up to strength. Daniel came home yesterday, and although he was a little tired, he had a great day. He is getting more mobile by the minute. He has several things planned for today, not the least of which is a trip to Chicago's for the lunch buffet. Chicago's is second only to White Castle on his list of favorites. His Mom will then take him by the high school for a few minutes to visit, and his day will culminate by visiting his brother Anthony's classroom at Creekside. Daniel and I had a long talk yesterday before the surgeon came in with MRI results. He has had a terrific attitude all along given the circumstances, and we talked about turning this experience into a positive for our family and community. It has been mentioned several times that this is so unfair for the Mercer family. Daniel and I spoke yesterday that in some strange way we might have been the right choice for something like this for a couple reasons. First, cancer will have no tougher opponent than Daniel and his family. Second, we must use this unfortunate event to exhibit Daniel's faith, strength, and determination. We hope as a result, that our entire community can draw strength from observing, praying, and supporting us in this battle. Again, many thanks to all who have lent their support, prayers and assistance. It is appreciated more than you know.

November 11, 2004
What started as a pretty good day for Daniel ended up being a terrific day. Dave Taylor (founder of the Indiana Bulls baseball organization), and Scott Rolen (St. Louis Cardinals) visited the house to provide well-wishes and encouragement to Daniel. Fortunately, a number of Dan's friends were there and had the opportunity to meet and talk to Scott. What a great evening.

Appendix

Journal Entries

November 13, 2004

Saturday is a day we hope to forget.....quickly. Daniel's incision began leaking so we took him to the emergency room at Methodist where they stitched the remainder of the opening. He almost instantly began getting sick as the pressure in his brain became unbearable. No sooner than we got him home we had to rush him back to the emergency room. He spent nearly 5 hours in the emergency room and was then transferred to the critical care unit. I don't know that I have ever seen someone in so much pain. My admiration for the way Daniel handles this continues to grow. He never once cried or yelled out, it's like he just kind of went to another place in his mind. The pain medication was virtually useless, and so were we as parents. We have never felt so helpless in our entire lives. So frustrating and heartbreaking.

November 14, 2004

Sunday began with more of Saturday. Daniel had intense pain followed by vomiting, which in turn made the pain worse. His incision was swollen from the pressure and you could track his heartbeat in the swollen area. Each beat produced a pulsating action. He had a terrific nurse who worked all day to control his pain. However, about 9:00AM further complications appeared. His temperature began rising about 1 degree per hour due to what they suspect is infection. He topped out at 103.1 in combination with the pain. At a time when things couldn't have gotten much worse, a ray of sunshine peeked through the clouds. All the work of his nurse began to pay off. His temperature began dropping, his pain level went way down, his blood pressure become much better.....thank God. By 5:00PM he was resting comfortably, and he was hungry.....a good sign.

His neurosurgeon came in, on his day off, to check on Daniel. He inserted a tube through the side of his head to drain fluid and relieve some of the pressure. He also told us that they would have to insert a shunt once Daniel fought off the infection. The shunt is a tube inserted internally that diverts fluid from the brain into the abdomen. His body is just producing more spinal fluid that it can absorb. It looks like Daniel will be there most of the week as we get him squared away. We expect to receive our pathology results this Wednesday and that will tell us what we are dealing with and how it will be treated. In the meantime, our sincere appreciation and gratitude to all that have done so much to assist us.

November 15, 2004
Daniel has begun to feel better. The pain is beginning to subside a bit, and he has been allowed to eat again which is great news for him. He even managed to choke down the White Castle's which he requested, and I brought him. I'm beginning to think that we should hold out for some sort of endorsement deal with White Castle like Jared did with Subway. If the White Castle's cure the tumor, you can bet my first call will be to the White Castle corporate office (Ha!). The doctors have started antibiotics that will fight the infection in Daniel's brain. Once the infection is gone, the doctors will decide if Daniel is going to receive a shunt to divert fluid from his brain to his abdomen. He had a few visitors this evening, and he was very happy to see some of his friends.
I even think he is beginning to miss school a bit.....this brain surgery is having a more profound impact than I thought. Is there a "school" section in the brain? If so, we may need to consider tweaking it again.

November 16, 2004
Daniel felt great today. He is 100% more coherent than before. He has begun to remember specific assignments from school, and has started to worry about how he will get caught up. His vision appears to be improving as well, which is a good sign. Daniel had quite a few visitors tonight. He was in the height of his glory. He is still unable to move around as he is limited by the tube in his brain, but they have indicated that they will hook him up to a pump soon that will allow him to get up and move around. Hopefully, to a shower.....and soon!

We meet with the neurosurgeon Wednesday at Noon to go through the pathology report. We will learn of the type of tumor we are dealing with and how we intend to proceed. Pam stopped by the Chapel (at the hospital) for a moment. As she approached the altar she noticed an open bible. It was open to "The Book of Daniel".
Coincidence.....maybe.....or maybe not.

November 17, 2004
Daniel continues to feel better as he fights infection. He is eating well and tired of laying in bed. Pam and I met with Daniel's neurosurgeon today regarding his pathology report. We did not get the news we wanted. Daniel has an ependymoma. This type of tumor responds to treatment if it can be removed completely. If not, the odds go way down. Daniel's tumor is located so deeply in the brain that the likelihood of taking all of it out is slim. His doctor is sending his results to St. Jude Hospital in Memphis, TN.

for further study. St. Jude is the foremost expert on pediatric tumors in the world. Daniel, as per usual, is handling this news with great courage. His faith and determination were evident yesterday as we began to deal with the reality of our situation. Pam and I are incredibly proud of our son. He is a special young man. Now on to better thoughts. At this moment Daniel doesn't need our sympathy, he needs our love, support, encouragement and prayers. He will not give up, and neither can any of you. Your calls, notes, and visits will continue to lift his spirits. We hope to have him home by Thanksgiving where he can enjoy his family, the outdoors, and most importantly, the food!

As always, thanks so much for all that each of you has done and continues to do.

November 20, 2004
It's never good when the phone rings at 2:00AM. Daniel's drainage tube stopped working, and the pressure in his brain went back up. His neurosurgeon happened to be on call this weekend, which was sheer luck, so he came in about 8:00AM and replaced the entire apparatus. It is a very painful process, but Daniel handled it well. He was quite sore all day, but by evening he was in less pain. We did receive some encouraging news from the neurosurgeon today. He and his partners have been looking at the MRI, and they believe it might be possible to access the tumor from another direction. As you may recall, this type of tumor needs to be removed completely. So, maybe they will be able to get to it after all. We will continue to pray that the doctors will develop a plan that will include successful removal.

November 23, 2004
After being given little hope for surgical removal of Daniel's tumor at our meeting last Wednesday, Dr. Turner informed us yesterday that upon further study of his MRI"s and CT scans that they believe they can get to it. It will involve entering Daniel's brain from the back as opposed to the top. While Daniel isn't particularly excited about the prospect of having his head opened up again, this is GREAT news for us. Dr. Turner feels good about the chances of getting the tumor out, which as you may recall was necessary in order for a positive prognosis. Surgery is tentatively scheduled for this Friday. Daniel will get to enjoy Thanksgiving dinner with his family, albeit at the hospital, but we have much to be thankful for. The surgery will take about 4 hours, and while there is always risk involved, it isn't a huge concern for the doctor. The normal recuperation period is 4-5 days if all goes well. He will be back in critical care for a few days

until he feels well enough to be moved. We wish everyone a wonderful Thanksgiving, and I hope to have a "good news" update next Monday.

November 26, 2004

Reflecting back on the news we received one week earlier, today is a blessing. Just knowing we have a chance to remove part or all of the tumor gives us hope. Complete removal of an ependymoma improves chances greatly. Partial removal gives us a better chance than we had one week ago. Daniel is scared to death, as we all are. He read Sherri Coner's Daily Journal article about himself this morning....he cried....so did we. Sherri did a really nice job, but I think the reality of the situation is now upon him. As they took him to surgery several of his nurses from the past two weeks came in to wish him well. They have been so kind. Coach Pieper and Mike Carter joined us and our family as we took him to surgery. It was great to have them there for support, and to lighten the moment. As they were shaving electrode circles on Daniel's head, Mike Carter reminded Daniel "not to pay for that haircut". His hairstyle is sure to be quite unique for a while. They took Daniel to surgery at 8:35AM. It took them until 10:00AM to get him prepped. At 10:05AM they began work. As you might expect it was highly computerized and the technicians later gave us a CD of what the doctor used to guide his progress. Every hour they called to update us. I have never been more nervous in my entire life. Sectional championships are a piece of cake compared to this. At about 1:20 they called to let us know the procedure was complete and they were just finishing up. At about 2:00PM the surgeon, Dr. Michael Turner came out and informed us that he was able to get the vast majority, or all of the tumor. He would know more after the next MRI. He said it went as smoothly as possible. Daniel remained in recovery until about 4:30PM. He arrived back in critical care a short time later, and I must admit he didn't look very good. However, he could see and he could move his arms and legs....Thank God! He was sick most of the evening. Primarily from all the medication I expect. They were a bit concerned at about 9:00PM and took him for a CT scan to check for internal bleeding. It came back clean. He rested pretty well the rest of the night.

November 27, 2004

They kept Daniel very sedated the entire day. He did come around long enough to tell me he was in a lot of pain, and that "I want out of here". He took no visitors today, and even seemed agitated when the nurse or I came into his room. So, I would check in on him every 30 minutes or so, but I didn't go into the room. About 2:00AM or 3:00AM

Appendix

Journal Entries

they became a bit concerned that he was sleeping too much and they began to cut back on his pain medication.

November 28, 2004
He woke up, with help, at about 10:00AM, and actually spoke pretty coherently. He brushed his teeth by himself although he missed the mark a bit. He also had 2 cups of orange sherbet. About 10 minutes later he asked for food....good sign. He ate a little bit and then went back to sleep. Later in the evening he ate a grilled cheese, macaroni and cheese, and an orange sherbet. The nurses and doctors are very pleased with his progress.

December 03, 2004
Daniel has gone 29 hours with his drainage tube clamped, and his intercranial pressure down which is terrific news. Maybe we can avoid having the permanent shunt? According to his Mother and nurse, he is much more coherent today. He was awake for five hours this morning, ate normally, watched TV, and played a football video game. It is so nice to see him returning to his normal disposition. He has begun his exercise routine to prepare him to move around normally. If all goes well today they may take out his drainage tube tomorrow. At that point Dad will become his worst nightmare. If I have to physically carry him up and down that hallway, we're going to get him moving. His eyes appear to be moving together for the first time in a week. Knock on wood, but this has been our best day in a week, maybe in a month. I truly believe all the prayers are continuing to work as his body comes back together. Here's one from the really cool column, Don Fischer (voice of IU athletics) sent an email to Daniel and indicated that he will recognize him tomorrow on the radio just before tipoff of the IU vs. Connecticut basketball. We will make sure we have a radio in his room at game time. This has been such a "great" day!!!

December 06, 2004
Daniel's doctor returned from Mexico City today and stopped in this morning. He has determined that Daniel will need to have a shunt installed. The surgery is scheduled for Tuesday afternoon. If everything goes well we can think about getting Daniel home toward the end of the week. Keep your fingers crossed. Daniel is not excited about another surgical procedure, but he understands that the intercranial pressure issue is not going away on its own. His motor skills have improved greatly in the past few days. He is now able to use his left hand pretty well, which was not the case earlier in the week.

His eyes have gotten better, but he has a long way to go. I think this will serve as a source of great frustration before were done. While Daniel is improving physically we need some work on the mental side of things. He has had enough of the hospital and the pain. I must say, I don't blame him. However, that is our reality, so we can sit and complain about it, or we can focus on the light at the end of the tunnel. For now, that will be a return home to celebrate Christmas.

December 8, 2004
Daniel underwent surgery last night to install the shunt. He was in a great deal of pain when he arrived back in his room in critical care. I went home last night to pick up the little boys and came back first thing this morning. Needless to say, I didn't know what I would find. It was with much trepidation that his brother Jeff and I peeked into his room. What I found was that "my kid was back". Aside from the soreness of multiple incisions he feels so much better. He has been out of his bed this morning, sat in a chair and ate breakfast, and is intending to walk around the ward this morning. This is one of the happiest days of my life. I am so excited to see him feeling better! This has been the greatest challenge our family has ever faced, but all of us are so appreciative that we have not traveled this path alone. Our faith, family, friends and community have made this past month bearable. While we have a long way to go, I believe we have taken the first big step. We expect to bring Daniel home this Friday. He can't wait to see everyone. He even looks forward to being around his younger brothers....miracles do happen. Thanks to you all!!!

December 10, 2004
Thirty-five of the past thirty-seven days have seen Daniel lying in a bed in Methodist Hospital. Today, he comes home. Dr. Turner stopped in early this morning, indicated that Daniel is doing very well, and that it was time to get him out of here. I can't even begin to express the emotional rollercoaster that has accompanied this ordeal. From the lowest of the lows, to the jubilation of the past few days culminating with the "good news" phone call from Pam at 6:50AM this morning. We do realize that this is merely step one in what will certainly be a multi-step process. However, I think I will enjoy this one for a few days. Life holds many realities for the Mercer family. First, Daniel faces radiation and chemotherapy beginning in the next couple of weeks. He also has vision challenges, and will for awhile. He is extremely weak and will require months to regain an acceptable level of conditioning. In addition, we have his "reverse mullet" to contend with for the next several weeks while his hair grows back. A contrasting set of

realities have become evident as well. If there was ever a question as to where Pam and I should have chosen to raise our children, it has been forever answered in the past five weeks. To contemplate the amount of time, energy, and money our community has committed on behalf of Daniel and our family would be staggering indeed. We cannot begin to repay the kindness and generosity that has been shown to our family. We do however, have the opportunity to use this experience for the benefit of others. Daniel can, and will, exhibit strength, courage and determination to stand as a shining example for what can be achieved through faith, family, and community. And, when it comes down to it, we may have needed to remind ourselves of that in this holiday season anyway.

God Bless everyone, and on behalf of the Mercer family we wish you all a most joyous holiday season.

December 14, 2004

Daniel spent less than one day at home before we had to return to Methodist. Severe headaches were the culprit. We were in the emergency room from 8:30AM until about 6:00PM on Saturday while they ran tests and tried to get his pain under control. If I haven't said it before, the emergency room is not a fun place to be, especially on a weekend. Those folks earn their money. I'm glad they do what they do, because this is the third time we have put them to work on a weekend. Daniel was transferred to the 7th floor on Sunday. There is some concern about a possible infection in his brain, so they continue to read the cultures from his tests. He is actually feeling pretty well physically. Last night he took a shower by himself, and took three laps around the ward. His vision seems to be improving as well. The challenge now is not physical. He seems to have reached his hospital tolerance level, and then some. He is discouraged. As parents, we struggle knowing when to pat him on the back, and when to give him a swift kick. We sympathize with all that he has gone through, and we wouldn't wish it upon anyone. However, lying around worrying about the next procedure, needle stick or whatever else isn't getting us any closer to normal life. I hope Pam or I come up with a bright idea in the next day or two. Although, I feel the "Coach" in me beginning to emerge. It's much like I used to tell my players, "If you're waiting for tomorrow to start competing...mistake...tomorrow has already arrived." Daniel needs to see firsthand the way that his family, friends, and community have been competing on his behalf. When that happens I believe we will begin to see that "Grizzly Spirit" that he has always exhibited. Unfortunately, he has spent so much time in a hospital bed that he is not fully aware of the incredible level of support that has surrounded him since this all began. I could be misjudging his character, but I don't think it will be long before he begins to kick this illness in the teeth. Behold the hand of God at work.

December 15, 2004

We're back on the rollercoaster, but hopefully the downhill side this time. The doctors have indicated that Daniel has a late stage infection in his shunt/head, however they decided against drawing fluid off Daniel's brain, for which Daniel is eternally grateful. 10-15 needles to the head is enough for a lifetime, much less 3 days. They have chosen to place Daniel on oral antibiotics in hopes that it will take care of the infection. Daniel's spirits and attitude were lifted on Tuesday night as Scott and Nikki Rolen, Dave Taylor, and John Thiel stopped by. Scott brought Dan a game jersey with the inscription "Small Victories". Scott coaxed Daniel out of bed, took him on a four lap jaunt (the most he had ever done), and shared with him the meaning of "Small Victories". He told Daniel that being scared was OK, but to hold on to all those around him who love and support him in this situation.   He also told him to be proud of his small victories, whether that was walking the ward for four laps, or going outside, or whatever. I had the good fortune to push the IV cart while Scott worked his magic with Dan. It meant a lot to both of us. Scott is a terrific ballplayer, but more importantly, a terrific person. It could be coincidence, but Daniel was released from the hospital on Wednesday morning, insisted that we go straight to Chicago's Pizza before we went home, and in general had the best day at home probably since this ordeal began. He ate dinner at the table with his family, enjoyed seeing Emily, Ashley, and Michael, and even played Madden 2005 with his brother Joe. Thank goodness for "small victories". His pain, at the moment, is limited to the area on his head where they performed the needle "tap dance". That is to be expected, and should go away soon. The real positive is that there are no pressure headaches, and we are praying that it stays that way. If things continue to go well we hope that Daniel can stop by the basketball game on Friday and the County wrestling on Saturday. He is cautiously optimistic, but very excited to see all his friends. We hope to see many of you there. Keep your fingers crossed.

December 20, 2004

Well, we made it through Saturday without having to make a trip to the hospital.   I'm sure Methodist had brought in an extra crew in anticipation as we have kept them quite busy on the weekend.   Daniel had a terrific end to the week.   He has really done well. He is virtually pain free and getting stronger each day.   On Thursday he went shopping with his Mom for a bit (he must have had surgery or something for that to have ever

Appendix

Journal Entries

happened). Friday we went to the high school basketball game. As we were standing in the hallway ready to go into the gym someone came running out and told Daniel they had just announced his name, and that he needed to go in. The entire gymnasium gave Daniel a standing ovation. He walked to the scorers bench and stood there while they played the national anthem. What an unbelievable show of support, and one of the first he has had the opportunity to witness. He was really touched, and so were we. Anthony, our 9 year old, said afterwards "Mom cried the whole time", and I said "she wasn't alone". Daniel got really tired, but just had to stay to the end of what was an exciting game. On Saturday Daniel went to the Johnson County Wrestling meet. It was great for him to see all of his wrestling buddies, teammates and opponents. He went to the locker room with the team for the pre-meet "pep talk", Coach Hasseman let him go out for the captains meeting, and John Rigney (AD at Indian Creek and family friend) had a nice presentation for him prior to the start of the meet. It was a huge poster signed by the different wrestling teams. On Sunday, Daniel went out with some of his friends for awhile, and went to Emily's to watch some of the Colts game. It's great to see him slowly returning to his regular activities. We were somewhat thrilled that Peyton didn't break the record against the Ravens, because Chris Lynch (wrestling coach) has tickets for Daniel to attend next Sunday's game against the Chargers. He even has field passes for Daniel. The Dome will never be the same! His mother and I have been so pleased to see Daniel's personality returning as well. He was upbeat and funny this weekend, and that's really the first time since November 4th that he has been that way. This will be our best Christmas ever. It certainly brings to light "the true meaning of Christmas". One of the boys asked me what I wanted for Christmas, and I said I already received my present. It weighs 200 lbs. and has a funny haircut. Here's wishing you all a very Merry Christmas!

December 22, 2004

Daniel is continuing to progress. On Monday he worked out at Franklin College with his brothers Jeff and Joe, and family friend Levi Smythe. He rode a stationary bike for 10 minutes, walked for 10 minutes, shot baskets, and even did some light bench presses. I think he may have overdone it a bit as he crashed in the evening. He is getting out of the house every day now to go eat or go shopping. He looks and sounds so much better. On Tuesday evening Coach Vittorio (baseball coach at the University of Dayton) and his wife Heather stopped by for a visit. We laughed and laughed at Daniel describing the 15 needles to the head ordeal that he went through last week. It's great that he can laugh about it now, because it was no laughing matter when he was going through it. Dan is really looking forward to having his family over for Christmas Eve, and traveling to his Grandma and Grandpa Kieffer's on Christmas Day. It will be the first time since this began that his cousins will see him while he is feeling well. I'm sure they will notice a big difference. Pam has informed all of us that tonight is reserved for the movie "It's a Wonderful Life". That picture takes on a new meaning this year, and for the first time I don't think the boys will even complain about having to watch it.

December 29, 2004

Daniel had a terrific holiday. He enjoyed spending Christmas Eve with the Mercer side of the family, and had a great time on Christmas Day with the Kieffer side of the family. The Christmas Day trip to his Grandparents house was the first extended trip away from home in months, but he felt fine, ate an inordinate amount, and in general had a wonderful day. On Sunday, December 26th he attended the Colts game with Coach Lynch, Michael and Bart. Coach Lynch had field passes for the boys and they were really excited about being close to the action. What a great game! Dan was somewhat shocked that the lady sitting next to him, whom he did not know, asked if he was the boy with the brain tumor that she had been reading about. He has touched more lives than he realizes. On Monday he attended the Pacers game, thanks to Dean Abplanalp. He was right behind the Pacer bench, and was stunned by the whole experience. He didn't arrive home until nearly 11:00PM, and was more interested in talking about the game than going to bed...now there's a change. Dan went to his first physical therapy session and has been given a series of exercises designed to strengthen his core areas. He has been doing them religiously as I think he is becoming more determined to regain his strength. Yesterday, Jeff brought Daniel to LTD (Baseball Facility). Dan hit off the tee for a little bit, and played catch with his Dad. He can't see to catch very well yet, but his arm strength was fine. I felt kind of like Kevin Costner in "Field of Dreams" when he was able to have a "catch with his dad". It's something that we tend to take for granted - not anymore.

January 04, 2005

Daniel continues to get stronger. He feels good. He's taking no pain medication, and hasn't for three weeks. Daniel and his mother met with Mrs. Hopper (guidance director at Franklin High School) yesterday to discuss his return to school. Mrs. Hopper has been extremely helpful in facilitating this whole process. Dan's schedule has been altered slightly to provide some accommodation for his challenges (fatigue, vision,

Journal Entries

etc.). He starts today for a brief period of time, and will probably increase as the week goes on. We expect that he will resume a nearly full day of classes as early as next week. We meet with his surgeon at lunch time today to check on his infection and possible next steps related to that. Hopefully, there won't be any next steps. We anticipate a call from his Oncologist in the next week or so to schedule a meeting to discuss treatment. We have placed that reality far from our minds for the past couple of weeks so that we can get Dan's strength and spirits up. That has happened, so I think we're ready for the next step. Huge "thanks" to all for your continued support, especially through the holidays. It has meant a great deal to all of us. Dan has written a "Heart" which will appear in next weeks "Hearts and Darts" section in the Daily Journal. It really captures the feeling that our entire family has toward our family, friends and community.

January 05, 2005
We met yesterday with Daniel's surgeon (Dr. Turner). We were there as a follow up to the infection that Daniel is being treated for. The jury will be out for another 2-3 weeks on the infection in order to give the antibiotics a chance to work, and the infection a chance to gain strength. At that point we will know whether another procedure will be required. Basically, it will involve replacing Dan's shunt if they can't control the infection. In addition, and more importantly, Dr. Turner informed us that the pathology report on Daniel's diagnosis has been changed. As a result of the tissue sample taken during the surgery on November 26th the report is now suggesting that Daniel has a Central Neurocytoma, and not an Ependymoma. A Central Neurocytoma is a benign tumor fairly common in young adults. The initial treatment involves resection (removal), which has been done. Follow up treatment could include simply monitoring future growth, or potentially radiation. Chemotherapy is used very little to not at all with this type of tumor. The following direct quote from Dr. Turner was prophetic, "I don't know if you guys have been praying or what, but this diagnosis is about 1000 times better than what we had before". My initial thought was, "as a matter of fact we have been praying....by the hour, and so have thousands of other people in Franklin and across the country". I will repeat a statement I made in an earlier update, "Behold the hand of God at work". I know no other way to explain it. Every single event that has occurred since we received the initial gloomy diagnosis has shown improvement. We thought they couldn't remove the tumor...yet they did. We couldn't resolve the intracranial pressure/pain issue...yet they did. The diagnosis of an Ependymoma, even after a biopsy, is changed to a Central Neurocytoma. Maybe it's just coincidence, maybe it's just luck, or maybe it's the consistent prayer and support of literally thousands and

thousands of people, and an outstanding medical team who have combined to make a significant contribution to the recovery of this young man.

January 19, 2005
Daniel has continued to progress very well. He attended school every day last week, and made it through the full day - every day. He has some short term memory issues that will require him to be a good list maker, and his vision continues to frustrate him although it is perfectly normal given the procedures performed on him. Daniel enjoyed spending last Saturday with the wrestling team as they won the Mid-State Conference tourney. Coach Hasseman even let him sit next to him for a few matches to provide some additional karma. Must have worked since we won, but I'm not sure that coaching is in the cards for Dan. He didn't appear to be offering much good advice, at least as far as I could tell. Daniel worked out with the baseball team Monday and Tuesday night. He ran, did sit-ups, modified pushups, leg lifts, and even played boredom ball. Last night he threw with one of the coaches, fielded some ground balls and took some short hops. It's just nice to see him back out with the guys again, and I could see the competitive juices flowing when it came time for him to run and try to keep up. We go back to see Dr. Turner next Tuesday to check on Dan's infection, or hopefully, lack thereof. Dan can hardly wait to have his "shunt tapped" again. St. Jude Hospital has sent Dan's tumor specimen to Johns Hopkins Univ. for a second opinion on diagnosis and suggested treatment.

January 26, 2005
Daniel visited his surgeon yesterday. Dr. Turner drew fluid off Daniel's brain to check for any existing infection. If there is infection then Dan will have to undergo surgery to replace the plastics in his shunt. He is feeling really good so Dr. Turner was hopeful that maybe there is no infection and that procedure can be avoided. We should know by Friday. A bit of news that we did not want to receive is that Dr. Turner believes the pathology report is going to revert back to the Ependymoma diagnosis. You may recall that the Indianapolis pathologist changed his diagnosis to a Central Neurocytoma. However, just to get a second opinion, we had his specimen sent to St. Jude in Memphis. They were unwilling to make a call, so the specimen was sent to Johns Hopkins in Baltimore. Their preliminary report is leaning toward an Ependymoma. We should know officially in the next few days. This has been an emotional rollercoaster of epic proportions. We will continue to hope for the best.
February 01, 2005

Appendix

Journal Entries

Emory Austin (motivational speaker) once said, "Some days there won't be a song in your heart. Sing anyway." That's kind of the way I feel about the last couple of weeks. We have tried, sometimes unsuccessfully, to be upbeat and positive regarding Daniel's unknown prognosis. It's really a challenge, the not knowing, the constant worrying, the inability to control anything.....except your attitude, and sometimes not even that. Therefore, I have decided to commit to copy my resolution to "Sing anyway". For Daniel to be strong of faith, body, and mind he will need our family and each of you to reinforce his terrifically positive attitude. I ask that every single person that reads this, sees Daniel, or has a moment to offer a thought or prayer, do so with a song in your heart.   Yesterday we met with Dr. Jeffrey Goldman (oncologist). As has been noted before, Daniel's diagnosis was changed from an ependymoma to a central neurocytoma. Dr. Goldman felt we should get a second opinion and we agreed. Daniel's tumor specimen was sent to St. Jude in Memphis.   St. Jude was unwilling to make a call on the tumor type, so they sent it to Johns Hopkins in Baltimore. The doctors at Johns Hopkins have determined that Daniel has a tumor referred to as a high grade glioma.   If that is the case, which we believe it probably is, then the tumor is malignant and will require appropriate treatment. Because of my baseball background and the fact that I don't like ties, we have asked to play best two out of three with the Mayo Clinic in Minnesota. Dan's tumor will be sent out tomorrow and we will wait for confirmation. In the meantime, we intend to get Daniel started on his treatment. The plan calls for radiation 5 days per week for 6 weeks. They tell us the treatment daily will last about 15 minutes. He will then have 4 weeks to recover before starting chemotherapy. The chemo, which will be taken orally, will consist of 5 consecutive days every 28 days, and this will last for 1 year.   On a more positive note, Daniel feels good. His strength is coming back little by little. He continues to be the strongest member of our family mentally, except for maybe his Mother. If his approach is any indication of what's to come.....strap in big "C" you're in for a heck of a fight!

February 07, 2005
Last week was a roller coaster for Dan. He had some really great moments, and some moments of real reflection. I think Daniel has done remarkably well for someone who has had to face all that he has. As was expected, some of the tough questions are being faced now. This is a time to ask for strength via your faith, your family, and your network of friends. His faith is strong, his family is determined, and his friends are committed. On a positive note, Dan was named Snowcoming King at the basketball game on Saturday night. He received a standing ovation when his name was announced. He

thought that was pretty awesome...so did his Mom and I. His Grandma and Grandpa, Aunts, and cousins were all there to share in the excitement. He had a great day yesterday as his family came over for a Super Bowl party. Dan had more energy than I have seen since November. We did some skeet shooting in the afternoon, and as per usual, Dan beat everyone...impaired vision and all. We go to Riley tomorrow night for an MRI. The pictures will give the radiologist and the oncologist a baseline for beginning treatment. My thought is that maybe the tumor will be gone...dissolved by all the prayers which have gone out on Daniel's behalf. Here's hoping!

February 11, 2005
Daniel's tumor is back...and bigger than before. He will have surgery next week to remove as much of the tumor as possible. After about one week of recovery he will begin radiation, followed by chemotherapy. Dr. Turner says that while the tumor is bigger it actually makes it easier for him to get to. In addition, he suggests that radiation seems to work pretty well on tumors multiplying at this rate. Dan, to his credit, is doing very well. He was his normal chipper self last night despite the discouraging news. He even went to school today, which in my mind is incredible given the number of times he will be faced with his reality via questions, etc. In case you haven't been able to tell through other updates, I am very proud of my son. He is the toughest person I know and a heck of a lot tougher than me right now. It looks like surgery will be next Thursday followed by 6-7 days in the hospital and then on to radiation. We're planning on spending a lot of time with Dan over the next several days. We want to do some things that he will enjoy. That may include a trip to Grandma and Grandpa Kieffer's, a visit to see his brother at the University of Dayton, spending time with the Mercer family, and maybe some other "special" activities. A number of people have said to me, "this is God's way of testing you". I don't believe that. God would have no part of something that hurts so many. Instead, in my minds-eye I see some little gremlin at work here. And, let me promise you this, if I ever catch him, I will pinch his head off (So let it be written, so let it be done). God will, however, be there to help us put Daniel and our family back together. On one of my morning walks last week I asked God for strength to guide Daniel and my family through this ordeal. The following message came to my mind, "worry not my son, for the Lord thy God will bring peace unto you." Maybe I dreamt it, maybe I made it up. I don't know. I do know this; however, God will be with Daniel and our family regardless of the outcome. Many, many thanks to all of our friends and our community who have continued to support us either in person, or through messages, cards, etc.. A huge thank you to all the students and teachers in

Appendix

Journal Entries

Franklin Community Schools who have been incredible in their support for Daniel. He has drawn such strength from the wristbands, comments, hugs, and extra help that you have provided. God Bless you all!!!

February 15, 2005

Yesterday morning Daniel woke up with a severe headache and began vomiting shortly thereafter. I brought him to the emergency room at Methodist at about 9:30AM. We spent the better part of the day in emergency while they tried to get his pain and nausea under control. By last evening Daniel was feeling better and began eating. Dr. Turner put him on steroids to reduce any swelling in his brain. Apparently, the tumor has caused some swelling and therefore it was prohibiting his shunt from working properly. According to the CT scan they did yesterday, the tumor has not grown any from last week, and Dan's ventricles are about the same. Dr. Turner said the tumor has pushed his shunt up a bit which is causing the problem. Dan is feeling better today and there has been some discussion about sending him home tomorrow if he has the pain under control. If not, he will stay in the hospital until surgery on Friday, which is scheduled for 12:30PM. Daniel is upbeat, playing lots of Playstation, and eating and eating and eating.... (steroids will do that to you). Dan is really disappointed that he will be unable to attend the wrestling state finals this weekend. He is so proud of the fact that we are sending 5 guys to state, and he wishes each one the best of luck. Please know that his heart will be with the team even though his body can't. For Wes, Michael, D.J., Philip, and Cody...carry his strength with you, and give it everything you have, as we know you will. Providing everything goes well on Friday, Dan should be in the hospital for 6-7 days. I will keep everyone posted on his progress over the next several days. Thanks so much for your continued prayers and support.

February 19, 2005

After a very poor start to the week things are beginning to look up a bit. Daniel's condition declined steadily from Monday to Thursday. From Wednesday at about 6:00PM until his surgery on Friday he didn't eat anything. He was asleep most of the time, and continued to have substantial pain issues. He did come around a bit on Friday morning and was pretty coherent prior to surgery. Dr. Turner estimated the surgery would take about 6 hours. They took him back at about 1:00PM and after all prepping was complete they began surgery at 2:10PM. At 4:15 Dr. Turner came out into the waiting area. My heart sank as I expected him to say something had gone terribly wrong. Instead, he said everything went great. There was no scar tissue to work through, the tumor was very soft and they were able to suck it out easily. In addition, there was minimal blood loss. Dr. Turner indicated that they were able to remove the tumor down to clear margins except for the piece of tumor attached to an artery. At about 6:00PM they took Dan to his room on the Critical Care floor. Pam and I expected to see Daniel like he was after the first surgery, which included, poor motor skills, eyes gone haywire, and virtual incoherence. Instead, we found his eyes were the same as before surgery, excellent motor skills, and he was able to carry on a conversation. He is in a great deal of pain as was expected, but we hope that his shunt will take care of the fluid pressure issue so that all we have to worry about will be the pain from the surgery. If the shunt does not work properly they will have to insert a temporary drain, and that is no fun. When I went in to see Dan at 5:00AM this morning he said two things, "My head hurts, and I'm starving", the latter being a good sign. I know I have said it many times before, but I am so proud of my son. He is the toughest kid I know. Yesterday prior to surgery as we were saying our goodbyes I was quite upset. I stood there not knowing if that would be the last time I ever see my son alive. I keep seeing images of Dan as a little boy full of energy and mischief, and what I wouldn't give to return to those days, without the pain, without the cancer. After I hugged him and told him that I loved him I stood up to leave, and he said "don't worry Dad - I'll be alright". I thought to myself, here goes my kid...whose life hangs in the balance, and he is more worried about me than he is himself. Incredible! My kid is incredible!

February 21, 2005
Daniel had a rough start to the weekend. He hadn't eaten anything since last Wednesday, and his pain level until noon Sunday was 8 or 9 (on a scale of 10). He had slept virtually non-stop, and I was convinced that his shunt was not working properly therefore causing tremendous pressure in his head. I had all but resigned myself to another surgery this week to repair his shunt. I went in to spend a few minutes with him about 3:00PM, at which time he was unresponsive. Pam went in at 3:30 to find him wide awake. His first words were, "I'm hungry, can I have a grilled cheese"? He went on to eat two, watch the Indiana game with his brother and I, and request a Playstation. When the nurse asked him his pain level at 6:00PM he said, "I don't really have any pain right now", and this was in spite of not having pain medication for over 2 hours. I can't really explain what happened. To go from hurting so bad to virtually no pain, from being too nauseated to eat to eating grilled cheese all in the span of a couple hours. Incredible when you consider that he had major brain surgery less than 2 days before. Despite the rollercoaster of emotions one thing has remained constant...prayers, and lots of them.

Journal Entries

We were especially touched by the students, faculty and staff at St. Rose. During the day on Friday, all of the children were taken, by class, to the church where they prayed for Daniel. In addition, I have received countless emails and calls indicating that Daniel is being lifted up in prayer. I asked Pam last night if she believed the prayers had played a part in his turn around, and she said "I've learned that nothing is impossible". I think I agree with her. As of Monday morning, Daniel is scheduled be moved to the 7th floor, they have removed his catheter, he has been up sitting in a chair, and he was highly agitated that they forgot part of his breakfast. They left off his Rice Krispies and orange sherbet from a menu that included a sausage biscuit, 6 pieces of bacon, and 3 pieces of toast. Sounds like the breakfast of champions, but at this point the boy can have what he wants...he has earned it.

February 24, 2005
Daniel continues to make outstanding progress. He is down to oral pain medication now and is generally taking that only as a precaution. He is eating well...as if that was ever a problem, his motor skills are excellent, and he has begun physical therapy. He even went down to the play room yesterday and baked cookies with the little kids on his floor. It is cute to see this big, hulking guy surrounded by 5-10 year olds. The kids really like Daniel, and it seems as though he has a renewed interest in little ones as a result of his ordeal. Daniel continues to be one of the nurse favorites. I think in part because he can actually carry on adult like conversations...at least sometimes. I expect he will probably be released from the hospital today if all continues to go well. He actually needs to come home to get some rest. In addition to the regular nurses coming in, he has been part of the student nurse program this week. Let's just say they have made sure he has been attended to...like every 15 minutes. As I try to tell Daniel, that's the way they learn. However, it will be nice for him to piece together more than a ? hour of sleep at a time. Especially since I fully intend to get his big carcass moving as quickly as I can. One thing I have really enjoyed watching since November is his transformation to a young adult. He tells me he loves me 10 times a day, and he constantly reminds me to be "very careful" as I traverse to Methodist and back. The other night he told me to be "very careful" before I left the hospital, he called to tell me again before I got out of the parking garage, and he called two other times before I got home. Who says miracles don't happen?

February 28, 2005
Daniel arrived home last Thursday. He attended pieces of the home basketball game

Friday and the Wrestling State Finals on Saturday. He is feeling fine, but is sleeping a good portion of the time. Some of that, I am sure, is from the trauma of the surgery, and some is from the medication. Hopefully, he will begin to become a little more active soon. We meet with the oncologist and radiologist on Wednesday, and I would expect treatment to begin early next week. While Daniel's situation has consumed most of our attention for obvious reasons, the other boys had a terrific week. Anthony's basketball team finished their season 9-1, Joe won his 2nd varsity wrestling match at Custer Baker, and Jeff had the game winning hit on Sunday against 19th ranked Notre Dame. I just have to include an exerpt from an email Jeffrey sent home last week. He reminds us that there are positives all around...we just need to take the time to see them.

Just to let you know I am sending you this from Arizona. We just got in a little bit ago and grabbed some food from Waffle and Steak. Flying out here was an incredible site, we flew over mountains the entire way. It was beautiful, just like you said it would be. It's in the 70's here, which is nice because it just snowed 6 inches in Dayton last night; and we are supposed to have a home game on Tuesday. This is all so unbelievable that it's almost surreal. Notre Dame is so good. There will be so many pro scouts there that it's not even funny. If I get to play I might swing at every pitch they throw (ha ha). All the endless hours I've spent working out, and all the sacrifices I've made are starting to pay off. Knock on wood, but I don't think I could ask for much more at this point in my life. Daniel is doing great and came home today; I'm in Arizona playing against Notre Dame on the Cubs spring training field, and I might actually get to play. This is what life is all about.

Jeff's email reminds me of a quote by Jorge Luis Borges, "Any life, no matter how long and complex it may be, is made up of a single moment...the moment in which a man finds out, once and for all, who he is." Just like Jeff, I think a lot of us have had that moment in the past 4 months.

March 4, 2005
Daniel has been improving slowly. He has ventured out to some basketball games and wrestling matches recently, and he seems to be getting more alert daily. He has been a little down and discouraged lately, but appears to be improving in that area as well. We visited the oncologist and radiologist on Wednesday and received our treatment plan. On March 14th Daniel will begin 42 consecutive days of chemotherapy in addition to 6 weeks of radiation (5 days per week). He will then get a month off, and do 5 days of chemotherapy every month for 10 more months. The radiology guy wasn't overly prom-

Appendix

Journal Entries

ising, and that bothered Daniel a great deal. I explained to Dan that they have to share the worst and hope for the best. I do wish that they would speak to the parents first before dropping a bombshell on a 17 year old kid. One of the many things we would have preferred to NOT experience throughout this process. One of the things that we continue to be appreciative of is the support that Daniel receives daily. His friends continue to call and make it a point to touch base regularly, he receives cards and well wishes every day, and so many family members and friends continue to make themselves a part of Daniel's life. A huge thanks needs to go to Mike Carter, Chris Lynch, Joe, Michelle, and Emily Fox for going way above and beyond the call of duty. We continue to feel really blessed by all the support. One item from the really cool column, thanks to Maria Coudret, the Archbishop himself is wearing a pink Daniel bracelet. Move over Scott Rolen, now we're calling in the really heavy hitters!!

March 8, 2005
Daniel is getting stronger every day. He is awake and alert for the better part of the day now. He has even begun exercising some. We tend to forget, at least I do, that he is less than 3 weeks removed from major brain surgery. His attitude and demeanor have improved in the past few days. He is returning to the "happy go lucky" kid we are used to. Daniel even made a list of all his activities scheduled for this week - Mrs. Hopper you would be proud. He is looking forward to a bunch of fun events and activities. He went on Monday to be fitted for his radiation body mold, and is set to begin that at 1:00PM next Monday. He will begin his chemotherapy that day as well. It should make for an interesting week as we observe how he reacts to the treatment. We are hopeful that he will be able to return to school very soon, but much of that will depend on his tolerance of the medication. On Friday of this week, Daniel and I are going to visit the University of Dayton, hopefully to watch Jeff play baseball. The weather doesn't look too good but regardless, we will have fun spending time with Jeff and the team. This may be the last time Daniel sees Jeff for awhile depending on how he feels. So, at minimum, we wanted to take a couple days to visit. This past weekend our family attended the county Middle School wrestling tournament at Greenwood Middle School. Daniel and the rest of us were pleased to be able to watch Joe and the Custer Baker team compete. Beyond the fact that we won, which was great, a really special thing happened. Five young boys, 4 from Franklin and 1 from Indian Creek spent the better part of the day selling "Daniel bracelets". More than the very caring act of helping Daniel in his hour of need was the fact that Daniel was able to see it first hand. These boys sold 225 bracelets over the course of the day, and they did it for no other reason than to help

Daniel. They donated their entire day to this cause. It was all I could do to hold it together as I came back from lunch to see these boys outside the gymnasium, bracelets in hand, selling them for Dan. I think its further evidence of the terrific young people we have in this community. Thank you boys!!!

March 14, 2005

We received a phone call last Thursday that the cancer has spread down Daniel's spine. He went back to the hospital on Thursday to prep for his new radiation treatment. They will now have to treat his spine in addition to his brain. Obviously, this is not the news we were hoping for. No one, especially a kid, should have to go through this.

However, it is the hand we've been dealt so we will deal with it the best we can. We left town on Friday for Nashville, Tennessee to watch Jeff play baseball. It came at a good time and allowed us to briefly take our minds off our problem. We had a terrific time. It was so much fun to spend time together laughing and watching baseball. I have to share one story that is vintage Daniel. We went to Ryan's dinner buffet last night in Bowling Green, Kentucky on our way home. Daniel, due to the steroids has been eating a great deal and as we were about done with dinner Daniel walks across the restaurant and finds our waitress. We asked him what he had said to her, and he responded that he had asked for more dinner rolls. His Mom got on him because he had already eaten about ten. In a matter of seconds we realized what he had done, because here comes five waitresses to sing "happy birthday" to Anthony, despite the fact that it wasn't his birthday! The weekend was made better by the fact that Dayton won all four games. Daniel got a kick out of spending time with his brother and the team. As always, Coach Vittorio (Dayton head coach) was terrific with him and continues to encourage Daniel to be strong through this process. Only once since last Thursday has Daniel given in to his feelings. His Mom and I took him to lunch on Thursday and he made the statement that "I don't think I have much longer to live". All of our parenting skills were put to the test at that moment. I don't know that I have ever faced a single tougher moment in my life. Despite the hope that we continue to have, there are no guarantees at this point. The best we can do now is to have faith that God has a plan for Daniel, and maybe that plan allows him to continue in this life. We hope he can continue to bring joy to those that know and love him, continue to be an inspiration to his family, friends, and his community, and continue to be a son that any Mom and Dad would be proud to call their own. We so appreciate your prayers, and ask that you continue to ask for God's blessing.

Appendix

Journal Entries

March 17, 2005

Daniel continues to be a source of great strength for me and our entire family. Despite long and very arduous sessions this week to prepare for radiation treatment, he continues to be very positive and courageous.   Treatment, which was scheduled to begin on Monday, was postponed until Tuesday. The radiologist wasn't comfortable with the alignment of radiation to the treatment area. Therefore, Daniel spent 3+ hours on Monday and Tuesday strapped to a table in what is called a CT simulation. It requires a body mold which holds one in place. It was not fun, but we do realize the importance of aligning the treatment to the affected area. Radiation and chemotherapy began on Tuesday. Thus far, and we do realize it is early in the game, Daniel has experienced little to no side affects. As I share with him, for every one day that you don't feel poorly, it's one day closer to being done (2 down and 40 to go). Yesterday, Daniel asked if he could drive his truck, to which I replied "absolutely". So, we took a test drive to pick up Anthony.   Daniel did very well so we let him drive to baseball practice last night. He used only back roads all the way to Franklin. I mention that in case any who reads this might be concerned that we need to blockade St. Rd. 144 while he drives into town. Actually, I think with a good "tail wind" I could have outrun him to town in his truck, but I would much rather he exercise a good deal of caution. It was great to see him exert a little bit of independence. He really feels pretty good right now. He had a great time at practice while stretching, doing his arm exercises, throwing, and walking. Coach Luse has been terrific in welcoming Dan back into the mix. In fact, he even made Dan go help the young catchers during their specialty practice period. I was happy to see him push Daniel to find a way to help out and be a contributor to the team. I don't know what we would do without the wrestling and baseball programs providing encouragement for Daniel to stay involved and active. We have had several discussions with Dan regarding what he controls, and what the doctor's control. Dan understands that he controls his attitude, and keeping his body as fit as possible through exercise and nutrition. The doctors control the treatment which will allow us to beat this disease. So, Dan worries about what he can control and he's leaving the rest to the trained professionals. I would conclude by saying this, "the doctors better do their job, because Daniel will most certainly do his."

March 22, 2005

Daniel has completed one week of treatment. He currently has not experienced any significant side effects other than some fatigue. For that we are extremely grateful. As I have said to Daniel, "for every day you aren't sick it's one day closer to being done, so be thankful for every good day". Dan has been driving himself to town and attending baseball practice almost every day. He is increasing his workload daily and seems to be handling it pretty well. His vision prevents him from catching or hitting a moving object, but he has been throwing a bucket of balls each day. We are working on his schooling options for this year and beyond, and should be making some decisions soon with the help of Mrs. Hopper (Guidance Director). Daniel continues to be very upbeat and positive, and it's good to see him returning slowly to his normal activities. He is quite excited about Easter and spending time with his family. It's amazing what you are grateful for when things aren't guaranteed. Daniel was disappointed to see Coach Coudret (football coach) was leaving for Beech Grove at year's end. He, like most other kids has a great respect for Coach Coudret and will miss his positive approach to life. Hopefully, the new coach will allow Daniel to be around the team next season in some capacity. For now, we are taking one day at a time and enjoying the journey along the way.

March 24, 2005
Daniel continues to progress well through treatment. He has some fatigue but no nausea thus far. They have made some adjustments to his radiation treatment as they are treating three separate sections of his spine. Dan is settling into his daily routine which includes X-rays, radiation, chemo, blood work, and physical activity. He is prepared to add school back into the mix after Spring Break. We have decided as a family that it would be best for Daniel to repeat his junior year. Pam and Dan met with Mrs. Hopper yesterday and worked out a schedule that will allow him to attend ? days for the rest of the year, and then hopefully he will be set to return full time next August. We just don't feel that he will be academically prepared to begin college after next school year. You just can't miss 60% of Algebra, Chemistry, English, etc. and expect to move on normally. Daniel was very interested in graduating with his class, but he decided that this new direction would be best. In addition, he holds out hope, as do we, that he will someday be able to play baseball. This extra year will allow his body and vision a chance to recover to the point that he can compete. If not, that's OK, but it is something to shoot for. Life's priorities have had a way of taking on a decidedly different emphasis. Dan is just happy at this point to be here and pain free...anything beyond that is a bonus. Have a wonderful Easter, and take time to remember the many blessings that have been bestowed upon each of us.

Appendix

Journal Entries

March 29, 2005

Daniel had a really enjoyable Easter weekend. He went to Dayton to watch his brother play baseball and then on to his Grandma and Grandpa's house for Easter. He played Euchre for hours on end and relished in the fact that he only lost twice. He and Uncle Bob made a pretty good team, though I have serious questions about the level of competition (Ha!). Dan continues to respond well to treatment. He has yet to be sick and he still has his appetite. We have noticed that his throat is beginning to get a little sore, and that is probably from the radiation. His back is giving him some trouble as well. I think that is a combination of things; tumors in his spine, extra weight, lack of activity, etc. It seems as though his back is fine until he sits in a hard chair for an extended period, and generally every evening he has some discomfort. But, by the next morning it feels fine again and then we start the process all over. Today is an especially tough day for Dan and all of us really. The baseball team leaves for Kentucky this morning on their Spring Break trip. Daniel can't go. He has radiation every day this week and the 7 hour round trip drive is more than his back can take in 1 day. I don't think things would be quite as bad if he could just make the trip. However, not being able to play nor make the trip is really difficult. We certainly wish the team the best of luck as they take on the boys from Kentucky. Dan's heart and spirit will be with you even if his body can't.

April 4, 2005

Daniel's lack of reaction related to treatment is unfortunately disappearing. As of the middle of last week several things have cropped up; his hair officially started falling out, and his back has been giving him moderate to serious pain as have his knees. So, we have just dealt with those realities by shaving his head and making sure he has a soft chair to sit in virtually all the time. As for the knees, we are scheduling an MRI to determine the problem. Daniel has been blessed that he has not been ill and his blood/platelet count has been good thus far. In a weird sort of way you almost hope for the treatment to show some signs of working (ie. hair falling out, etc.). In reality, those symptoms actually have no relation to the success or failure of the prescribed treatment. This past weekend we took the family to Dayton to spend Friday evening with Jeff and watch the University of Dayton games on Saturday. Daniel can only take so much riding in one day so we had to split it up. While we enjoyed spending a couple days with Jeff we didn't get to see any baseball because the games with Rhode Island were rained out. It was fun though...or as fun as 5 people in a motel room can be. I think Daniel visiting Dayton also took his mind off of the fact that he couldn't travel with the high school team. He sure missed not being with his teammates, but radiation Monday thru Friday prohibited that as did the long drive. Mike Carter, Coach Luse, and his buddies kept him posted on how things were going. Dan hopes to attend the Franklin vs. Center Grove game tomorrow if his knees feel up to it. It should be a good game, but more importantly it will be nice to see some of the kids from Center Grove who have been very supportive of Daniel throughout this ordeal. Of course, he is really hoping to sit in the dugout with his teammates and make some sort of a contribution...like chewing sunflower seeds and saying dumb baseball stuff. Daniel has the ability to add a new dimension to a dugout atmosphere. He is one of a kind...and I realize that more and more all the time.

April 11, 2005
Daniel continues to persevere through his treatment. His knees and back are aching a bit, but small doses of pain medication have helped a great deal. He will begin treatment for his knees tomorrow. The intraveneous fluid is designed to counteract the effects of the steroids which have caused the problem. His blood work continues to be good, so no transfusions or other remedies are needed at this time. Dan was able to get out to some of the Franklin ballgames last week. Center Grove and Franklin Central baseball teams both took time to recognize Daniel before the games. It means a great deal to him to have the support of kids he has played against for so many years. We went to Dayton on Sunday to watch Jeff and the Flyers play Temple Univ. It was a great day all the way around. First, the Dayton Daily News ran an article on Jeffrey and Daniel on Sunday morning. It was a terrific article that really focused on what is important, relationships and living, and how these two boys have handled this challenge. If you can navigate the registration process it really is a terrific article (written by Tom Archdeacon). Secondly, Pam's Mom and Dad, two sisters and a nephew were able to come see Jeff play. It was has become another of those "it was almost meant to be" moments, Dayton was trailing 5-1 going into the bottom of the 6th inning. Up to that point the Flyers had only three hits and it looked like it was going to be an "off" day. Lo and behold, and off the same pitcher, Dayton gets 8 hits in a row and takes a 10-5 lead. Aside from the fact that we want Dayton to win, a large lead in a conference game also increases the chances that Jeff will get into the game. So, in the bottom of the 8th inning Jeff is scheduled to be the 5th hitter. With two outs and an 0-2 count on Joe McSoley (Cathedral H.S.), the hitter just before Jeff, Joe grounded a single up the middle. Then, Jeff on a 2-1 count lined a single to left-center. After another hit and Jeff advancing from first to third, Coach Vittorio seemed more excited than anyone when he

told Jeff "it was meant to be, it was meant to be". It was a perfect ending to a perfect day.

April 13, 2005

Good news and bad news for Daniel today. The good news is that today is Daniel's last day for radiation on the spine. While the radiation itself is not painful, the position and face mask he wears are. For the next two weeks he will be in a different position while they radiate the brain only. The bad news is that Dan's blood counts are low and as a result the oncologist has temporarily halted the chemo. Dan goes back in Friday morning for further blood tests. In addition, the nurses were unable yesterday to start an IV for the drip treatment on his knees. Dan was stuck five times with no success. Therefore, it looks like he will have a port placed in his upper chest to accommodate blood draws, IV's, treatment if necessary, etc. He is a bit discouraged at this point as I think he was hoping to make it through without significant complications. However, as we shared with him last night he really has been pretty fortunate with regard to treatment. To date, he has not been sick a single time, and the back and knee pain are manageable at this point. So, it could be considerably worse. But, try telling that to a kid that has been through as much as he has been through. We are trying very hard to focus on things he can look forward to. Prom is at the top of the list, although as Dan suggests, his dancing prowess will be greatly diminished this year with his vision and balance issues (kids beware...of a runaway truck). In addition, he is looking forward to a planned trip to St. Louis to watch Scott Rolen and the Cardinals. We find that giving him something to point toward helps him to take his mind off the present. One other thing that has been noticeable is Dan's competitive fire creeping back into his life. He has been a reading machine lately. He has finished a book given to him by Doug Feyerabend, and is nearly done with the new Jose Canseco book, and is planning on several other baseball books. This may not seem significant, but for Dan to read a book is like the sky falling in, and furthermore he is relishing in the volume of pages he is reading daily. I know in his own way he is competing against an imaginary opponent. That's good...we need that fighting spirit to remain alive and well.

April 14, 2005

Daniel went in for radiation today at 8:00AM, he arrived home at 6:30PM. The minute he walked in for his blood draw the doctor ordered a blood transfusion. Dan was very weak and pale. His blood count was down again, and his immune system is at zero. They hope to improve his strength before tomorrow's surgery to install his port. Dan will be very limited in what he can do until the blood counts improve. He has to wear a mask when he goes out, and any unprotected contact with someone who is sick can create real problems for him. This is not totally uncommon for someone who has gone through so much, but it is scary nonetheless. I can't believe how quickly this hit him. Just last night he seemed good, a little tired, but good. Today when he arrived home he was shaking (cold) and barely able to hold his eyes open. I hope tomorrow is a better day.

April 18, 2005

We made another midnight run early Friday morning, 1:30AM to be exact. Dan had a fever and severe head pain so I took him to Riley Hospital. By about 5:30AM or 6:00AM they were able to get his pain under control. He is really over this pain, and I don't blame him. His blood counts came back even lower than the day before and he is very susceptible to any type of infection. On Saturday they inserted a "pic" line in Dan's arm so they could quit sticking him all the time. They also tapped his shunt to look for infection in his brain. This is normally a very painful process, but this time the doctor retrieved the fluid in one stick, for which Dan is eternally grateful. The preliminary results show no infection, which is good news. They gave Dan three more units of blood on Saturday in hopes of raising his blood counts. By Sunday his counts were coming up slowly and he was feeling a little better. I even took him outside in a wheel chair just so he could smell the fresh air. He is unable to eat much right now as the low blood counts and stray radiation have irritated his throat. The doctor said it is called "thrush", and should go away as his body is better able to heal itself. Poor little Anthony wasn't allowed in to see Dan yesterday because he recently had strep throat...he cried as he so wanted to see Daniel. But they spoke on the phone from 100 ft. away and that seemed to help Anthony. Pam has decided to take the rest of the school year off as it has just been too much on her and her students at Whiteland, with all the on again - off again. A huge thanks to Mrs. Harlow and Mrs. Dunn for coordinating the absences and making sure that Pam's classes ran smoothly. We expect Dan will get to come home sometime this week but it will really depend on how his immune system responds. We'll keep our fingers crossed.

April 22, 2005

Daniel came home late Wednesday afternoon. It was actually quite a surprise, but his ANC reading (infection fighting count) went from 40 on Tuesday to 380 on Wednesday. In general he has been very tired and if he is not sleeping he is certainly laying around.

Appendix

Journal Entries

It's great to have him home. He continues to be very weak for obvious reasons, but the soreness in his throat is keeping him from eating which doesn't help in regaining strength. It does seem to be getting better, but very slowly. Dan's brother Jeff gets to come home this weekend as the University of Dayton cancelled their baseball games due to inclement weather. Coach Vittorio is allowing Jeff a couple days off to spend with Daniel and our family. We are very appreciative as I think this is the first time he has been home since Dan's surgery on February 18th. Dan is excited to see Jeff, as is everyone else. Daniel is really looking forward to prom next Friday. I hope he will be up to it. He has been nominated for Prom Court, and while he doesn't say anything about it I think he is really honored to be considered. Daniel has just 6 more radiation days, and if his blood counts continue to move up they may restart the chemotherapy. While we will be happy to have this phase concluded we are certainly apprehensive to see how the treatment has gone. It will probably be the end of May before we know. Continued thanks to all who remember Daniel and our family in their prayers, or with cards and letters. A special thanks to the Perry Meridian baseball team for an awesome poster signed by the team and sent to Daniel in the hospital. We wish he could have been at the game, but the poster was the next best thing.

April 26, 2005

Daniel has made steady progress since coming home last week. The soreness in his chest and throat is all but gone thanks to Dr. Goldman who suggested that hydrating Daniel with fluids might have a positive impact on his throat. He couldn't have been more correct. For the past 4 days Dan has been hooked up to an IV at night for 10 hours. The two liters of fluid daily have made a world of difference. Although his appetite isn't back to normal, he is now able to eat without pain. He has been resting a lot as I think the radiation has just caught up with him. Friday is his final day of the initial treatment period. We will be happy to leave the radiation behind, but pray that it has done its job. The doctors will do an MRI in about a month and make a determination regarding next steps. If the treatment has not been effective then they will change his chemotherapy. If it has been effective then they will put him on a maintenance plan. Dan is looking forward to tomorrow when he will be inducted into the National Honor Society at Franklin High School. He may be the first kid ever to repeat his Junior year and still be inducted into NHS? In addition, he has Prom on Friday so this will be a big week for him. It will probably result in him collapsing into his bed for the entire weekend, but what the heck. It's great to see him feel well enough to attend normal 17 year old activities.

April 29, 2005

Today is Dan's last treatment day...hurrah!! Pam and I took him out to breakfast to celebrate. He is in good spirits and feels relatively well except for the fatigue. He is resting up today to save his energy for the Prom tonight. He is going to the Prom in style...he and 19 other kids are riding in a stretch Expedition to dinner and the dance. Heaven help that restaurant, it may never be the same (Ha!). Thanks to the family who is providing the limo...you are the best!!! Dan is pretty excited about the whole deal. Oh, to be 17 again. The doctors are going to give Dan's body some time to recover, and therefore he will have very little done for the next month (we hope anyway). He will have a follow-up MRI toward the end of May and then we will know our next steps. We'll put that on the back burner for awhile and enjoy the next month. He's got all kinds of neat stuff coming up between the community concert next Friday, the trip to St. Louis, trips to Dayton to watch his brother, a trip to the Colts complex, and any other trouble we might get into. Life is good...and we plan on it staying that way, because as an ancient poet once said, "While there's life, there's hope".

May 2, 2005

Daniel had an exciting end of the week last week. First, he attended the National Honor Society induction and enjoyed it very much. Although as a 17 year old male you are not allowed to show emotion connected to academic achievement, I know he was excited to have earned this award.   Secondly, he had a great time attending the Prom on Friday. He and twenty other kids went to dinner and the dance together. He had a wonderful meal made more enjoyable by the company. Pam went to the Prom for a short while to take pictures and stayed long enough to see Daniel named Prom King. A tremendous honor indeed. I wish I could have been there, but I was hanging out with Anthony, in the rain, at the ballpark. All was not lost however as Anthony's team played very well. Dan ventured out a little on Saturday to watch Joe play baseball against Whiteland, but he quickly tired and I took him home. He feels really good except that he is tired constantly. He could sleep for 15 hours and wake up just as tired as when he went to bed. We knew this would happen as a result of massive amounts of treatment, but it has reached its peak. Thankfully, round one of his treatment ended on Friday and his body will have a chance to recover somewhat. Dan checks in with his oncologist on Tuesday to see what his blood counts look like.   Hopefully, they will be decent and we can avoid any additional transfusions...well see. Time for rest and healing for a month. We're all looking forward to that.

Appendix

May 9, 2005

Daniel had quite a weekend. First, the concert that the community hosted on Daniel's behalf was held on Friday night. There was a terrific show of support for Daniel and our family, and we are humbled and tremendously appreciative. Both bands were excellent, and the Blind Side Band featuring Coach Pieper played several of their own songs, four of which will be featured in films in the near future. So many people spent so much time putting this special evening together that I can't begin to thank everyone, however a special thanks goes out to Gretchen and Greg Robinson, Ann Gordon, and the Franklin Baseball Team. For all those who worked behind the scenes...a huge thank you as well. Daniel joined the band to play the tambourine during one number, and then later spoke to the crowd. Daniel's brother Jeff accompanied him onto the stage for a few remarks and thanks, and at one point it looked like Jeff might have to take over, but Daniel composed himself and finished nicely. His last comment says a great deal about the man Daniel has become. After he thanked his friends, family, and community he concluded by saying, "I can promise you this, I won't be down for long". I guess at this point I wouldn't bet against him.

Dan rested up on Saturday as he was completely spent from the night before. Michael and Ashley did come and spend the evening with Dan as they so often do. On Sunday, Daniel, Pam, and Anthony took off for Dayton to watch Jeff play baseball. Jeff managed to win the starting first base job this past week so it was nice for them to see him play.   Jeff contributed a double and an RBI as Dayton rolled to a 14-2 win over Duquesne. It took Dan about 15 minutes to fall asleep once they returned home, and I'm sure today will be spent resting. Our family has been invited to be the guest of the Colts this week at their complex and we are very grateful, and very much looking forward to that. In the meantime, Daniel is exercising a little more each day and is trying his best to build up his stamina. He continues to be relatively pain free and very upbeat.

May 18, 2005

Daniel has responded very well during his initial post-treatment phase. His back pain is completely gone. He has no pain in his head at this point, and the difficulty in swallowing is now gone. The only visible remnants of treatment continue to be a loss of appetite and fatigue.   His spirits have been good and he seems ready to return to some of his normal activities like hanging out with his friends. He has been to several ballgames both at Dayton and Franklin recently. Last night the Beech Grove team honored Dan with a post-game prayer joined by the Franklin team. Nearly all of Franklin's opponents this season have done something special for Daniel, and we are very grateful. Dan had a big day this past Sunday. His Uncle Bob took him turkey hunting early on Sunday morning. I'm not sure how he did it, but Bob managed to coax 3 toms into gun range for Daniel. As you can imagine, Dan is not mobile at all, and therefore it makes hunting a wary turkey very difficult. Nonetheless, as if it was almost meant to be Dan killed his first turkey that morning. The tom weighed 17 lbs. and had an 8" beard. Not a great big one, but a real trophy anyway. Many thanks to Bob for going way beyond the call of duty and making that day a very special one for an excited kid. Last Wednesday Daniel and our family were honored to be the guests of the Indianapolis Colts at their training facility on 56th Street. The Colts sent a limo to collect our group, and the boys thought that was really cool. Tom Zupancic coordinated the visit and was incredibly kind to take time from his busy day to spend with us. Bob Potter, and Kevin Kirkhoff also played a key role in pulling this off. For those who may question the financial value of having an NFL team in our city, let me confirm that there are many ways to play a significant role in being a good community participant. The Colts are the epitome of a class organization with class people, and there are none better than Tom Zupancic. Tom allowed us access to the training room, meeting rooms, video and radio studios, the weight room, locker room, and the indoor training facility. Along the way the boys met Gary Brackett, Jason David, and Cato June. These players took time from their workouts to say hello and sign autographs. Tom said he had never seen players do that before, because the players view this as their office and they really don't want to lose their focus. These guys were great representatives of the Colts organization, and we appreciate them very much. Our next big event takes place on May 26th as Daniel has his MRI. This will tell us how he has responded to treatment. Believe me, we have cranked up the prayers in anticipation of that day, but regardless we are committed to battling this with everything we have.

May 23, 2005

Quite a weekend for Dan. On Saturday, Daniel and Jeffrey were able to sit in the dugout as the Franklin baseball team won the Johnson County Tourney for the first time in 32 years. What a great day for all involved. Daniel was given a Johnson County medal to represent the championship, and he immediately pinned it to his letter jacket and proudly pointed it out to me. If we have to wait 32 more years I hope Daniel has the chance to be in attendance...maybe to watch his son play. On Saturday night we held a surprise 18th birthday party for Dan. Joe and Michelle Fox were kind enough to let us use their lovely property for the event as it was just too big for us to host at our house. Dan

Journal Entries

was totally in the dark. I have no idea how we were able to keep it from him...luck I guess, and the fact that we didn't tell Anthony. Everyone had a great time, especially Dan who didn't get home until about 11:30PM. Daniel scared Jeffrey by riding four-wheelers in the dark and weaving in and out of the trees. I have to admit it's probably best I didn't know, but on the other hand you have to be pleased that he's trying to return to normalcy. Dan, Jeff and I went shopping on Sunday at Gander Mountain for his birthday. Dan had a bit of a headache and was worn out but enjoyed it very much. Of course, we have the MRI on Thursday about which we are praying mightily. On Saturday we leave for St. Louis to spend the day with the Cardinals. Scott Rolen has been kind enough to invite us, and although Dan is disappointed that he won't be playing (due to injury) he is really looking forward to going. Also, from the "very cool" column, Daniel has been invited to throw out the first pitch at the Indianapolis Indians game on Saturday, June 18th. While he thought that was pretty cool, he wonders if he can get the ball to the plate. Don't worry "D" the catcher can block your 57 footer if need be just like you have thousands of times before.

May 27, 2005
It's difficult to describe the emotions that precede a single conversation where your child's life hangs in the balance. I think maybe I have matured as a father and person through this, but I still didn't handle the waiting and worrying very well as we were summoned by Dr. Goldman. Daniel tried to keep things light by making several funny comments. God love him...I don't know how he did it knowing what was at stake. Pam, as usual, was a rock. For a person who has spent most of her life as an emotional wreck during trying situations, she has been unbelievable. Mother bear syndrome I think. Whatever it is, it has sure made handling this much more manageable. Dr. Goldman asked Dan how he was feeling, and Dan responded "really well but that might depend on what you are about to tell me". Dr. Goldman after what seemed like an hour of agonizing suspense and 20 questions said, "the cancer in the spine is gone...completely, the tumor in the brain is tough to read because the spot is actually larger than before, but often when radiation is recently completed the area swells. It appears that there are cysts in the mass and often they accompany the tumor dying". While Dr. Goldman can't be sure that the tumor in the brain isn't growing he was encouraged by the fact that Daniel feels good, and that his hair is still falling out. The loss of hair indicates that the radiation is still present and burning the tumor. One additional positive is that radiation to the spine finished two weeks prior to finishing the brain. So it is quite possible that the tumor is still reacting to the radiation. Daniel was his normal stoic self...very little

emotion. When Dr. Goldman left the room I gave it a loud "Yessss" while pumping my fists in the air, and Dan sat quietly although he did crack a smile at Dad making a fool of himself. So the plan now is that Daniel will begin his oral chemotherapy this coming week. He will go for 5 days and then take 23 off, and repeat that for 6 months if all goes well. We will have another MRI in five weeks of his head only, and that will let us know how the tumor is responding. All along I have just been praying that God would give Daniel a glimmer of hope, because I know that his toughness and resolve will kick in and we can give this cancer a run for its money. My prayers and the prayers of thousands of our friends, family, and supporters were answered in part yesterday. While we are far from beating this thing altogether I know that "a journey of a thousand miles begins with but a single step". Yesterday was the first step and the first confirmed bit of good news we have received since this ordeal began on November 4th. Oh, we've had the misdiagnosis of a benign tumor and things we had hoped were positive, but none that truly were...until now. God bless all of you who have continued to pray on behalf of Daniel and our family. I believe it has made a huge difference in yesterday's report, but I know it has made a huge difference in our ability to push on with a positive and determined attitude.

June 6, 2005
Daniel completed his first round of secondary chemotherapy on Saturday night. His dosage level has doubled from before since he will only take it for 5 days at a time. He hasn't responded very well this time. After the first day he began feeling sick and began vomiting multiple times daily. In addition, he has been unable to eat or drink much of anything. One complicating factor is that every time he gets sick it makes his head hurt. Fortunately, the pain seems to be short lived and is controlled with Tylenol. So, right now pretty much everything in our lives is controlled by how Daniel feels, and making sure that one of us are always present. Daniel was able to go lift with his brother Jeff a couple times last week, but both times were followed by him getting sick. He also made it to one graduation party over the weekend but that was all he could do. Yesterday was spent totally in the bathroom or on the couch. We hope that he will begin to feel better in the next couple of days.

June 16, 2005
Last week was not good. Daniel was very ill and was eating virtually nothing. It seemed as though whenever he ate or drank anything he would immediately get sick. Of course, every time he got sick it made his head hurt. We finally took him to Riley on Friday

night to see if they could provide any solutions. They took a CT scan and found that there was nothing going on with his shunt or tumor that should be causing him to be ill. They determined two things, first, they put him back on a small dose of steroids to reduce the swelling in his brain, and they also decided that the morphine injections designed to reduce bodily aches and pains could be making him sick. So, bring on the steroids and so long to the morphine. Within two days Daniel was a new kid. By Sunday he had begun eating again without getting ill, and by Monday he was back in the weight room with Jeffrey and Joe. On Wednesday when I came out of the shower at 6:30AM there sat "pumpkin head" at the breakfast table. I said, "Daniel what in the world are you doing up at this hour", and he replied, "I wanted to get my lifting in before my doctors appointment at Noon". I can safely say that this is a first. He hasn't been up that early, nor felt compelled to lift since last November. He ended up having a really good day. He drove over to football lifting, met the new coach, and did his workout. He also rode his stationary bike at home...twice. Hopefully, today will bring similar results. Dan is looking forward to Saturday when he gets to throw out the first pitch at the Indianapolis Indians game. It's Franklin Night at the ballpark so I'm sure lots of our friends will be there to cheer him on. It should be fun.

June 24, 2005
I have learned through all of this that you never take anything for granted, you never assume, that nothing is ever as good as it seems...nor as bad...but somewhere in between reality falls. However, with all that said, Daniel feels really good. This is the best he has felt since this all began. He has more energy, he is more alert, he is more committed to recovery. He has been lifting with the football team on Monday, Wednesday, and Friday. He is getting out of bed, on his own, at 7:15AM to get he and his brother Joe to the workouts. In addition, he has been riding his Aerodyne bike 20-30 minutes a day. This is incredible progress given the fact that two weeks ago he couldn't even get out of bed. We are really proud of him. The past week was filled with activity and we are so thankful that Dan felt up to participating. He threw out the first pitch at the Indians game last Saturday...strike by the way...albeit 40 mph. Thanks so much to all who took part in setting that up. Dan was thrilled to see so many friends and supporters from Franklin, as well as, his teammates and families from the Indiana Bulls who made the trip to be with him.

Also, our family took a couple days and went to Monroe Reservoir. We went fishing, swimming, and eating...not necessarily in that order. We had a great time, and Daniel took part in all of it as he felt really good. I must admit that his fishing acumen was called into question a few times. He caught the first fish of the trip, which ended up being his last fish of the trip. That's OK, we had fun nonetheless. Dan goes on Monday for his brain MRI. They will be checking the status of his tumor and swelling. It may mean nothing, but he feels so good that we are hoping that is a good sign. He will begin his chemo next week, and his MRI will determine which type. It could be that we continue on Temodar or change to something else. At this point we are just thankful for all the good days recently, and we will keep praying for good news.

June 29, 2005
As Knute Rockne once said, "we've got to get em on the run boys, and then we've got to keep em on the run". Our meeting with Dr. Goldman (Daniel's oncologist) yesterday confirmed what you, and we, had been praying for. We've got the cancer on the run. The swelling in Daniel's brain has decreased, and while the tumor size is roughly the same as before there are 3 or 4 spots in the tumor which appear to be black (dead). While this is not quite an affirmation that the tumor is gone, it is a step in the right direction. Daniel picks up cycle 2 of his chemo this week, and the positive part of that is the fact that they are leaving his treatment the same. In effect, it is an indication that they think this treatment is working. We hope that Dan will not experience the nausea that he had with chemo cycle 1. However, we are prepared in the event that he does. We have fluids on hand to keep him from becoming dehydrated, and we had asked to double his anti-nausea medication.

Daniel has decided to have a port installed in his upper left chest. That will take place on July 19th. The port will allow blood to be drawn, intervenous fluids to be given, etc., and all without any restriction to physical activities. Currently he has a pic line which is a tube inserted into his right arm. The pic line prevents swimming, aggressive contact, and it makes showers difficult as well. Needless to say we are happy he has made this decision. It is a surgical procedure, but a minor one. Daniel is continuing to progress. He has been to lifting three days a week, and he is riding his stationary bike or walking twice a day. He is visibly stronger, more agile, and walking with a more normal gait. We have a big weekend planned with lots of activity. Hopefully, Dan will feel up to participating.

Appendix

Journal Entries

July 6, 2005

Daniel completed his second round of chemotherapy last Saturday night. As you may recall he was very ill the first time, and as you might expect we were braced for the worst. One thing we have learned through all of this is that through observation you can make a difference in the outcome related to medication. When is he taking too much, not enough? What works well and what doesn't? This time we asked the doctor to double his antinausea medication in hopes of avoiding the illness. We also asked for fluids just in case he became dehydrated. Our preparations seem to have paid off as Dan did not get ill a single time. He has been fatigued from the chemo, but he has felt really good and is eating normally.

Daniel continues to lift, walk, and ride his stationary bike. He is increasing his work-outs with regard to maximums, which is a very good sign. I know he very much wants to get back into shape and he feels like he is moving in that direction. Jeff has been a big motivator and takes Daniel to workout when he is home. We had a big weekend over the 4th and Daniel was the biggest duck in the puddle...staying up til all hours of the night playing euchre at his Grandma and Grandpa's house. He still gets beat regu-larly, so I guess practice isn't making perfect, at least in his case.

His blood counts came back very good yesterday. In fact, they were higher than they have been for the past couple of months. He, as well as Pam and I are very pleased with his progress at this point. I think he is even looking forward to starting school in August...boy did I really say that! He has met with our new football coach and dis-cussed briefly ways in which he can stay involved in a non-playing capacity. I think it would be good for him to stay around it. Who knows, maybe he can be a kicker some day? Kick the ball and sprint off the field...yeah right...he would have to lay a hit on some poor unsuspecting soul. Ah, just like old times.

July 16, 2005

Daniel continues to do well. Aside from a short spell this week when he was really tired, he continues to increase his activity level. He lifts, rides his stationary bike, and walks about an hour a day. He threw a baseball a little bit on Thursday, and I think is looking forward to getting his "pic" line out of his right arm so that he can begin throw-ing and swinging a bat. Dan has surgery on Tuesday to insert a port into his chest, and this will allow him a great deal more freedom (showers without getting his arm wrapped up, swimming, etc.). While the surgery is considered minor, he isn't looking forward to being back in the hospital.

We have been discussing trip dates to Fenway Park (Boston) with the "Make a Wish" Foundation. They are a wonderful organization and have worked very hard on Daniel's behalf. Dan would very much like to meet David Ortiz while attending a Red Sox game. Hopefully, we can get things worked out. In the meantime, we just live one day at a time and thank God that Dan feels good and can conduct life fairly close to normal.

July 21, 2005

Daniel had surgery this week to install his port. The port will allow him to get rid of the pic line in his arm, become much more mobile (throw a ball, swim, etc.). The surgery went fine and Dan came home the same day. He is a little sore but otherwise is progressing nicely. Daniel continues to work out as much as possible given his limitations this week due to surgery. He is very fatigued and is hoping to have more energy soon. I think the fatigue is due in part to his no longer taking steroids.
Pam, Dan, and the other boys are off to Holiday World on Sunday and Monday. They should have a great time, and I know they are all looking forward to it. We are still working on a date for the Make a Wish trip to Boston. In the meantime, we are happy to take one day at a time and be thankful to be pain free.

July 30, 2005

Daniel has responded well to his port installation. He went in this week to have blood drawn and fluids injected. His port worked fine. It hurt a little bit, but nothing major. He is into his 3rd month of chemotherapy. He was a little sick on day 1, but has done really well that last couple of days. I think we are getting a handle on what needs to be done.

Dan continues to work out, lift, ride his stationary bike, walk, etc. He has lost 25 pounds since May. He is nearly down to his presurgery weight. Some of it is located in the wrong spots, but he is working to redistribute it. Daniel went swimming twice this week, and I think he is enjoying his new found freedom due to his port.
We were notified this week that the "Make a Wish" foundation has scheduled our Boston trip for August 6-9. We will be attending the Red Sox vs. Rangers game on the 8th. Dan will also get to meet David Ortiz, which is a big part of his wish. Our most heart felt thanks to the Make a Wish Foundation for making this a reality. Beyond that, Daniel continues to work hard and exhibit a terrific attitude..."one day at a time".

Appendix

Journal Entries

August 12, 2005

We returned from Daniel's "Make a Wish" trip to Boston late Tuesday afternoon. What a wonderful time. My business background truly appreciates the level of efficiency in the Make a Wish organization. Every "i" was dotted and "t" was crossed. For a family from little Bargersville, Indiana to be able to navigate Boston so smoothly it is really a testament to how well prepared the Make a Wish folks were.

Daniel had a great time. He felt good the whole weekend, and aside from a muscle problem he has in his hip which makes sitting for extended periods difficult, everything went very well. We arrived late Saturday night and checked into the Marriott in downtown Boston (near Chinatown). Sunday was our day to explore Boston, and explore we did. We took the "Duck" tour around Boston. The Ducks are WWII amphibious vehicles that run on land and water, so we took the land tour and then splashed into Boston Harbor. Anthony, and Daniel were invited to drive the Duck in Boston Harbor. Captain Foghorn made the ride very enjoyable and was one of the highlights of Dan's trip. We also rode the "T" which is the subway. The boys either hadn't ever ridden on one, or it had been many years. We also went to the aquarium where they a really neat display with sharks and barracuda's, etc.

Monday was our big day. At 1:30 a limo arrived at our hotel and took us to the Hard Rock Cafe. The Hard Rock picked up the entire tab and allowed us to order whatever we wanted from the menu. The entire group at the Hard Rock could not have been nicer, our server was terrific, and they even gave Daniel two Hard Rock shirts to commemorate his experience. At 3:30 the limo delivered us to Fenway Park for the 7:05 game. Julie from Make a Wish, and Jennifer from the Red Sox organization were there to meet us. We took a tour of the Green Monster, and the Hall of Fame Club and then we went to the field to watch batting practice. Vanessa with the Red Sox took all the boys into the dugout to meet the players and watch BP. All of the players were incredibly gracious with their time. Jason Varitek, Trot Nixon, Johnny Damon, John Olerud and several others came over and spent time talking with Dan and his brothers. Dan had all of them sign a ball, and Anthony was so excited that Johnny Damon signed his "Johnny Damon" shirt. David Ortiz came out and sat with the boys for several minutes, and as you may remember, that was Dan's wish...to meet David Ortiz. He was as delightful in person as he is on TV. As Pam and I stood and watched the boys it occurred to both of us just how lucky we are. People care enough to make this sort of experience possible for a kid from Bargersville, Indiana. This trip coupled with our trip to see Scott Rolen in St. Louis had made for a memorable summer.

Aside from the fact that the Red Sox won the game and we all had a great time, I have to share just one more of those "goose bump" moments that we have experienced through this ordeal. Of course Daniel was just thrilled with meeting David Ortiz and the rest of the guys, but in the bottom of the first David Ortiz came to the plate with a runner on. In retrospect, I think of the Babe Ruth story where he promised to hit a home run for the sick child. Well, David didn't promise to hit a home run, but on the first pitch that he swung at in his first at bat he deposited a home run deep into the seats in right. As luck or fate would have it I turned the video camera on just before he swung, and I thought as he was rounding the bases how symbolic the home run was of the support that has been offered to Daniel and our family. A great ending to a great experience.

August 25, 2005
Daniel is about to complete his second full week of school. Aside from our trip to his oncologist on Tuesday he has made it everyday. That's the good news. The bad news is that Dan's tumor is growing again. It is not significantly bigger, but it is bigger. His treatment is being changed starting next Tuesday. This treatment is more aggressive and we pray will arrest the development of the tumor. Daniel's surgeon has indicated that surgery is not an option at this time, so obviously we hope this treatment works.

Dan, as usual is handling this with tremendous strength and courage. After Dr. Goldman (oncologist) told Daniel of the situation this Tuesday he began his standard check-up...testing his strength, sight, and movement. Part of the routine is to have Daniel smile in order to check the muscle control in his face. As Dr. Goldman finished the check on his face Dan said, "I'll bet you've never seen anyone so good looking"? It even made Dr. Goldman laugh. That is indicative of the way in which Dan has handled every bit of bad news. I continue to be so proud.

We were able to put off the start of his new treatment until next Tuesday so that Daniel could enjoy his first ever concert...Kenny Chesney (his favorite), and the Dodge ball Tournament that the Fox's are hosting in his honor at Franklin High School. He is quite excited for the weekend, and I am excited for him. Please continue to pray that the treatment works and Dan can continue to spread his positive message across our community.

Appendix

Journal Entries

September 13, 2005

Daniel began his newest round of Chemotherapy on August 30th. It involves 3 separate medicines, 2 of which are administered intervenously and 1 which is oral. He has completed fifteen days and has handled it relatively well. As Dr. Goldman put it, we have brought out the big guns for this round. Interestingly enough, one of the side effects of one of the medicines is that "if" it leaks out of the intervenous line it will burn your skin. Imagine what that's doing on the inside. Daniel has had some jaw pain, as well as a sore throat, but other than that he has responded pretty well. In fact, the last three or four days he has felt about as well as he has for several months. I hope that is a good sign.

Dan has been nominated for homecoming king this Friday night. He is looking forward to the parade and dance. He has even indicated that it might be time for him to display his acumen on the dance floor...that should be a sight to behold. For now we are just approaching one day at a time, enjoying the good days, taking the bad days in stride, and praying for a solution to our life's greatest challenge.

October 10, 2005

Daniel continues to persevere through treatment and side effects. He is attempting to conduct life as normally as possible, and for the most part he has been successful. Aside from fatigue and the accomodations that comes with it he is doing pretty well. He received his grades this past week and he has amazed even himself. He had 5 "A's" and 1 "B+". I told him that maybe Dr. Turner didn't tweak the "school part of his brain" completely hence the B+. He didn't think that was too funny. We were really proud of him and very appreciative of all the help he received from his teachers and Mrs. Hopper (his guidance counselor).

Dan has been deer hunting recently and has gotten up on his own at 3:45AM to get into his stand. Thanks to Joe Fox and Dennis Henderson he has a terrific set-up and any failure at this point will be because Daniel can't shoot straight with his crossbow. He is really excited to get back into the woods and he looks forward to every opportunity.

Tomorrow he begins his second round of the new Chemotherapy. It takes about 15 days to work through the entire process, and probably will result in some difficult days. He is scheduled for another brain/spine MRI in about 6 weeks. We will know at that point, or before, if this treatment is working. Please keep him in your prayers.

November 8, 2005

I have been somewhat negligent in forwarding updates, I suppose in part because I hope it signals a return to normal. In part it also means that Daniel is just busy living life to its fullest. He has made it through another round of chemo. He was more fatigued this time, and I expect that is a reflection of the volume of treatment that is beginning to add up. He has felt better in the past several days, and in fact, he and I played catch last night which was a first in the last six months or so. Dan continues to make it to school nearly every day, and he has again done well in his classes with a great deal of help from his teachers and Mrs. Hopper, his guidance counselor.

A couple highlights in the last month. Daniel shot a deer on a trip with his friend Michael and his Dad. Unfortunately, the deer was never found. Which leads one to wonder what exactly he did shoot...he swears it was a deer. I do know that after he shot and went to look for his arrow another deer (8 pointer) walked by and Daniel hugged a tree to try to disguise himself...yeah fat chance. Also, Daniel received a huge honor last Saturday night at the Scott Rolen Foundation Dinner. Scott annually presents a "Hero" award to a child who has exhibited strength, courage, and integrity in the face of a serious illness. Daniel received that award, and by the way, was completely shocked and very humbled. He received a really cool trophy complete with one of Scott's game used gloves. In addition, the Indiana Bulls retired his number 54 jersey and presented it to him in a beautiful framed enclosure. Dave Taylor (Indiana Bulls) and Scott Rolen have done so much to keep Daniel's spirits high, and it has made a huge impact. They are wonderful people who truly care about others. We feel blessed to know them.

Daniel has another MRI on the 28th of this month. We will get an idea at that time for what the tumor is doing. Please join us in praying that it is gone, or at least substantially reduced.

November 30, 2005

We received preliminary results from Daniel's MRI yesterday. The MRI of the spine was not clear and will have to be redone tonight. The MRI of the brain showed the following: The original tumor appears to be more "cystic" which means it is less dense and that is good news, but the bad news is that there is another growth. We go in tomorrow to get the details as well as charting the plan for how we proceed.

Appendix

Needless to say, we are very disappointed. However, Daniel handled the news remarkably well, and continues to display courage well beyond the level at which I currently operate. I am so very proud of the man he has become. Jeff is staying home from school this week to be with Daniel, and that has been comforting to all. In the meantime, we will continue to forge on, undaunted by life's challenges. As I stated early on, "cancer will have no competitor any tougher than this kid and our family".

December 5, 2005
We have had a rough couple of weeks with Daniel. First, he had an intestinal virus which caused severe stomach cramps and illness. Then, he contracted a bacterial virus which is a blood disorder. He has been in the hospital three times in the last week. Finally, we received the results from his latest MRI. The film of his spine is inconclusive...it appears in one dimension that the cancer has returned, but it does not appear in the second dimension. This means that he will have another MRI in a couple weeks to try to determine the status of the spine. The initial tumor in his head appears to be better, but now there is a new growth. It appears the new growth is an outcropping of the original tumor.

The status of future treatment is as follows...we have asked that he be accepted into the Proton Therapy program in Bloomington. This is similar to radiation, but not completely. He is not eligible for any more radiation so we hope the Proton Therapy will be an option. If that is out then we are looking at experimental chemotherapy and/or surgery. We certainly want to avoid surgery if possible. Daniel continues to face this with much courage. He's one tough kid. Please keep him in your prayers as we search for a solution to this situation.

December 8, 2005
Daniel had a tough couple of days. He has been in and out of the hospital with several "midnight runs" to the Methodist Hospital Emergency Room. The pressure has returned to his head due to the growth of the tumor. Last night at about 6:00PM they did surgery to modify his existing shunt to assist in the drainage of spinal fluid. It went well and he is pretty comfortable today. No pressure headaches just the normal surgery pain. Daniel has been selected as the last trail patient on a new experimental chemo designed to block the growth of anaplastic astrocytomas. It has shown some success in other cases. We begin on Monday. It is comforting to know that at least we have an additional option. Thanks so much to all who have called, sent emails or

cards. Your support is so appreciated. Please keep Daniel in your prayers.

December 11, 2005
We brought Daniel home from the hospital yesterday. It was good to get him back where he belongs. The surgery to add to his shunt is minor in comparison to some of his other surgeries, but it's not minor anytime they open your head. We have noticed significant weakness in his left side. He has lost a lot of feeling and is having a hard time holding on to things. I hope some of this will dissipate with time. By and large he isn't feeling too bad. His head pain is level 1 or 2 on a scale of 10, and that is much improved from last week when it was 8 or 9. He continues to be nauseated and that makes it hard for him to keep up his strength and hydration. I really don't know why he is sick other than he has so much medication still running through his system.

Tomorrow, Daniel begins an experimental chemotherapy. It is not designed as curative, but rather as a blocker. Which means that hopefully the treatment will block his tumor from growing further. He will go in on Monday and Tuesday this week and then every Monday for another five weeks. At the end of that time they will do another MRI to check results.

As you might expect, Daniel is discouraged but he continues to exhibit great strength and determination. This is a time that we hope his friends will make the effort to be around him, call, and/or visit. He needs to stay connected since he won't be able to return to school before Christmas. I hope he will get to feeling better through the holi- days. He so enjoys seeing his family and spending time eating and playing cards. Let's keep our fingers crossed and say a little prayer that he will be able to enjoy the month.

December 14, 2005
Daniel's day went from bad to worse yesterday. He began his experimental chemo on Monday, but during the day he began having severe head pains so he was admitted to Riley Hospital. They grew progressively worse through Monday night and Tuesday, and were nearly uncontrollable by Tuesday late morning. The lack of attention shown to him at Riley was very disappointing and prompted us to transfer him to Methodist in the afternoon. They quickly stabilized him and he rested pretty comfortably Tuesday night. Unfortunately, swelling in his brain has forced us to begin steroids which dis- qualifies him from the experimental chemo program. We are nearly out of treatment

options. Daniel continues to be a trooper through all of this. I don't know that I have ever seen anyone in so much pain, except for Pam and I as we feel totally helpless. Many of Dan's friends came to visit yesterday, and that provides him much pleasure and a momentary release. We should know later today if the steroids are helping much. I am confident they can't make anything worse.

There was an unfounded rumor on Monday night that Daniel had passed away. It is interesting how things like that take on a life of their own. While we were quite distressed that so many friends had to go through that we are thankful that Daniel and our family is so loved.

December 28, 2005
The past week was a mixed bag of emotions. Thursday night found us back in the hospital with severe head pain. Daniel and I were up until nearly 6:00AM when they transferred us into a room. We slept until about 9:00AM, and I can promise you that 3 hours sleep at my age just doesn't cut it. However, I'll live and I was happy see Daniel's pain under control. Dan spent the night at the hospital again on Friday as Jeffrey went out to join him. The doctors were terrific in trying to find something that would work so that we could get him home for Christmas Eve. Fortunately, we struck on a combination of three types of morphine that seemed to do a pretty good job, and they released us to go home at about 12:30. We made it home just in time for my family's arrival to celebrate the holiday. Dan, although very groggy, enjoyed himself immensely. On Christmas we traveled to Pam's parents and Daniel made it through Christmas and an additional day. Again, he had a great time playing cards, eating his Grandma's good food, and spending time with his family. He even slipped outside long enough to down a squirrel with his .22 rifle. Took him three shots using his Dad's shoulder as a rest and his brother acting as his dog, but by golly, he got the job done.

We have been fortunate that his doctors have now armed us with the medication to keep him comfortable. Pam and I keep a constant vigil surrounding his medication times and doses, and thus far it has worked pretty well. Daniel has continued his experimental chemo in hopes that we find something to stop the growth of his tumor. We continue to pray and ask for strength, and our spirits are ever lifted by the many cards, calls, and visits from our friends and family members. Here's hoping that everyone who takes time to read this message had a wonderful holiday, and please accept our best wishes for a joyous new year.

January 17, 2006

For all of you who continue to check the website for updates I want to thank you for thinking of Daniel and to apologize for the lack of new/recent information. No excuse other than these are harder and harder for me to write. This forces me to reflect on the hand that Daniel has been dealt, and if seeing it everyday isn't enough, having to write about it has only made it more difficult. In the past few weeks we have been faced with numerous obstacles. Daniel has been unable to take his chemo because his blood counts have been too low, he has battled some serious depression issues (although medication has helped tremendously), and as of this past weekend he has basically lost the use of his legs.

It just seems that everything that could have gone wrong has. The worst part is the feeling of helplessness that accompanies our reality. When Dan asks, "Dad can you help me"? What can I say? Trade my life for his...do it in a minute. Take away the pain? Make his legs work? Allow him to return to being a normal kid? We have prayed for miracles, we have prayed for strength, we have prayed for skilled doctors and surgeons. I guess we just need to pray that we can do our level best to be good parents to Daniel and the other boys, and trust that God will provide the answers for us all...in his time. In the meantime, please continue to keep Daniel in your prayers as he goes through this battle. I will leave you with a vintage Daniel. The other night Pam and I helped Daniel into the restroom and after 40 minutes he still hadn't finished. Pam said to him, "are you done yet"? To which he replied "No". She said, "well I thought you might be ready to quit"? He said, "Mom, this is Daniel, and I never quit". Buddy, how right you are...We love you "D".

January 18, 2006

Stop the presses...hold the phone...we're not done yet. Given the tone of my January 17th posting one could conclude that we were pretty discouraged, and one would be right. We anticipated that Daniel would go to Riley for his chemo only to be told that his blood counts were too low for him to continue in the study. Unfortunately, that did occur. However, as a conclusion to the study that had to do an MRI on his brain. When the doctor returned to discuss the MRI he did so with a big smile because the tumor has in fact decreased significantly in size. Don't ask how given that Daniel hasn't had any chemotherapy treatment in nearly a month. Attribute it to prayer, attribute it to the right chemo, at this point I don't really care. Nonetheless, Daniel still has some very real physical issues so we met with the surgeon today and he explained that

Appendix

Journal Entries

in essence the tumor has decreased so significantly that the brain has collapsed on top of Dan's shunt thereby prohibiting it from working properly. This has caused a fluid build up that could result in his left side not working properly. So, tomorrow (Thursday) Dan will have surgery to install a new shunt and have two small holes drilled in his head to allow excess fluid drainage. We are hopeful that this will decrease his head pain and allow the left side of his body to begin functioning normally again.

This is the first bit of good news we have received in nearly a year. Thank you to all who continue to include Daniel in your prayers. I honestly believe it has made a difference. I cannot explain why this has happened, and quite truthfully I believe it even has the doctors at a loss.

January 22, 2006

Daniel's surgery went as planned on Thursday. It took about an hour and fifteen minutes. They replaced his shunt with a new programmable type, and they drilled two holes in the upper front of his skull to dissipate pressure. While he was in significant pain after the surgery he has steadily improved the past two days. His left side which was virtually non-functioning prior to the surgery has begun to work again. This was a real blessing as he was so worried that he would be paralyzed and unable to be the active, vibrant young man that all know him to be. I called Pam from the hospital last night to give her the news about his left side...she cried...I would have too, but I was too busy devising his workout plan for how we might get full strength back. Always the coach. It appears as though we might keep him in the hospital for the time being as we hope to have the physical therapists work with him prior to returning home. We'll see how things go.

January 28, 2006

Daniel is improving slowly following his return from the hospital last Thursday. He can now walk with the aid of a walker and is much more mobile and coordinated since the surgery. He is still somewhat loopy and forgetful due to the pain medication and seven surgeries. I am hopeful that this will lessen with time and a decrease in medication. He is nearly free of pain in his head, but has replaced that (to a lesser degree) with muscle aches and pains due to inactivity. Dan has regained 10 lbs. since one week ago. It's good to see him eating normally again. His brother Jeff is of course staying home with Daniel and playing Physical Terrorist...I mean Therapist. He is putting Dan through the paces. Daniel legs were so sore and weak this morning that he collapsed three times. Ever try to catch 170 lbs. of dead weight in a free fall? Shortly I may be the one in need of a Physical Therapist. Daniel did not receive chemo last week because his platelets were too low. We are praying that they will be up this coming week and we can get started again.

February 4, 2006
Daniel continues to feel better and better. He is now walking with and without the aid of his walker. We have pretty much done away with the wheelchair. It has been a struggle for him to get stronger as the heavy doses of steroids decrease bone density throughout his body. His oncologist describes his body as that of an 80 year old woman. Fortunately, as they wean him off the steroids his bone density will return and his ability to regain strength will too. For now, he is doing his stretching and flexibility work as well as walking and riding his stationary bike.

As far as his attitude is concerned I think it is as good as I have seen it for quite some time. He has begun talking about what he thinks he might like to pursue as a career, and we really haven't talked about that in a long while. He is very interested in getting out now and attending events. He is going to the wrestling regionals today and is really looking forward to seeing the "good matches". He has begun to talk about hunting again and how he really looks forward to getting started. All these things add up to a real change in approach...I guess that's what a little good news will do for a person.

We met with his oncologist yesterday. They have taken Dan out of the experimental study due to his low platelet counts. However, there is a counterpart drug that is available and they have started Dan on that. According to the doctor it is the same type of agent but is taken as an oral medication rather that IV. Actually, we feel fortunate that he was taken out of the study because we have just been sitting idle. This new medication will not be impacted by platelet counts so we can start immediately. Join us in saying a prayer or two that this works as well or better than the last treatment. It was interesting yesterday...Pam asked the oncologist if he was surprised that the tumor had decreased so significantly in size when the previous treatment was only designed as a blocker and not a curative agent. He said, "yes...very surprised". Maybe we all have a few more surprises in store?

Appendix

Journal Entries

February 18, 2006

We had to bring Daniel back to the hospital last Tuesday night with severe abdominal pain. Tests showed that Daniel was bleeding internally. Initially it was thought to involve his pancreas, which is extremely serious, but it appears to be a "spontaneous bleed". A spontaneous bleed can be caused by low platelet counts. In other words, due to all the treatment Daniel has received a hemorrhage that for most people would clot normally, cannot in his case. Therefore, the bleeding continued until he began showing signs on Tuesday. They have given him lots of transfusions but his counts are still dropping slowly. I think they will use a scope today to look for the cause and then attempt to cauterize it.

Daniel was really looking forward to attending the wrestling state finals on Friday and Saturday, but unfortunately that could not happen. The doctors told him that transporting him to Conseco for the event could endanger his life should he begin to bleed internally. However, the Franklin Athletic Director (Noel Heminger) and the Franklin wrestling coaches (Bob Hasseman and Chris Lynch) saw to it that Daniel was recognized during the Parade of Champions. There was a two-minute tribute to Daniel at Conseco when the Franklin boys were introduced. Although Pam and I were unable to attend, our sons Jeff and Joe were there and filmed the highlights from the evening and weekend. Apparently the entire Fieldhouse (10,000+) gave Daniel a standing ovation as his teammates carried a poster with his picture and his accomplishments were read. Thanks so much to Noel, Bob, and Chris for including Daniel. He, and we, were very touched. Jeff is going to bring the film to the hospital today for Daniel to see. He can't wait to see the matches his teammates wrestled in, and he was ecstatic that 3 of the Franklin kids finished in the top 4 in the state.

We expect Daniel to be in the hospital most of this next week. They have to stop the bleeding and he has to start manufacturing his own platelets. For his sake I hope that is soon. He is very weak and his body just needs a break. Today Daniel's personal prayer team again swung into action as Pam and two of her sisters attended church services where Daniel is being recognized. They each have an incredible amount of faith and are totally convinced that Daniel will recover and will serve as a testament to the power of faith and prayer. I am confident that if anyone can overcome the myriad of challenges that this young man has been faced with...it is Daniel. Thanks so much to all who continue to support Daniel and our family with prayer and best wishes.

February 25, 2006

There is no easy or good way to share that Daniel is in very critical condition at Methodist Hospital. This past Wednesday he his body began to shut down. His blood pressure dropped to 60/33 and the doctor on call responded with a "Code Blue". That's a first for me and I hope it's my last. Fortunately, they were able to stabilize Daniel over the next day. What we found was that he had contracted a blood infection (sepsis) which is very serious, especially for someone in such a weakened state. Daniel eventually experienced great difficulty in breathing and Saturday morning they placed him on a ventilator. Frequently when someone is placed on a ventilator they don't come off. However, he has responded pretty well and is doing some breathing on his own. In essence what has occurred is that the infection attacks your internal organs which requires great effort from the organs to fight it off. Daniel's heart rate shot through the roof and his blood pressure bottomed out. When that occurs they have to pump huge volumes of fluid into his body to get his heart rate down. The fluid then results in leakage into the lungs which caused his breathing difficulty.

While Daniel's breathing, heart rate, and blood pressure have all stabilized, his platelets (which cause the blood to clot) have dropped to virtually zero. His is at huge risk for spontaneous bleeding. If that occurs he, nor the doctors, have any way to stop it. They are giving him platelets but his body is not doing a good job of accepting them. We continue to pray for strength and courage as Daniel fights the good fight. He is a terrific kid and I hope that God has a plan that will allow him to continue to stay with us.

March 3, 2006

Daniel is like a cat with nine lives. Forget that he has used up 4 or 5. He has made remarkable progress on many fronts and they have stopped his ventilator as of this morning. He is breathing completely on his own and if things continue to go well they will remove the tubes today. He is alert and is able to communicate with pencil and paper. He is not in any real discomfort other than he needs to brush his teeth...REAL BAD. God love him, I can't wait to help him brush his teeth and shave. He seems to be somewhat down and discouraged...who wouldn't be given all that he has gone through? He asked Pam and Jeff yesterday if he was going to die. We've decided that God can't have him yet...how do you like that for an executive decision...God will just have to find another catcher/linebacker/189 pounder...oops make that 152 pounder.

Appendix

Journal Entries

We've received many cards, emails and well-wishes. We appreciate the continued concern for Daniel and his recovery, and I know it helps keep his spirits up. Thanks to all of you who continue to hang in there with him and us.

March 15, 2006
Daniel has had a challenging couple of weeks in the Critical Care unit at Methodist. His blood counts are still very low, his blood sugar is all over the map, and he just isn't eating much at all. You can just tell he doesn't feel very good. On the bright side though he has become much more coherent. Once they were able to regulate his sodium we could carry on a normal conversation, or at least as normal as we were every able to carry on with Daniel. He does march to the beat of a different drummer, but that's probably been a good thing through this whole ordeal.

God love him...he is still pretty positive and has begun showing signs of his personality returning. You'd have to see him, but he is skin and bones and yesterday one of the nurses was explaining to Daniel what they were doing (i.e. giving him some insulin, changing his antibiotics), and she finished by saying, "do you have any questions"? In a voice barely audible, he said, "can you tell me why I am so big and studly". She burst out laughing and said "now that's the Daniel I know".

My niece, her two kids, and her mother-in-law stopped by to visit yesterday. Daniel absolutely loves those two little ones and you should have seen him light up. It certainly made his month. The doctors believe Daniel's colon is acting up and they will begin treating him with antibiotics. That means he won't be able to eat for a few days...which is not good. Dan had a group of ladies visit last week from Terre Haute who were there expressly to pray for him. They said they had been called to pray for his healing. The woman who kind of took charge said that is the 24th healing she has performed. Ladies, thank you so much...and Ma'am I hope you are correct.

March 30, 2006
"Great occasions do not make heroes or cowards; they simply unveil them to the eyes of men. Silently and imperceptibly, as we wake or sleep, we grow strong or weak; and at last some crisis shows what we have become". Brooke Foss Westcott

I certainly could not have said it better...so I didn't try. The events of the past two weeks have demonstrated what Daniel has become. It seems we take one step forward and two back. Yet, through it all he remains steadfast in his determination to survive. He has experienced continued bleeding in his abdomen with a pocket of fluid 8" by 10". He has another bleed near his left lung. He has had difficulty breathing. He has again contracted sepsis (blood infection), and now they tell us he has pneumonia. Tuesday night of this week he was completely incoherent...he could not respond to any stimulus at all. I really thought that maybe we had reached the end of the line, and I was as close to losing my composure as I have ever been. By Wednesday morning, after a hefty dose of antibiotics he had again returned to close to normal. He knew who I was again and began eating a little bit...let's see part of a popsicle, most of a cup of orange sherbet, two bites of a Reese's cup, 1 bite of pizza, and a bowl of Lucky Charms. I know...I know...where is the nutritional value. At this point the kid gets whatever he wants and if they need to give him a shot of insulin then so be it.

Our extended family and community continues to keep watch over Daniel, Pam and I and the boys. We are so grateful for all who have stayed with us. They are too many to mention for fear of leaving some out, but we are truly blessed. Father Tom (St. Rose) stopped by at 11:00PM last Friday...how long was his day??? We continue to receive lots of spiritual support from the St. Rose community, Pam's sister Ann, and a whole host of folks...many whom we don't even know. It certainly provides comfort that everyone is doing all they can to see Daniel through this fight. Must go for now as I'm off to the hospital. Please keep Daniel in your prayers!

April 15, 2006
Daniel continues to feel better each day. His stomach hurts less and he has gotten a little stronger. These gains are relative however as he is incredibly weak and is virtually incapacitated. Dan continues to be fed through a tube with an occasional bite of real food. He still receives quite a lot of pain medication and is now on insulin due to the steroids and tube feedings.

Daniel weight is down to about 140lbs. His muscles are completely gone as you might expect from someone who has laid flat on his back for 60+ days. Despite the challenges though he continues to have that same positive attitude. He regularly makes the nurses laugh hysterically about something he says or does. I don't know how he stays so upbeat.

Appendix

Journal Entries

It appears as though he will be coming home in the next week or so. While we are thrilled that he gets to come home he will require constant attention. We have been undergoing training over the past few days for some of the many things we will be required to do. The one upside to getting him out is the possibility of taking him to the Proton Institute in Bloomington for treatment. An MRI was taken this weekend and it shows the tumor has grown again. We need to get him started in treatment ASAP.

Lots of people continue to hang in there with us, and for that we are truly grateful. That may seem like such a small thing, but when you've been in the Critical Care Unit as long as we have you see so many kids who have virtually no one there in support of them. We are very fortunate.

May 2, 2006
We have continued to operate in a holding pattern for the better part of two weeks...one step forward and one step back.

We anticipated getting Daniel home at some point last week but that did not happen. His liver numbers came back high at one point and there was some concern, but just as quickly as they went up they came back down. His stomach continues to be the major issue as he just can't eat or even receive tube feedings. They did order a CT scan of his stomach and it showed large pockets of air in addition to the fluid collection. This probably accounts for some of his stomach pain. Also, due to high volumes of morphine his bowels aren't operating normally and that only complicates matters.

We are somewhat hopeful that Dan may come home this week sometime, but who knows? He continues to be positive and complains only when something hurts. He still hasn't shown signs of the depression that many would exhibit given his reality. For that we are grateful and very proud. He is still convinced that he can get out of the hospital and get himself back in to some sort of shape...at least enough to lead a semi-normal life. We'll see how things progress. As soon as he arrives home I will add a post with an update on condition.

May 8, 2006
Nearly 90 days after this journey started Daniel returned home yesterday afternoon. He was transported via ambulance to our Sunroom which had been made ready with all the conveniences of Methodist Hospital. His departure from Methodist was truly a cele-

bration for all. The nurses and doctors all had noise makers and blew to their heart's content as Daniel was wheeled down the corridor. Tears flowed everywhere...except for Daniel...I think he was just happy to be going home.

I am happy to report that the first 24 hours have gone well and he seems to be adjusting nicely. A huge "thanks" to all our kind friends who have provided meals, cards, visits, etc. over the past three months. God Bless you all.

May 17, 2006
Monday morning at 3:30AM Daniel was returned to Methodist Hospital. He has severe abdominal pain and just didn't look good. It was determined upon arrival that he has acquired sepsis once again and that additional bleeding has taken place near his stomach. As generally accompanies these events his blood pressure dropped low and his heart rate went up. The medical protocol requires that they treat this with lots of fluids through his pic line. When they do that it affects his breathing because the fluid fills up his lungs...it'a a vicious cycle which we have repeated frequently.

We hope to stabilize Daniel quickly and then I expect some decisions will have to be made related to surgery to stop the bleeding in his abdomin and remove the collected fluid. We are reaching a point where something must be done or we won't be able to treat the problem...which continues to be a brain tumor. Through it all Daniel doesn't complain about his plight other than to tell us that something hurts. God love him...I don't know how he avoids throwing in the towel. I guess it's because he wants to live so desperately. He asked his friend Emily last night if there was anything he had to do for Senior Night. She of course said no, but I disagree...your job Daniel, should you choose to accept it, is to LIVE...LIVE Daniel LIVE!!!

May 25, 2006
Daniel celebrated his 19th birthday was this past Sunday in Methodist Hospital. He was surrounded by friends and family, and his nurses made and hung the letters "Happy Birthday Dan" from the ceiling. It was a very bittersweet day for me. On the upside, the Archbishop himself came and visited Daniel at the request of Dan's Aunt Ann, cousin Linda, and friend Maria. In addition, Dan's friends headed up by Emily and Katrina, made a happy birthday video which included well wishes from tons of friends. All those things were wonderful, but unfortunately about all I could dwell on is the utter and complete unfairness of this entire situation. Daniel should be at school with

his friends, he should be planning his graduation party, he should be finishing finals and enjoying the completion of high school, he should be participating in the terrific season the baseball team is having, he should be looking forward to attending college next year.

I realize that may appear like sour grapes, but I feel so sorry for all that he has missed and will miss. As strong and determined as he has been I still long for him to return to the activities of a normal teenager, despite the fact that I know it will never happen.

Dan's doctors have told us that the infections in his body are at this point more life threatening than the brain tumor. I think they believe the liklihood of overcoming those physical challenges are virtually zero. To complicate things a bit Daniel has been asleep for the past three days straight. We don't know exactly what is going on, but I am certain it is not good. In the meantime, we are doing our best to wade through this sense of helplessness and hopelessness. We continue to have tremendous support from family, friends, and community and for that we are ever so grateful. Please continue to pray that Daniel is able to sustain himself and his faith through this most difficult time.

May 29, 2006
Shortly after midnight on this 29th day of May, Daniel Patrick Mercer touched the face of God. He drifted off peacefully while surrounded by family, friends, and his caring nurses and doctors. The past few days have been vintage Daniel. Knowledge that the end was near has brought scores of friends and family members. As I observed the scene around us I thought how much Daniel must be enjoying the stories being told about him...the baseball games on TV...and Kenny Chesney in the CD player. After some initial sadness the conversation inevitably turned to something off the wall that Daniel had said or done during his short life here on earth. He was a "piece of work". Like the time when he was 4 or 5 and said "Dad" 86 times in an hour and fifteen minutes on the ride home from Grandma and Grandpa's. Gaining 16 lbs. in one day after nearly starving himself to make weight in wrestling...probably at Chicago's Pizza while being served by his favorite lady, Petunia Daylilly (a name that of course he had given her). Or, the time that he got his truck stuck in a ditch backwards, at midnight (after curfew), while trying to shine his truck lights on several deer standing out in a field. I still remember standing in a pitch black kitchen waiting for him and what was sure to be a creative excuse.

As a good friend reminded me recently, amid all the sadness how very lucky we have been to have had Daniel for 19 years. Conversely, how lucky he is to have been so loved by so many. Some people, in a full life, never experience one-tenth of the joy and happiness that Daniel did.

As a family, we have been so fortunate to have been surrounded this past 18 months by so many wonderful friends and family members. They have given and given and continue to offer help in any way necessary. Even though we haven't been able to thank each one of you personally...please know that we love you for all you have done. Our friend Mike Carter once said "you are the richest man in the world if you have five friends you can truly count on". Mike is probably right, but it occurs to me that his assessment must make us the richest family ever. I cannot count the number of people whom I know we could have depended upon at any time...day or night.

I encourage each and every one of you who reads this note to always remember Daniel. Not for him, or for us, but for what the journey had meant to each person it touched. We have been reminded of what is truly important in life, and it's not winning or losing, making money, or even getting a car on your 16th birthday. It's about enjoying every day you have with family and friends. It's about telling those you care about that you love them every chance you get. It's about giving life everything you have during the time you are here. Daniel taught us that and more every day for the past year and a half. Daniel you were one of a kind, you are one of my four best buddies and I will forever love and miss you.

Johnson County
Community Foundation

398 S. Main Street, PO Box, Franklin, IN 46131
Phone: (317)738-2213   Fax: (317)738-9113

☐ **YES,** I would like to support the Daniel P. Mercer Fund

In honor of their late son, Daniel Mercer, and some of the activities he loved best, Jeff and Pam Mercer of Franklin recently launched the Daniel P. Mercer Family Fund.

The Daniel P. Mercer Family Fund will in part make an annual award of $1300 to the Indiana Bulls for a teenager to participate in one of the Indiana Bulls teams.   In addition to ear marking monies for the Indiana Bulls baseball scholarship, the Mercers also bestow a second annual award to a local youth athletic program or organization.

First Name_____   Middle Initial_____   Last Name_____

Address_____   Apt. No._____

City_____   State_____

Zip_____

- -

Gift Amount $_____   Joint Gift With:_____

Payment Information:

Form of Payment: _____ Check   _____ Visa   _____ Mastercard

Credit Card Number: _____   Expiration Date: _____

Signature: _____   Date: _____

Please remit to:
Daniel Mercer Fund,
c/o Johnson County Community Foundation,
398 S. Main St.,
P.O. Box 217
Franklin, IN. 46131

Make a difference...Daniel did.

Printed in the United States
110835LV00002B/113-1000/A